In *An Aesthetics of Morality*, John Krapp reappraises the value of ethical criticism in our time. Allying himself with those who, like Wayne Booth and Martha Nussbaum, believe that there is room for attention to moral considerations in literary criticism, Krapp argues for the possibility of speaking about the ethical dimensions of reading without reducing the discussion to dogmatic declaratives. Focusing on instances of moral pedagogy in novels by Thomas Mann, Albert Camus, Joseph Conrad, and Fyodor Dostoevsky, he suggests that literature uses an aesthetic portrayal of personal relations to introduce scenes of moral tension that illustrate the way ethical claims are made and validated.

Krapp describes current theoretical attitudes about ethical criticism, distinguishes ethical criticism from the more prevalent political criticism, and locates his own less widely attributed views within the landscape of literary studies. Diverting attention from moral themes and toward aesthetic structures, he provides refreshing discussions of *The Magic Mountain, The Plague, Heart of Darkness, Lord Jim,* and *The Idiot* that include his assessment of recent rhetorical and critical positions on these texts. Citing specific examples of how literature can be morally momentous without promoting a particular moral outlook, Krapp pays special heed to each of the four writers' second-order remarks on the linkages between art and morality. He supplements those comments with an appreciation of the dialogue among "ethically invested voices" presented by their characters and narratorial positions. As he considers why some ethical voices are more pedagogically effective than others, Krapp argues that moral dialogue in literature may be studied as a paradigm for ethical literary criticism.

D1525153

AN AESTHETICS
OF MORALITY

AN AESTHETICS
OF MORALITY

Pedagogic Voice and Moral Dialogue in
Mann, Camus, Conrad, and Dostoevsky

JOHN KRAPP

University of South Carolina Press

Published in Columbia, South Carolina, by the
University of South Carolina Press

Manufactured in the United States of America

06 05 04 03 02   5 4 3 2 1

Library of Congress Cataloging-in-Publication Data

Krapp, John, 1965–
   An aesthetics of morality : pedagogic voice and moral dialogue in Mann, Camus, Conrad,
and Dostoevsky / John Krapp.
    p. cm.
  Includes bibliographical references and index.
  ISBN 1-57003-448-6 (cloth : alk. paper)
  1. Literature and morals. 2. European fiction—19th century—History and criticism.
3. European fiction—20th century—History and criticism. I. Title.
PN49 .K72 2002
809'.93353—dc21   2002001052

     Part of chapter 3 appeared previously in *University of Toronto Quarterly* 68, no. 2 (spring 1999), and is reprinted by permission of University of Toronto Press Incorporated 1999. The author also acknowledges permission to quote from the following works:

     Lord Jim, by Joseph Conrad, edited by Thomas Moser. Copyright ©1996, 1968 by W. W. Norton & Company, Inc. Used by permission of W. W. Norton & Company, Inc.

     Heart of Darkness, by Joseph Conrad, edited by Robert Kimbrough. Copyright ©1988, 1971, 1963 by W. W. Norton & Company, Inc. Used by permission of W. W. Norton & Company, Inc.

     Reflections of a Non-Political Man, by Thomas Mann, translated by Walter D. Morris. Copyright ©1983 by the Ungar Publishing Company, Continuum International Publishing Group. Reprinted with the permission of the publisher.

     The Idiot, by Fyodor Dostoevsky, translated by Constance Garnett. Copyright ©1981, 1958 by Bantam Books. Reprinted with the permission of Bantam Dell Publishing Group.

     The Plague, by Albert Camus, translated by Stuart Gilbert. Copyright ©1948 by Stuart Gilbert. Reprinted by permission of Alfred A. Knopf, a Division of Random House Inc., and by permission of Penguin Books Ltd.

     The Magic Mountain, by Thomas Mann, translated by H. T. Lowe-Porter. Copyright ©1927, 1955 by Alfred A. Knopf Inc. Copyright ©1952 by Thomas Mann. Reprinted by permission of Alfred A. Knopf, a Division of Random House Inc., and by permission of Random House Group Limited.

for my family

CONTENTS

Acknowledgments / ix

Abbreviations / xi

1 Ethical Literary Criticism Today / 1

2 History and Pedagogic Voice in *The Magic Mountain* / 35

3 Time and Ethics in *The Plague* / 70

4 Marlow's Moral Education, from *Heart of Darkness* to *Lord Jim* / 99

5 Reading *The Idiot* as Ethical Criticism / 134

Notes / 171

Bibliography / 199

Index / 211

ACKNOWLEDGMENTS

Many people contributed to the completion of this project, providing opportunity, encouragement, counsel, or some combination of all three.

My institutional debts are legion, but it would be unconscionable not to recognize several here. Ignacio Götz is most responsible for bringing me into this field as a student and has continued to help me mature, now additionally as colleague and friend at Hofstra University. Conference with him opens new ways of thinking about things that would otherwise likely remain inaccessible. In the Department of Comparative Studies at Stony Brook, Sandy Petrey saw this manuscript originally take shape and then, with an uncompromisingly firm and generous hand, helped form it into a more lucid and cogent expression of ideas far exceeding its beginnings. Also at Stony Brook, Michael Sprinker served both as a scrupulous editor and as a critical benchmark for much of my argument. The pedagogic example they both set while I was writing was invaluable, providing a model of how, never what, to think and do in the course of such intellectual work. My citing their involvement with this enterprise is slight return for their investment. I am also grateful to John Lutz for his generative criticism and commentary. Finally, I thank David Christman for creating a professional environment at Hofstra University in which all things of the mind are possible.

I cannot imagine having better fortune than to be publishing a first book under the guiding hand of Barry Blose, acquisitions editor at University of South Carolina Press. From the moment of my first correspondence with him, he has been the most congenial lifeline imaginable. There is no adequate way to thank him for his kind, forthright, and timely attention, assistance, and counsel during the production of this manuscript. For their months of care in supervising the production details of this project, I also thank Barbara Brannon, Scott Evan Burgess, and Skot Garrick.

Finally, I owe my most comprehensive gratitude to my family. My parents, Josephine and Robert, provided me the opportunity to begin this book and offered ceaseless encouragement along the way. Their enthusiasm was equaled by my wife, Lisa, who, along with my son Nicholas, also displayed heroic patience when deadlines disrupted the normal routines of our household. As a group, they characteristically reminded me of the light when I had begun even to lose sight of the tunnel.

Hempstead, New York

ABBREVIATIONS

Primary sources cited in the text are identified by the following abbreviations:

LCE	Albert Camus. *Lyrical and Critical Essays*.
MoS	————. *The Myth of Sisyphus and Other Essays*.
P	————. *The Plague*.
RRD	————. *Resistance, Rebellion, and Death*.
HoD	Joseph Conrad. *Heart of Darkness*.
LJ	————. *Lord Jim*.
NLL	————. *Notes on Life and Letters*.
I	Fyodor Dostoevsky. *The Idiot*.
MM	Thomas Mann. *The Magic Mountain*.
RNM	————. *Reflections of a Non-Political Man*.

An Aesthetics
of Morality

1

Ethical Literary
Criticism Today

■

These residual humanists—they must *prove* they are more than
residual.

Paul Bové, *In the Wake of Theory*

The burden of proof [is] on anyone who now wants to divorce
poetry from the pleasures of moral education: if genuine "literature"
should be read as offering no unequivocal advice about "real life" . . .
then centuries of informed witnesses have deliberately deceived us
—or they have been self-deceived.

Wayne Booth, *The Company We Keep*

Perhaps the seminal voice of ethical literary criticism in the Western cultural tradition belongs to Plato, who dismissed imitative poets from his
Republic on the grounds that mimetic poetry conveys a morally deleterious message to its readers.[1] Two critical moves generate Plato's estimation
of literary mimesis. First, and most important, Plato self-consciously
acknowledges that a fictional text can be a receptacle of morally instructive
significance. Second, Plato's detection of literature's moral significance is a
forthright demonstration of ethical textual practice. Plato's methodological
example yields a skeletal definition of ethical criticism as the reflexive
process by which a text is consciously read for its potential to yield some
standard for human conduct, a standard that then becomes the locus for
further critical scrutiny.

While Plato may have sincerely feared that ethical criticism had the
potential to corrupt the moral education of Greek culture, such criticism
was practiced as a matter of course until this century. Indeed, when literary
theorists like Horace, Sidney, Johnson, Shelley, and Arnold took the primary
functions of literature to be delight and instruction, they were duplicating
the critical gestures acknowledged in Plato's formula.[2] Its commonplace

practice for nearly twenty-five hundred years notwithstanding, ethical literary criticism is now at a crucial juncture, having suffered charges of illegitimacy for most of the twentieth century.[3]

The charges against the practice of ethical criticism generally incorporate one or more of the following basic contentions: (1) ethical criticism is monologic, reductive, and proselytizing and thus does violence to the aesthetic complexities of literature in order to promote a critic's moral agenda; (2) ethical criticism covertly endorses elitist and/or oppressive ideologies; (3) ethical criticism has no claim to objectivity and can never end in anything but opinion, which is not knowledge; (4) in its attempt to find a stable ideological position in a medium as indeterminate as language, ethical criticism ignores the rhetorical dimension of signification; (5) ethical criticism tries to standardize interpretation by threatening the exegetical freedom burgeoning from literary modernism and anti-essentialist philosophy.

A common denominator of all of these objections is what they perceive as ethical criticism's tendency to thematize interpretation, to make reductive, dogmatic, monologic claims about the moral content of a literary text. This fear is indeed legitimate, but if one looks carefully, it becomes quite clear that the word *ethical* might be replaced with a variety of other theoretical qualifiers that are popular in today's critical landscape without altering the general tenor of the objection, which merely adduces the characteristics of any irresponsible textual practice. Irresponsible criticism is irresponsible criticism, regardless of the stakes, and no amount of it should be permitted to threaten the validity of a textual practice that labors to avoid such pitfalls. Nevertheless, what makes the objections of ethical criticism's opponents valuable is that they assist a dialogue that takes the moral component of literary studies as its theoretical and practical object.[4] The contemporaneity of this dialogue between ethical criticism's opponents and its espousers is an invitation to develop a particular idea about how to define and perform responsible ethical criticism on literary texts.[5]

What I understand to be responsible ethical criticism is not exclusively thematic in scope or agenda; neither is it monologic. Responsible ethical criticism is not an eternal paean to an ideal, whatever that ideal might be. Rather, it is the record of the way critical codes influence interpretive judgments of both literary documents and commentary on those documents.[6]

Correlatively, responsible ethical criticism is intrigued as much by *how* the ethical component of a literary document signifies—both as a self-contained aesthetic object and as a pedagogic instrument—as by *what* it signifies. It neither subordinates the aesthetic to the moral, nor the moral to the aesthetic; instead, it keeps both categories intact in its choice of forms and methods necessary for textual practice.

Responsible ethical criticism does not pretend to find *the* moral of a story; it can, however, fairly discover *a* moral that does not betray the story's aesthetic modality.[7] As Christopher Clausen explains, "Moral criticism requires agreement that the moral values and judgments asserted or implied in a literary work are worth noticing, examining, and evaluating. It does not depend on acceptance of any particular moral code, or on any particular view of the status of moral judgments."[8] It is nonsense to dismiss all ethical criticism on the grounds that the worst of it monologizes a polysemous document; such objection is nothing more than the same kind of univocal interpretation of a text that the bringers of the argument find so offensive about ethical criticism in the first place. *Univocality in exegesis*—the idea that there is one "correct" way of interpreting a text—is a chimera to which few literary critics would hold today; *verification of exegesis*—the idea that different readers sharing the same critical apparatus and conditions for textual practice can find their way to a similar interpretation of a text —seems to me an intelligent and principled aspiration of the critical profession. The two, however, are not identical. And there is no reason to think that all ethical criticism must treat them as though they were.

Ethical criticism is most persuasive when it remains in dialogue with what may be called the aesthetic structures of a text. The tension between these aesthetic structures and a text's ideological components solidifies a production of textual meaning. Attention to these aesthetic structures may profitably contribute to a nonmonologic, nonthematic ethical criticism by demonstrating how to read literature for insight, not into the kinds of ethical claims a text might convey, but into the way ethical claims may be expressed and validated. This is not to say that ethical themes can be sifted completely out of the process of ethical reading, but these themes need not be taken as the exclusive object of study; rather, they are understood as simply an ideological effect of an equally important signifying process. On this view, the structural example of ethically charged voices engaged in moral dialogue within a text may serve both as the object of ethical criticism and as a morally instructive model for one way critics may articulate their own nonmonologic interpretive claims about a text's moral component.

This latter goal is desirable because one of the primary difficulties in practicing ethical criticism inheres in the *voice* of criticism, in the way literary critics express and seek to vindicate their claims about texts. One of the literary critic's roles is to explain what a text means. Literary critics do not tacitly declaim their interpretations as unworthy of serious consideration; rather, they express a *pedagogic* voice that implicitly seeks some measure of authority in the process of presenting an argument for the legitimacy of a given interpretation. However, in the process of developing literary readings, critics always have the potential to ignore significant exegetical voices that might undermine, or even refute, the reading they are trying to authorize. While ethical critics must indeed be responsible for directing a particular interpretation of a text's moral dimension, they must also keep their interpretive voices in the foreground of their textual readings so that their own methodological biases do not distort the nuances of a text's moral dynamic into totalizing moral lessons or tidy epigrams.[9]

As Don Bialostosky contends, studying the way epistemological claims speak to one another provokes critics to become self-conscious contributors to the critical community that enables and challenges their cultural practices.[10] This process makes them directly answerable to the dynamics of reading and writing.[11] Promoting recognition of other critics' positions as the necessary condition of our own positions leads us to expect that whatever we have said will give others more to say.[12] As a consequence, the "truth" relevant to literature and criticism becomes a function of their shared subjectivity, and their shared concern with value and ethics becomes a corollary to their dialogic status.[13]

The dialogue among critical voices *on* a given topic of literary investigation is analogous to the dialogue among competing ethically pedagogic voices *within* a given literary text. In each, the narrative record of the contingencies of temporal experience foregrounds the contingency of truth claims. Exposing the process of this record makes it possible to elaborate the concept of a responsible critical voice that is indeed ethical, without promoting a univocal code of values. As readings of moral voice and dialogue in Thomas Mann's *The Magic Mountain*, Albert Camus's *The Plague*,

Joseph Conrad's *Heart of Darkness* and *Lord Jim*, and Fyodor Dostoevsky's *The Idiot* will show, it also makes it possible to figure pedagogic voice and moral dialogue as objects of ethical criticism.

A fair objection to the use of narrative texts to explain the role of ethical voice and moral dialogue in ethical criticism is that, because they are already dialogically rich in a way that *La Commedia* or *Chanson de Roland*, for example, are not, they already produce the values that I wish to attribute to ethical criticism.[14] Yet this objection need not threaten the theoretical claims advanced above. Certain narrative texts do indeed tend to reflect a plurivocality perhaps not immediately apparent in other literary genres; they do characteristically avoid ideological closure. Nonetheless, it is far from certain whether they necessarily engender a nonmonologic critique. Fredric Jameson's narrowly focused Marxist analysis in *The Political Unconscious* of anticapitalist themes in Conrad's *Lord Jim*, one of the canonical masterpieces of literary modernism, suggests that they do not. Readers of texts, not the texts themselves, produce values.

Moreover, as Mikhail Bakhtin has persuasively argued, once we understand that the vocal utterance is a dialogized social phenomenon through its entire range and in each and every one of its factors, then a precise form and content distinction is impossible to maintain. Although the novel represents a "deepening of dialogic essence," that essence exists, if perhaps less transparently, in virtually every literary genre available for ethical interpretation, a corpus that would not exclude medieval poetry and romance.[15] Finally, sustained engagement with several texts is, in some ways, less likely to distort the accuracy of methodological claims: it is often easier to pick and choose one illustrative example from a broad variety of texts to make a theory appear sound than it is to submit a small selection to a thoroughgoing critique, the sum of which may inevitably contradict a theoretical position.

Whose Ethics? Humanism, Politics, and Relativism

In a 1989 essay, Martha Nussbaum delineated the history whereby literary theory "lost [its] practical dimension," concluding that such a history would include "a critical look at some writing about literature that did, during this long period, keep ethical concerns in view. For much of this writing has understandably given ethical writing about literature a bad name, by its neglect of literary form and its reductive moralizing manner."[16]

Had Nussbaum required an example of reductivist, monologic, and/or thematizing ethical criticism to illustrate her point, she would have found a good one in John Gardner's *On Moral Fiction*. Gardner, too, offers a history, one that bashes virtually every kind of literary criticism but that which he practices. The following is a typical summary of his argument:

> The first great evasion [of moral criticism]—though it was not originally intended as an evasion—was the New Criticism, which studied works of art as if they existed independent of the universe, outside time and culture, as self-sufficient organisms. That school of course served as an invaluable corrective to the almost universal nineteenth-century evasion, which avoided talking about the work by talking, instead, about the man who created it. . . . A number of equally ingenious evasions rose in furious reaction—Marxist criticism, generic criticism, various forms of historical criticism, the present fad of structuralist criticism, destructionist [*sic*] criticism, and the safest, easiest approach of all, "hermeneutics," or opinion, bastard grandson of the eighteenth century's rule of taste.
> None of these really qualifies as criticism.

True criticism, according to Gardner, is simply that which detects and praises true art. And true art is that which "clarifies life, establishes models of human action, casts nets towards the future, carefully judges our right and wrong directions, celebrates and mourns." For Gardner, both true art and criticism serve a moral end, which he describes as "nothing more than doing what is unselfish, helpful, kind, and noble-hearted, and doing it with at least a reasonable expectation that in the long run as well as the short we won't be sorry for what we've done, whether or not it was against some petty human law. Moral action is action which affirms life."[17]

It is one thing to subject such Enlightenment, humanistic themes to rigorous critical scrutiny and then to conclude that they may be legitimate standards for moral behavior by specific agents at a specific historical juncture; it is quite another simply to honor them as authoritative, essential, immutable Truth. The former represents a mode of judgment that may be classified as a critically responsible textual practice. The latter is an unapologetic homage that reductively and dogmatically serves an agenda because it fails to foreground the methodological justification for its truth claims; rather, it pretends to have arrested an absolute Truth that enjoys a privileged position outside historical time. While not all exclusively thematic ethical criticism goes to quite this monologic extreme, the tendency

among ethical critics to rally their interpretations around a particular ideological code at the expense of competing codes is sufficiently prevalent to
have necessitated my investigation into a less thematic, more structural
approach to ethical criticism.[18]

Gardner takes for granted the credibility of a nonideological critical
perspective that is not implicated in the mundane sociopolitical effects that
inflect perception. While Peter Brooks is not entirely willing to concede
the validity of an ideologically neutral critical voice, he remains quick to
condemn a fairly comprehensive stratum of criticism wherein he diagnoses
"a measure of moral arrogance . . . that derives, *grosso modo*, from Foucault,
who often gives the impression that we, as analysts, know better—better
than the deluded discourses we are unmasking. . . . Virtuous philosophiz-
ing really undoes the work of situating knowledge, and the knower in relation to it. It tacitly assumes a place of privilege—within contemporary
American academia, of all places—from which it proffers its discourse."
Brooks is particularly wary of the kind of critic—he mentions Raymond
Williams, Terry Eagleton, and Fredric Jameson—who "can, and must,
position him or herself as analyst and actor in an ideological drama [since]
not to do so is simply to be a bad faith participant in hegemonic cultural
practices."[19] On Brooks's account, not only is certain ideological criticism
morally delimited and delimiting, but it is also representative of an elitist
discursive community that has no real connection with any but a professional academic audience.[20]

Tobin Siebers expands the category of potentially bad ethical criticism
to include that which "establish[es] an artificial (and moralistic) distinction
between ethics and politics based on the belief that politics is more concrete
and historical than ethics, and therefore less prone to mystification and airy
theorizing." Siebers also interprets Jameson as exemplifying a highly dubious
interpretive method that privileges political critique but then ineluctably
smuggles in ethics to serve some agenda.[21] This is a position with which
Simon Stow would agree: "Political commitments . . . provide the framework and set the limits on the ethical criticism debate." Moreover, at least
as far as the debate has been conducted thus far, Stow finds the role of politics "distorting," since it covertly makes "the *conversation about* the text,
rather than the text *itself*" the functional target of critique.[22] This need not,
however, necessarily be the case; indeed, Stow presents only one side of
the story of the relationship between political and ethical critique. At least

two others are possible. Both help clarify the distinction between the kind of politically inflected ethical criticism that continues to draw such fire and ethical criticism as I conceive it.

First, not all critics guided by political concerns attempt to weave a surreptitious ethical subtext into their work. Second, not every ethical critic aims to subtly promote a political position. Instead, some critics are quite up front about the program that might drive their work. For example, Michael Sprinker concludes a relentless critique of the shortcomings of contemporary cultural studies with the forthright injunction that it "come to terms with the necessity of overthrowing the existing relations of production, of transforming them in such a way as not to aid in the reproduction of capitalism." There is nothing indirectly political about this commentary, just as surely as there is nothing secretly ethical about his judgment that "cultural studies still stands in the shadow cast by its British originators. It is high time it came out of that shadow, in which its own political degeneracy has been successfully hidden, to face the responsibilities and risks of participation in a genuinely democratized cultural practice."[23] Politics and ethics are manifestly coterminous in this line of argument, as they are in much political criticism, particularly that which investigates the social determinants of racial, ethnic, gender, sexual, and class identity. Hence, Siebers and Stow are certainly not entirely wrong in assessing select criticism that conflates the boundaries between the ethical and the political.

Nevertheless, regardless of whether the link between politics and ethics is smuggled or paraded, all such political criticism must be distinguished from an ethical criticism that has no interest in advancing a political cause. Responsible ethical criticism is not invested in politics, if by politics is understood the strategies of authorizing and legitimizing modes of ideological governance. Moreover, and perhaps surprisingly, responsible ethical criticism is not invested in ethics, if by ethics is understood something along the lines of a code of values by which a certain kind of life—traditionally "the good life"—may be attained. What I call responsible ethical criticism could only be deemed political insofar as the claims identified on an ethical reading may possess a political import. But even when the ideological, or specifically political or ethical, significance of a claim is a matter of inquiry, it is, on my readings, always ancillary to the way the speaker of the claim constructs the pretense for the claim's validity. When ethical criticism targets the rhetorical structure of the claim rather than its content, political criticism and ethical criticism are no longer so easily made synonymous, and to attack the former is to leave the latter undamaged.

Allan Bloom's high-profile and highly controversial polemic *The Closing of the American Mind* depended on hostility toward ethical relativism to set the terms of the evaluation of the university's contribution to the late-twentieth-century American moral ethos. Characterizing the academy, Bloom writes: "Relativism is necessary to openness; and this is the virtue, the only virtue, which all primary education for more than fifty years has dedicated itself to inculcating. Openness—and the relativism that makes it the only plausible stance in the face of various claims to truth and various ways of life and kinds of human beings, is the great insight of our times. The true believer is the real danger." This inclination to relativism alarms a critic like Bloom, who then speaks fluently of "our" virtues, "our" values in articulating his encomium to reason, the quintessential Western gift: "The West is defined by its need for justification of its ways or values, by its need for discovery of nature, by its need for philosophy and science. This is its cultural imperative. Deprived of that, it will collapse. The United States is one of the highest and most extreme achievements of the rational quest for the good life according to nature. What makes its political structure possible is the use of the rational principles of natural right to found a people, thus uniting the good with one's own."[24]

Bloom cannot bear the thought that a student might leave the classroom ambivalent about all that the West, as conceived by Bloom, holds valuable. Those whose thinking is commensurable with his own he finds unobjectionable; those who think otherwise are guilty of relativism and are peremptorily dismissed. What Bloom apparently does not consider is that his position is also relative, that is, to his experience as a Western cultural critic. He would not likely hold this view were he an Indian Hindu. This is not to say that Bloom is wrong in his view as much as it is to say that his perspective has a context, a fact that does not seem to cause him much concern.

Bloom's tendency to normalize claims that are fundamentally relative to a context is common enough. Ironically, ethical criticism cannot expect to win sudden legitimacy even if it conquers the related charges of relativism and plurivocality. When ethical criticism attempts to disclose an

objective, or even stable, referent for textual analysis, it often opens itself
to the opposite charge—already de rigueur among those wary of moralizing and propagandizing—of univocality in interpretation. And if anything
is worse, in our contemporary critical idiom, than a hermeneutical relativism that cannot stabilize its truth claims, it is a monologic mode of textual practice that dogmatically impedes reinterpretation.

Richard Posner's "Against Ethical Criticism" is emphatic on this point.
Citing Nussbaum's ethical readings of Dickens's *Hard Times*, Forster's
Maurice, and Wright's *Native Son* as examples of what he rules an invalidat-
ing flaw in ethical criticism as it is commonly practiced, Posner maintains
that "the ethical position is in place before the examination begins, and furnishes the criteria of choice and shapes interpretation." Furthermore,
according to Posner, Nussbaum's example of how ethical readings load
their argument is evidence for why ethical criticism fails to demonstrate its
case that reading literature may have a morally edifying effect, for "if literature were really believed to be a source of ethical insight, the critic would
examine and compare . . . works of literature that reflected different ethical
stances."[25] Taking these two statements together, it appears that Posner's
charges are directed at a certain voice of ethical criticism, a dubious one
that plays it safe by interpreting a text that either felicitously yields a preconceived agenda or that accommodates the critic's impression of a moral
upon it.

Hence, between the freedom and the terror of literary readings, ethical criticism is ostensibly caught in a no-win situation. It is supposed either
to be plurivocal to avoid absolutizing, in which case it is considered merely
relativistic; or it must be univocal to escape relativism, in which case it is
dogmatic and improper.[26] Michael Bérubé recapitulates the assault on ethically informed textual practice as follows:

> We are being attacked over these exigencies of value not because we
> have vacated the terrain on which critics interrogate cultural values, but
> precisely because we have not vacated this terrain. To put this another
> way, the academic transvaluation of all questions of aesthetic and cultural
> value provides one of the primary reasons we are met with such hostil-
> ity and misunderstanding in the literary public sphere. For traditionalists
> and conservatives have succeeded in opposing the academic transvalua-
> tion of value by painting it as a radical relativism that refuses to believe
> in "values," thereby generating a moral panic that the institutional guardians

of culture have left their posts—or worse, transformed their posts into soapboxes from which they proclaim that there should be no guardians of culture, since everything is as beautiful and true as everything else.[27]

These are serious charges. They intimate an apocalyptic vision for the future of literary studies. And yet they are only half of the story. On the other side of the controversy over ethical textual practice are a camp of defenders who contribute to the possibility of a responsible ethical criticism that is neither monologic nor dogmatic.

DECONSTRUCTIVE ETHICS

Deconstructionist criticism has often been taken as having provided, intentionally or not, the most formidable conceptual ammunition in the last three decades to undermine the possibility of authoritative truth claims. With its insistence on the impossibility of an absolute, inviolable linguistic correspondence between words and the things or ideas they represent, deconstruction has asserted the constructedness of all knowledge. Categorical ethical claims are little more than pretense because all categorical claims are pretense. Every linguistic utterance is influenced by the context in which it is expressed. For example, deconstructionists might argue that what gives the Ten Commandments their absolute authority is not the power of their correspondence to an absolute standard of ethical conduct. What gives them their authority is the willingness of certain individuals to invest them with absolute authority. All linguistic meaning is human, thus temporal, thus in some measure indeterminate.

Assurances of the inevitable slipperiness of language tend, however, to be greatly exaggerated; moreover, deconstructive literary criticism reveals a more substantial moral component than has been acknowledged by its harshest opponents.[28] Indeed, rhetorical readings are an extremely effective conduit to a text's moral dimension. The process by which tropes are interpreted can yield evidence of ideological contradiction that in turn betrays moral pressure. Moreover, even deconstructive readings that are read as repudiating an openly ethical moment of interpretation are themselves open to ethical interpretation.[29] Finally, primarily via Jacques Derrida's engagement with the ethical thinking of Emmanuel Levinas and the commentary this engagement has been steadily inspiring, deconstruction has demonstrated its relevance to the conception of an ethics of responsibility generated in the encounter with the other.[30] On this view, language originates in responsibility as a response to someone else; thus, from the moment of its articulation, it is ethical.[31]

Murray Krieger speculates that recent literary theory has quite simply forgotten its implicit moral component: "We can find at work, even in those theories that are least permissive about what texts can tell us about their subjects, indirect claims for privileged moral and ideological meanings, even if they are negative ones representing unspoken negative visions. . . . Poetics cannot remain purely descriptive or semiotic; instead, it narrows into the realm of privilege and spreads into the realm of the thematic. It subliminally invokes attitudes that we can think of as moral." Krieger silhouettes poststructuralist critics of culture like Frederic Jameson, Michelle Foucault, and Edward Said—whom he judges to be openly moralistic in their criticism of different ideological mystifications, oppressions, and barbarities—against more language-centered theorists like Paul de Man and J. Hillis Miller, original members of the "Yale school of deconstruction" whose writings of the 1970s and early 1980s emphasize the rhetorical dimension of textuality while reputedly downplaying the text's openly moral significance. Krieger reads de Man the semiotician as unable to abandon de Man the existentialist; though de Man's criticism focuses on the "referential incapacity of language," it inevitably "thematizes itself by illuminating our 'temporal predicament' as existents." Similarly, Krieger sees in the writing of Hillis Miller a condition in which "the elusiveness of discourse traps and displays itself, so that the inevitable linguistic movement toward infinite regress slips into the concept of infinite regress— whose home is in the abyss—with its consequences for our moral view of the universe."[32]

Christopher Norris would ostensibly agree with Krieger's thematization of deconstruction, viewing the deconstructionists as critics of consciousness whose respective projects are "by no means incompatible with a broadly phenomenological approach" to textual practice. As Norris sees it, undecidability itself is the ethical premise of deconstruction. Norris unites Paul de Man with "moralists like Kant—or indeed with antimoralists like Nietzsche and Foucault, as well as strong revisionists like Freud and Lacan—[in] the fact that he mounts a resistance to ethics on terms that cannot in the end be other than ethical."[33] For Norris, de Man's corpus becomes simply one more piece of evidence to substantiate the latter's own claim that literary critics are often most blind to the kinds of critical insight that their texts engender. As a result of this methodological blindness, deconstruction may be judged a form of ethical literary criticism exactly insofar as it professes not to be.[34] Thus, for both Krieger and Norris, deconstruction maintains a precarious relationship to the anti-essentialist, poststructuralist ontological crisis that it simultaneously foregrounds and represses. But in the deconstructive criticism that chooses the latter response to ontological skepticism, the stories of this repression are themselves themes redacted as the narrative of their loss. If the legacy of Freud has taught us anything, it is that the more powerfully something is repressed, the more powerfully it inevitably returns in symptomatic form.[35]

Hillis Miller himself provides the most forthright and protracted elaboration of the moral component of rhetorical readings. He openly declares that "there is a necessary ethical moment in [the] act of reading as such, a moment neither cognitive, nor political, nor social, nor interpersonal, but properly and independently ethical."[36] He enlists de Man, whose project rarely reflects direct engagement with ethical criticism, for his emphasis on the need to stay with the letter of the text despite premature seductions of coherency.[37] Hillis Miller makes it clear that the ethical moment of reading is not merely an aesthetic exercise: "Each reading is, strictly speaking, ethical, in the sense that it *has* to take place, by an implacable necessity, as the response to a categorical demand, and in the sense that the reader *must* take responsibility for it and for its consequences in the personal, social, and political worlds."[38]

These two quotations hardly suggest the kind of interpretive nihilism in textual practice detected by deconstruction's opponents; still less do they indicate the repressed thematic textual implications of deconstruction observed by Krieger. Yet Krieger may be very much in Hillis Miller's mind as he pronounces the ethical command that follows the act of reading: "Do not make the thematic dramatizations within a work of literature the basis of ethical judgments and actions in the real world. . . . Withdraw. Abnegate. Give up." On Hillis Miller's account, the ethics of reading is finally tantamount to the inevitable recognition of both the text's referential undecidability and its incapacity to provide practical ethical knowledge: "This ethical judgment, like the ethical moment in reading generally, is aberrant in the sense of not being logically based on the knowledge I get from the work, since that knowledge is 'understanding' of my inability to understand, of my failure to read."[39]

Commentary on the ethical potential of deconstruction tends to conjoin the mandate for interpretive responsibility with the acknowledgment that reading can never produce normative, essential ethical knowledge; rather, it stresses the experience of intersubjectivity that must lie at the heart of an ethical practice consistent with deconstructionist strategies of reading. Invoked in support of this move is the work of Levinas, for whom alterity is the necessary precondition of ethics because responsibility is born in the moment of being placed face to face before another.[40] Such a condition of being compels a contingent ethics, whose site is the dialogue between individuals who are constantly negotiating their claims. Modeled on such a conversation, "the only path for criticism to take is to make its interpretation continual interruption. 'Theory,' understood as interruption, should make discussions that appear to be closed open, turn the expected into the unexpected and show the last word to be only the most recent word."[41] Ethics so understood is always incomplete and, if compared with traditional attempts to express "categorical" moral precepts, is also impossible.[42]

The challenge of a deconstructionist ethics is to acknowledge and assess the potential validity of relentlessly competing ethical claims in order to understand more clearly the dynamic of the process involved in the production of moral knowledge. Thus, deconstructive ethical criticism is obviously at considerable odds with ethical criticism as traditionally practiced. However, criticism of the ethics of deconstruction has shown that, though deconstruction might often be termed an aesthetic mode of textual analysis, the aesthetic is always shot through with the traces of ethical pressure; hence, it is not deconstruction itself, but distorted assessments of it, that lie at the beginning of its representation as an amoral, or even immoral, interpretive practice.

THE EITHER/OR FALLACY, CANONS, AND CLASSROOMS

Wayne Booth, perhaps the most vocal espouser of ethical criticism writing today, submits that the interpretive tension generated by linguistic ambiguity should be the locus of judgment for what makes ethical criticism an acceptable, inevitable, and valid form of literary practice:

Without denying the overwhelming evidence that readers do take explicit instruction from even the least sermonic works, I would argue that a much more important moral effect of every encounter with a story, good or bad, is the practice it gives in how to read moral qualities from potentially misleading signs. That training can be harmful, if our line-by-line progress through a work suggests that the good guys and bad guys can be readily discriminated. . . . But our best narrative friends introduce us to the practice of subtle, sensitive moral inference. . . . The reader—at least *this* reader—comes away from reading Henry James, or Jane Austen, or Shakespeare, emulating *that kind* of moral sensitivity— not so much the sensitivity of any one character (because sometimes there is no dramatized character who exhibits special moral insight) but, rather, that of the author who insists that I *see* what these people are doing to each other.[43]

Booth's injunction proposes a careful mixture of moral and aesthetic consideration in the creation and practice of a nondogmatic, nonreductive ethical reading. It is, in a word, sensible: it does not constrain the ethical critic of literature into a narrow, artificial choice between an ethical or aesthetic, a practical or formal, textual practice. This artificial distinction was very much at the root of ethical criticism's demise in the first place, partly because to negotiate one's way through this distinction requires a sensitivity to the relations between qualities or categories. The skill required to elucidate such conceptual relations is enormous.[44] At some point, critics must make certain methodological decisions on which to base their interpretive and theoretical projects, and it is far easier to choose between two clear-cut principles of criticism than it is to choose among degrees of those same principles.

Gerald Graff suggests an immediate arena in which the either/or underpinnings of evaluation may be detected in literary criticism, to wit, the classroom: "The initial questions we decide to ask in teaching a literary work, the questions that delimit what we will say about it, are always dictated in some part by the pressures of our time, our culture, and our sense of history: what is it in Shakespeare or Keats or Beckett that an age like ours . . . needs to relearn, consider imaginatively, or fight against?"[45] Graff is not insisting that only the moral dimension of a literary text be taught in a college classroom; the word *morality* does not even appear in his commentary, which in no way precludes an appreciation of the aesthetic technique(s) with which a given document signifies. But very few

English professors say anything like, "Surely I must put Shakespeare on my list of titles because of the way he changes his predecessor's conception of enjambment," and let it go at that. We may, indeed, be quite interested in this formal change, but the interest is likely based on the reasons for the change and its consequences for future dramatic verse. Once we start speaking the language of reasons and consequences, we are making a swift move away from the purely aesthetic into a critical realm that may fairly be titled ethical.

Nor is it always necessary to have to burrow beneath the surface of an apparently exclusively aesthetics-oriented classroom pedagogy in order to find quietly implied moments of ethical import. As with the examples of various schools of "oppositional pedagogy," or of teachers who use their classrooms as a forum for some form of ideological intervention or advo- cacy,[46] ethical considerations are sometimes pushed straight to the center of academic study, much to the chagrin of opponents who see the class- room as a site for learning the rules of intellectual inquiry and contest, not for advancing political or ethical credo. Since the specific object of these opponents' scorn is the same kind of reductive, monologic, and prosely- tizing tendency cited by detractors of ethical criticism in general, the question of whether ethical matters can be introduced into classroom dis- cussion without reproducing the pedagogic methods of critical ideologues continues to elicit a response from defenders of ethical criticism.

Booth has very recently interrogated this possibility. Grounding his reflections in John Dewey's thought that the goal of education is to build character, Booth begins with the very broad claim that "we should seek selves for ourselves as teachers that . . . will change students in ways that we are sure are most useful to *them*."[47] The commitment required of the teacher who seeks to execute this mandate successfully is complex. That Booth sees teachers of literature as teachers of ethical thinking goes with- out saying. What is most immediately striking about the ethically peda- gogic relationship between teacher and student is the notion that teachers reveal a certain preparedness before they begin to practice their vocation, a preparedness that must be subjected to constant autocritique lest the habit of inquiry demanded of ethical speculation grow weak. But what kind of "selves" represent the right kind of preparedness? Is this preparedness exclusively methodological (can any mode of literary critique ever be purely methodological?), or does it imply qualities of character that themselves may be highly questionable, threatening to become trapped in principled debate over which qualities are the better (the best?) qualities?

Booth acknowledges that the word *useful* is "deeply ambiguous," but he says little about the equally problematic word *them*—the recipients of the kind of ethical teaching Booth envisions. Who are "they"? It is common for teachers to lump students together as a homogeneous mass for one reason or another: "I don't know what else to do. They just don't get it," or "They don't get it because they just don't read." But such comments, which I suspect have been uttered in every university in the country at one point or another, are usually followed by an encouraging mention of the students who do get it because they do read, and hope is restored. The point is, there is no "they," unless "they" is actually intended as a collective reference to each student whose individual need Booth cannot describe in the space permitted by the journal's word limit. But the allure of characterizing students as an undifferentiated mass may encourage careless instructors to suppose that the measure of an ethical education's use value may somehow be standardized for too broad a sample of students. Such instructors consequently open themselves to the criticism that they oversimplify, or at worst monologize, the ethically educative capacity of literary themes.

Booth goes to considerable lengths to indicate that he wishes to encourage teachers to relay the sense of a particular kind of methodological experience of reading, one where students are enticed "not only into loving this or that book or fixed list but into loving *both* the seduction of story and the fun of criticizing those seductions." Lest this theoretical description sound too sanguine, Booth offers six practical suggestions on how these methodological goals might be met. Three are worth mentioning in anticipation of the forthcoming structural model of ethical criticism. First, Booth advises that literature instructors always teach at least one work whose ethical import they consider "extravagantly flawed," one that they suspect students will also find repugnant. Second, instructors should include at least one text that "reveals that first story's dangers or stupidities," so that students are compelled to deal with "value conflict." Third, instructors should include some story in which the implied author "rejects the values espoused by appealing characters or especially sympathetic narrators." On Booth's assessment, students engaged with such texts will learn not only how a text conveys ethical material but also how to compromise the neat transmission of an ethical position. This combination of "understanding with overstanding the ethical effects of narrative" will, ideally, inculcate a method of ethical thinking in students exposed to it.[48]

What is admirable about Booth's effort is his insistence on modeling *how* to think ethically, not *what* to think ethically. No one has yet been more persistently devoted to working through this problem than he, and no one sets the stakes, in terms of the function of literature and the future of its readers, of a solution so high. Nevertheless, Booth's writing on ethical criticism always seems to be trying to hide a subtext that holds certain values more sympathetic than others. Consider the teacher who desires to execute Booth's program for discussing ethics and literature in the classroom. By what standard does that teacher select works that are extravagantly flawed and morally repugnant? What, besides that teacher's biases, is most likely to determine text selection? And what if that teacher has, shall we say, an unorthodox sense of acceptable and unacceptable moral behavior? Will the selection of the rival text assure that the teacher's ethical affinities do not dominate the process of analyzing the representation of value conflict? It is hard to say. It may very well be that thematizing is unavoidable in ethical criticism. But it may also be possible to take steps to divest ethical criticism still further of its tropism toward a predominantly thematic engagement with literary texts.

The controversy over the process of canon formation is a second instance of the potential irrepressibility of thematic considerations in ethical criticism; it also illustrates the consequences of accepting an oversimplified "either/or" logic for any investigative practice. The canon's contemporary defenders are wont to argue that a superior quality of "literariness" justifies the selection of one text or another for inclusion within the traditional Western literary canon; texts are evaluated for the way their aesthetic dimension engenders and intensifies a powerful connection between the receptive reader and a broader humanistic sensibility that canonical texts represent. Little is made of moral import when this camp evaluates a text's candidacy for canon inclusion. By emphasizing the formal properties of the text in canon debate, defenders of traditional Western texts purport to steer clear of the kind of tendentious ethical considerations around which calls for canon revision frequently rally. Emphasis on a text's form allegedly transcends the "shameless" ideological investment detected in those politically interested theorists and critics.[49]

Though the defenders of the traditional Western canon may heroically labor to deflect attention away from their ideological investment in and toward aesthetic appreciation of the texts they celebrate, the labor only succeeds in hiding what everyone knows to be another valid stake in canon revision: canon wars are waged about the kinds of ideas that are to be considered either interesting or morally imperative.[50] So when Brooks rebukes Jameson, Williams, and Eagleton for their critical emphasis on textual ideology, what is particularly interesting about his argument is that all the critics he cites are Marxists, which in turn invites the question of the ideas he considers to be appropriate objects of literary study.

Richard Rorty is characteristically more forthright about the considerations of value that underpin canon formation, asserting that "the word 'literature' now covers just about every sort of book which might conceivably have moral relevance—might conceivably alter one's sense of what is possible and important. . . . Rather than detecting and expounding [a book's 'literary qualities'], the critic is now expected to facilitate moral reflection by suggesting revisions in the canon of moral exemplars and advisors, and suggesting ways in which the tensions within this canon may be eased—or, where necessary, sharpened."[51] For Rorty, any divorce of critical methods into the purely ethical and the purely aesthetic violates a basic symbiosis necessary for the production of textual meaning.

The tendency of contemporary literary critics to back themselves into an either/or methodological decision regarding the viability and value of ethical criticism is not entirely surprising. Opposition to ethical criticism solidified at the climax of the modernist movement in art, which had only intensified a retreat from morality shared by its formalist, symbolist, and impressionist counterparts. David Sidorsky explains how these artistic movements endeavored to escape engagement with the moral dimension of art by suppressing any sense of narrative telos in their respective projects. To this end, he recalls Virginia Woolf's comments on modernist narrative technique: "If a writer were a free man and not a slave, if he could write what he chose, not what he must, if he could base his work upon his own feeling and not upon convention, there would be no plot, no comedy, no tragedy, no love interest or catastrophe in the accepted style."[52]

Woolf's manifesto is provocative on at least two counts. First, the irony of self-limitation produced in the series of hypothetical considerations indicates that the compositional mode for which she longs is clearly out of reach: we are not free "men" in any sense of escaping the historically informed ideological determinants that constrain human creativity. Second, the inventory of plots, forms, and structures that would fall by the wayside, were escape ever possible, are all elements or variations of seminal literary themes. One might recall Krieger's contention that the need to thematize one's ideas inflects a moral dimension into even the most avowedly antimoral aesthetic textual practice. A collation of themes affords a textual narrative; and as narrative implacably betrays some teleological impulse, it can always be read as a record of existential choices in some way freighted with moral implications for reader and critic alike.

Narrative and Ethical Criticism

Much recent ethical criticism recognizes a debt to Alasdair MacIntyre, whose *After Virtue* is perhaps the major statement on the intersection of narration and moral instruction in the last twenty years. His account of the aesthetics of morality is worth quoting at length:

> Man is in his actions and practice, as well as in his fictions, essentially a story-telling animal. He is not essentially, but becomes through his history, a teller of stories that aspire to truth. . . . We enter human society, that is, with one or more imputed characters—roles into which we have been drafted—and we have to learn what they are in order to be able to understand how others respond to us and how our responses to them are apt to be construed. It is through hearing stories . . . that children learn or mislearn both what a child and what a parent is, what the cast of characters may be in the drama into which they have been born and what the ways of the world are. Deprive children of stories and you leave them unscripted, anxious stutterers in their actions as in their words. Hence there is no way to give us an understanding of any society, including our own, except through the stock of stories which constitute its initial dramatic resources. Mythology, in its original sense, is at the heart of things. Vico was right and so was Joyce. And so too of course is that moral tradition from heroic society to its medieval heirs according to which the telling of stories has a key part in educating us into the virtues.

Interestingly enough, MacIntyre confers no special contemporary value on narrative as an innovative mode of moral investigation; instead, he acknowledges narrative's pervasive presence in the Western ethical tradition from Homer to the late twentieth century. Narrative has always been the structure whereby consciousness has self-reflected its personal and interpersonal experience: "We always move towards placing a particular episode in the context of a set of narrative histories, historics both of the individuals concerned and of the settings in which they act and suffer."[53]

Nussbaum is a bit more specific in her assessment that a capacity to reflect, and to reflect on, history inheres in the teleological facet of narrative, observing that "a view of life is told. The telling itself—the selection of genre, formal structures, sentences, vocabulary, of the whole manner of addressing the reader's sense of life—all of this expresses a sense of life and of value, a sense of what matters and what does not, of what learning and communicating are, of life's relations and connections."[54] These statements provide a substantial theoretical point of departure for the primary reason why literary narrative is the aesthetic modality that best accommodates moral speculation: time is the prerequisite of ethics, and, as Paul Ricoeur succinctly explains, "*Time becomes human to the extent that it is articulated through a narrative mode, and narrative attains its full meaning when it becomes a condition of temporal existence.*"[55]

Literary narratives plot a series of contingencies created by an author as the fictive manifestation of human narrative; thus, literary narratives are the best representation of "moral personhood"—one is internal to the other.[56] It is not that literary narrative is a better medium for representing ethical claims. Rather, literary narrative often represents variegated ethical options on significant moral questions, options that a reader may choose to investigate seriously as possible alternatives to his or her extant ethical predispositions.[57] Moreover, and perhaps most important, narrative is the genre through which individuals characteristically express interpretive claims *about* literature, regardless of whether the literature under scrutiny may be categorized as narrative.

Richard Rorty appropriates many of the aforementioned moral implications of narrative in order to specifically endorse novels as the locus of future ethical textual practice. Rorty's ethical criticism hinges on his belief that, in the absence of categorical foundations for constituting self and society, human beings should become as fluent as possible in an array of cultural vocabularies so as to avoid the trap of blindly capitulating to oppressive cultural structures that pretend toward higher sanction. Ethics, if it can be passed off by family, state, or church as the genuinely "right" ethics, is one such oppressive structure to which we are accustomed to relinquish our personal liberties unless we have the intellectual apparatus to criticize the structure's truth claims.

According to Rorty, authority figures its power by professing the finality of its particular vocabulary; it labors to naturalize its foundational metaphors so that they seem atemporal and nonideological. Thus, the task of contemporary ethical criticism is to "drop the idea of 'intrinsic nature'" and "face up to the *contingency* of the language we use," since "a recognition of that contingency leads to a recognition of the contingency of conscience, and . . . both recognitions lead to a picture of intellectual and moral progress as a history of increasingly useful metaphors rather than of increasing understanding of how things really are." Rorty calls the people who are able to accept the contingency of descriptive vocabularies (including their own) and to work ceaselessly toward preserving it "ironists." In the struggle to explode ideological pretense in the name of ethical contingency, what ironists do best is read:

> Since there is nothing beyond vocabularies which serves as a criterion of choice between them, criticism is a matter of looking on this picture and on that, not of comparing both pictures with the original. Nothing can serve as a criticism of a person save another person, or of a culture save an alternative culture—for persons or cultures are, for us, incarnated vocabularies. So our doubts about our own characters or our own culture can be resolved or assuaged only by enlarging our acquaintance. The easiest way of doing that is to read books, and so ironists spend more of their time placing books than in placing real live people.[58]

In their mistaken search for universal truths, traditional metaphysicians have come up short as ethical critics; their philosophical texts reflect little more than rhetorically persuasive opinion dressed up as absolute knowledge. By contrast, ironists are as concerned with the process of moral speculation as with the product. The principles of redescription and revision, through which ironists conceive their moral identity, preserve the temporal dimension of moral development that is reexpressed in narrative; moreover, they furnish "a source of non–propositional knowledge characteristic of moral understanding."[59] Rorty insists that "ironists read literary critics, and take them as moral advisers, simply because such critics have an exceptionally large range of acquaintance. They are moral advisers not because they have special access to moral Truth but because they have been around. They have read more books and are thus in a better position not to get trapped in the vocabulary of any single book."[60] It might not be an exaggeration to say that, regardless of whether he is actually correct in his theory of the ironist as ethical critic, Rorty has done as much as any other academic philosopher writing today to popularize ethical criticism as a method and an object of literary study.

Much of the criticism against Rorty invokes the potentially oppressive and ethnocentric political applications of his idea that moral advice should issue from those with plenty of free time and money on their hands to become educated readers of frequently formidable literary documents. Yet an interesting facet of this strain of detraction is its repetition of Rorty's endorsement of contingency in moral thinking. Barbara Herrnstein-Smith, after dismissing most of Rorty's project as a "dubious" form of "self-privilege," nevertheless calls for the pursuit of "the continuous development and refinement of more richly articulated, broadly responsive, and subtly differentiated nonobjectivist accounts of, among other things, 'truth,' 'belief,' 'choice,' 'justification,' and 'community.'"[61]

Is this so different from Rorty's theory of methodological redescription? Indeed, it is possible—for the ironist it would be an obligation—to respect both Herrnstein-Smith's dismissal and her corroboration of Rorty's ethical criticism at the same time. We learn to meet Herrnstein-Smith's own ethical demands in the same way that Rorty says we become better moral thinkers: by reading, by learning to discern the subtle textual operations that convey a text's significance in any reading instance. The sociopolitical consequences of our knowledge of those operations is ultimately founded upon, but certainly not inseparable from, the ability to perform sophisticated readings in the first place. Put another way, just as interpretation needs to thematize its object, so themes need to be interpreted. The moral dimension of the text does not lie exclusively either in the thematizing or in the interpretation; it lies in the oscillation between these inextricable textual operations. The moment we reflectively choose the language with which we interpret that something—regardless of whether we are using an ideological, political, rhetorical, aesthetic, or other criterion for our judgment—we are solidifying an elaborate, value-laden scaffolding for the evaluations we produce.

To argue otherwise is to argue that, in the swirl of ideological determinants by which we are informed throughout our lives, we are able to avoid those that properly pertain to some standard of what is good and what is bad so as to remain ethically neutral; that is, by some heroic (miraculous?) act of will, we are able to flip the switch of ethical judgment to its off position before we begin to read and interpret a text. Neither of these contingencies is very likely. The validity of absolute knowledge, ethical or otherwise, may be undermined by narrative, but the narrative of an undermined knowledge's instability is still valid knowledge as long as it discloses the historically contingent conditions of its production.

PEDAGOGIC VOICE AND MORAL DIALOGUE

Ethical criticism, when responsibly practiced, can provide alternative ways of viewing moral problems and debate by investigating the aesthetics of literary narrative, a genre characterized by its ability to represent the dynamic among historically contingent ideologies that informs knowledge production. A locus of this approach is the structural tensions within and among literary characters' competing pedagogic ethical voices, through which both a literary text's dominant moral tenor and a model for moral thinking may be generated. As the sine qua non of fiction,[62] "character" figures prominently in the way pedagogic voices contest one another because, as MacIntyre explains, characters are "the moral representatives of their culture and they are so because of the way in which moral and metaphysical ideas and theories assume through them an embodied existence in the social world. *Characters* are the masks worn by moral philosophies. . . . The *character* morally legitimates a mode of social existence."[63] MacIntyre's description of character is felicitous for the emphasis it places on character as a socially informed ideological receptacle rather than as a predetermined and authoritative moral symbol.

The difference between a potentially satanic character and Satan neatly illustrates the difference between a socially informed agent and a symbolic representation, in this case of evil. A reader bringing the same Western interpretive proclivities to bear on an analysis of Satan in *Paradise Lost* and Kurtz in *Heart of Darkness* might draw the conclusion that, while Milton's Satan is a fairly transparent figure of evil in an allegorical Christian worldview reflecting absolute values, the adjudication of Kurtz's evil is far less obvious, depending as it does on the reader's attitudes toward both imperialism and Kurtz's inconclusive reproduction of imperialist values. Kurtz's character is the repository of a certain ethical ideology, but the import of that ideology is not predetermined by a set of transcendent interpretive coordinates of which the reader is expected to have knowledge; rather, it is overdetermined by the socially produced web of ideological determinants that inform the text and the reader's reception of it.

As part of a social organization, an individual character expresses one or more ethical positions among many historically contingent ethical possibilities. As the record of characters' lives, literary narrative typically maintains a tension among such possibilities.[64] The potential for the tension among characters to serve as an aesthetic paradigm for the production of moral knowledge is not so easy to dismiss on the grounds that, after all, the characters in literary narratives are just fiction. Nussbaum makes the case that novels enlist their readers as concerned participants in the adventures of their characters.[65] Appealing less to an emotional connection between reader and text than does Nussbaum, but contending nonetheless that the moral significance of literary characters is formidable, Frank Palmer asserts: "It would be illogical to suppose that we see fictional characters as half-people who perform half-deeds in a half-way house of existence. Within a fictional world the characters are responsible for their actions. They are moral agents."[66]

As agents, literary characters conventionally communicate their ethical positions through the medium of voice.[67] On the ethically invested structural function of this medium, Jeffrey T. Nealon writes:

> "Voice" can "de-essentialize" ethics precisely because it also highlights an emphasis on "response": "voicing" an opinion, for example, is not the same as "holding" an opinion. "Voice" becomes such an attractive concept because it is not tied essentially to one point of view; rather, one must learn to *find* one's own voice and to *hear* the voice of the other within a common social context. It is precisely in the movements of seeking, listening, and answering that an intersubjective ethics of response might be born. And this points to the distinctly *ethical* character of dialogics; if social space is understood as a rich dialogue of voices rather than a fight for recognition and domination, then the other is not necessarily a menacing or hostile force.[68]

It is possible to reconceive the limits of the social space cited by Nealon to include the landscapes created in the process of reading literary texts. The dialogues produced in the act of reading reflect (1) characters' intersubjective relations; (2) the relationship between the reader and the text; and (3) the relationships among critics of the text. Such dialogues thus afford enormous opportunity to debate nonnormative, nonfoundational ethical claims.

To read a novel is to be exposed to an array of voices, each of which conveys some measure of ideological significance within the text.[69] The easiest voices to identify are those that are the direct extensions of particular figures within the narrative itself. Reading these voices often provokes an interpretive connection between a specific pattern of textual significance and a specific character repeatedly associated with it. Thus, in *The Magic Mountain,* Settembrini comes to stand for the moral and intellectual principles of Enlightenment humanism, and he tends to speak authoritatively, with a voice whose legitimacy pretends to transcend historical pressures. If a reader who has assimilated Settembrini's ethical position happens to open the text randomly to a spot where an unabashedly self-assured encomium to Enlightenment ideas is given voice, the reader may reflexively associate this voice with Settembrini if there are no other textual clues present to identify the speaker. Whether or not the reader later learns that the identification is incorrect does nothing to change the fact that literary narratives often empower fairly stable connections between characters and readers through the signifying mechanism and thematic agenda of individual characters' voices.

Literary narratives also express a narratorial voice or point of view, conveying perspective on, and investment in, the tale being told. Narrative voice is a "fundamentally *composite* entity: a specific *configuration* of voices," and it is dangerous to presume that the absence of a "first-person pronoun as an indicator of narratorial agency" signals the absence of a narrative voice, since "all narratives are narrated, even if no distinct *teller–persona* can be identified (either pronominally or by means of stylistic expressivity)."[70] Narrators reveal different stakes and levels of complicity in the events they narrate. Because these stakes are cued by the text but ultimately validated by the reader, they create the potential for myriad shades of meaning, all of which contribute to the structural tension in which a literary narrative's moral component may be located. In some instances, the narrator's voice may even evidence internal tension. Such is the case with Rieux, who anonymously narrates *The Plague* until the epidemic wanes and he chooses to expose his identity. The experience of learning that the text's narrator had such an intense personal involvement with the crisis in Oran allows the reader to reconsider the objectivity of the narratorial report. In the act of reconsideration, the reader may subsequently add interpretive possibilities to those gleaned in the course of the first reading.

If readers carry some knowledge of a narrative's author into the process of literary interpretation, they may also find overt traces of the author's own theoretical voice represented somewhere in the text, whether directly through the voice of a single literary character, dispersed among the voices of several characters, or both.[71] It is possible to read Rieux as directly expressing Camus's resistance sympathies. Dostoevsky can be said to refigure his complex attitude toward religious faith in *The Idiot*'s dialogue between characters like Prince Myshkin and Rogozhin. Knowing something of Mann's ambivalence toward his brother Heinrich's penchant for using art to express political agenda sheds some light on the frequently self-contradictory ethics of Settembrini, who rhetorically extols a virtue that he has trouble translating into material practice. Authorial presence in textual voices complicates the import of a literary narrative and helps prevent the reader from reducing a text's moral component to a monologic position.

Furthermore, criticisms and evaluations of a literary narrative, if assimilated by readers before they actually read the text in question, may influence the process of reading in the form of any number of informing and directive voices on which readers may go so far as to confer authoritative status.[72] How many readers of *The Idiot* have scorned Petersburg society for crucifying its savior Myshkin without ascribing at least some of the responsibility for his ostensible pedagogic failure to the prince himself, because they were following the interpretive biases of some of the novel's earliest critics, who were themselves naïvely wedded to Dostoevsky's vision of Myshkin as a perfectly beautiful soul? That critics' authority can powerfully influence the reception of a literary narrative can also be seen in the majority of early writing on *The Plague,* which, after the seminal dismissal of the text's moral component by Roland Barthes and Jean-Paul Sartre, reproduces the contention that Camus deflects moral responsibility in the text by naturalizing evil.

Of course, even if readers are not aware of extant critical and interpretive work on a specific narrative, they are nevertheless reading that narrative through a critical sensibility that has been informed by a host of other evaluative structures. These structures may be categorized, somewhat broadly, as the ideological filters by which they have been interpolated in

specific historically conditioned and contingent contexts. Satan and Kurtz
are likely to be read, by critics informed by the same Western ideological
determinants, as representing conventionally different kinds of evil. But
Kurtz himself may be read at least either as the quintessential imperialist
or as a psychologically shattered apostate who has renounced the Western
imperialist dogma of "conquest in the name of progress." Different interpretive contexts and predispositions yield different interpretations, all of
which are valid data for criticism that attempts to make nonreductive
sense of a novel's moral dimension.

However monologic any of the above voices may seem, they are all
nevertheless overdetermined by what Bakhtin calls *"dialogic overtones,"* which
are a function of the context in which a voice speaks. In its context, a
speech-act reveals "traces of addressivity and the influence of the anticipated response, dialogical echoes from others' preceding utterances, faint
traces of changes of speech subjects that have furrowed the utterance from
within."[73] All of these voices have the potential to be pedagogic, but they
need not be entirely unreceptive to the morally instructive influence of
other voices with whom they are drawn into tension; they necessarily represent an ethical position, but the position they represent cannot always be
dismissed as monologic.[74]

A voice may be designated pedagogic from either a structural or a thematic perspective, or both. Thematically, certain voices are more instructive than others insofar as they contribute to what an ethical reading might
judge to be a literary narrative's dominant moral tenor. These voices may
typically convert other characters from one ethical position to another, as
in the way Marlow follows Kurtz's pedagogic example and at first views
with horror the London to which he returns. They may also be endorsed
by a narratorial presence in whom the reader has invested trust, much like
the morally inconclusive Marlow in *Lord Jim* may appear more trustwor-
thy after his unresolved moral crisis in *Heart of Darkness*. However, as the
readings in the following chapters suggest, it is quite possible to make
critical judgments regarding the structures of a text's pedagogic component without affording exclusive attention to the voices' thematic import,
this because a literary narrative's moral and morally instructive dimensions may be accessed and investigated as profitably through its moral
structures as through its moral themes. Structurally, the signifying mechanism of any voice that enters into the process of producing textual meaning

can be morally instructive to other characters and to the reader in that the way a voice signifies provides a particular model for the foundation and expression of ethical truth claims.

In general theoretical terms, a character's voice can signify either constitutively or referentially. The distinction between these modes of signification is neatly explained by Sandy Petrey, who invokes J. L. Austin's concept of speech acts. According to Petrey, for whom the word "constative" is synonymous with "constitutive," "the referential is the language of objective reality, the constative that of social convention." Referential language purports to describe the world in clear-cut terms of true and false, fact and fiction, because it claims for its denotative authority an absolute correspondence between an independent, objective ontological reality and the lexicon that signifies that reality. In referential signification, signs reflect the condition they articulate; the ontological condition itself is not much open to debate except for the discovery of the correct word to articulate it. Referential signification is not arbitrary but "inalienable." Referential signification thus can, and often does, assume a monologic, dogmatic representational power that forestalls the kind of critical and interpretive dialogue that I find necessary for a responsible ethical criticism.[75]

In constitutive signification, meaning is historically, not eternally, determined. On the constitutive model, words do not describe an eternally fixed, ontologically independent reality; rather, they stimulate a contextual interpretation of a referent, which may be designated as factual if the proper protocols of social performance, of public opinion, are realized. Constitutive facts, if the phrase may be admitted, are provisional, entirely dependent for their authority on "the sociohistorically variable conventions recognized by those for whom the constative is factual."[76] The epistemological claims deriving from constitutive language do not propose to be absolutely certain. Hence, they are open to discussion in a responsible ethical criticism.

Pedagogic voices that operate on a constitutive model of signification do not try to mask their shortcomings, internal inconsistencies, contradictions, and methodological limitations; they do not approach moral reflection as a reductive either/or operation; they are reluctant to claim authority for their ideological biases and predispositions, even though such a gesture would probably reduce painful moral anxiety; they are conscious of the historical pressures underpinning moral speculation; and they reflect the novel's generic characteristic of foregrounding the temporal contingencies that inform values and linguistic signification.

The interpretive chapters that follow elaborate strong models of constitutive pedagogic voices, several of which may be briefly delineated here. In *The Magic Mountain,* Hans Castorp does not univocally endorse any of the many and disparate ethical positions to which he is exposed while at the Berghof, and when he acts on the promptings of his moral consciousness, the text admits no single reason why he makes the decisions he makes. In *Heart of Darkness,* Marlow, prompted by the inconsistencies he witnesses in European social, political, and economic relations, maintains a painful relationship to what he perceives as the brutalities of capitalist ethics, despite the fact that his concession to these ethics would likely diminish his moral anxiety. In *The Plague,* Rieux's insistence that the town officials refer to the plague as plague, so that the appropriate legislation can be drafted to fight it, demonstrates his sensitivity to the material underpinnings of linguistic meaning.

In contrast to the constitutive, referential pedagogic voices presume to represent an absolute standard of morality; they characteristically eliminate the impression of ideological tension from their ethical positions, which are subsequently conveyed monologically and authoritatively; they affect a correspondence between unconditionally conceived abstract ideals and the socially determined, materially contingent contexts into which these ideals must always be expressed; and they vindicate their ethical claims according to atemporal, ahistorical foundations in order to reproduce the literally incarnationist operation through which language possesses a natural, organic, essential relationship to its object.

Constitutive pedagogic voices are likely to appear in literature more frequently than those voices that operate on a referential model of signification. I suspect the reason for this disparity inheres in the temporal logic of narrative, in which a historically contingent moral voice would arguably function more felicitously. However, by turns, both Settembrini and Naphta espouse ethical positions that each believes must be endorsed by all of humankind for the sake of its salvation. In *Lord Jim*, Jim appears to conduct himself according to an abstract moral code into which the more historically sensitive Marlow has little prolonged insight. Perhaps the most consistent exemplar of a referential pedagogic voice in these chapters is Myshkin; juxtaposed with the dynamism of Petersburg's chaotic inventory of materially contingent ethical positions, the transcendent foundation of the prince's moral voice is baldly exposed.

The structural example of a pedagogic voice that acknowledges its historical determinants supports the interpretive principle that there can be no final reductive word on a text's meaning. Such a statement may not seem all that controversial. But the purportedly referential, monologic signifying mechanism of irresponsible ethical criticism has very often been taken by ethical criticism's detractors as an invalid presumption of exegetical authority on a text's moral "lesson," based on which all ethical criticism is peremptorily dismissed. Since literary characters whose pedagogic voices seek legitimation by referring to absolute moral standards are conventionally undermined by the temporal pressures underscored by the logic of narrative, I draw the conclusion that they are often less pedagogically effective than literary characters whose pedagogic voices are sensitive to temporal pressures. This is not to say that all voices appealing to absolute ethical claims *via* linguistic correspondence are pedagogically impotent. As the example of Myshkin will show, a referential signifying mechanism that does not effectively indoctrinate other characters in transcendent, atemporal values can nonetheless provide a formidable structural model of how *not* to investigate, develop, or pronounce upon moral concepts. In short, such voices teach through what is characteristically their failure.

This conclusion about the internal tension necessary to a literary character's pedagogically effective ethical voice can—and perhaps must—also be applied to the voice of the ethical literary critic. In the act of interpretation, ethical critics read texts through a web of ideological structures that are historically determined. Critical judgment is therefore the expression of a temporally inflected process, not of an absolutely predetermined product. Neither the act nor the product of ethical reading can ever transcend the critical dialogues in which each finds itself. Indeed, no critical practice or product can. If, in fact, there is an outstanding precedent for an ethical criticism that monologizes the validity of its method and of the knowledge it produces, the very existence of my present theoretical claims about the possibility of nonmonologic, nonreductive ethical readings might be read as a testament to the historical contingency of textual practice: new historical context, new precedent.

Just as an analysis of the tensions *within* an individual character's pedagogic voice can be a morally instructive critical enterprise, so can an analysis of the tensions *among* competing pedagogic voices in a literary narrative's dialogue. Dialogue serves as another morally instructive structure because it underscores temporal contingencies that maintain tension among voices. Bakhtin furnishes a seminal statement on dialogue as a foundational structural feature of the novel:

> The novel orchestrates all its themes, the totality of the world of objects and ideas depicted and expressed in it, by means of the social diversity of speech types [*raznorecie*] and by the differing individual voices that flourish under such conditions. Authorial speech, the speeches of narrators, inserted genres, the speech of characters are merely those fundamental compositional unities with whose help heteroglossia [*raznorecie*] can enter the novel; each of them permits a multiplicity of social voices and a wide variety of their links and interrelationships (always more or less dialogized). These distinctive links and interrelationships between utterances and languages, this movement of the theme through different languages and speech types, its dispersion into the rivulets and droplets of social heteroglossia, its dialogization—this is the basic distinguishing feature of the stylistics of the novel.[77]

On my appropriation of Bakhtin, moral dialogue is informed by an array of pedagogic voices reflecting a broad range of ethical positions, from those that appeal to absolute moral codes and standards to those that affirm the historicity of knowledge production and ethical truth claims.

Within the dynamic of a text's moral dialogue, pedagogic voices frequently compete for privilege in the moral consciousness of other textual characters and of the text's readers. To recall David Parker, in the textual world of a literary narrative, characters take themselves as seriously as human beings do in the material world. World literature surely has its share of buffoonish figures; so does the human community. But when Settembrini and Naphta wage their rhetorical battle for the sake of Hans Castorp's approbation, they battle in earnest, as seduced by the validity of their own ethical positions as they hope to be seductive. Nor is it merely a felicitous coincidence that Marlow does not burst into laughter when Kurtz pronounces on the horror of the world. And it would seem unreasonable to argue that in no instance should readers allow themselves to be persuaded by literary characters who are themselves persuasive in their respective fictional worlds.

If moral development requires an acknowledgment of the way temporal contingencies force subjects to revaluate their commitments to moral reflection and ethical claims, then a reader who incorporates the moral import of a literary narrative's moral dialogue into his or her consciousness incorporates ethical options. The range of ethical options generated by moral dialogue constitutes one of the most intriguing features of the process of reading novels. There are times in *The Idiot* when Myshkin's implacable expressions of kindness evince empathy, and times when they evince confusion, perhaps even consternation. Similarly, Totsky's treatment of Nastasya Filippovna may seem reprehensible, commendable, or both, depending on the way the reader's sympathies toward each character develop during the reading process. The critically engaged reader of Dostoevsky's text may confer a value on any or all of these behaviors. None need be taken as the exclusive way to behave when confronted with a similar situation in the human community; however, any may be recalled to inform a particular moral choice at a particular historical moment.

Moral dialogue provides an aesthetic paradigm for the way moral consciousness may be developed and nourished in the competition among ethical positions. Thus, Marlow's moral consciousness does not uncritically capitulate to capitalist ethics because, his episodic contact with frank imperialist apologists notwithstanding, he also enters into dialogue with pedagogic characters like Kurtz, Stein, and Jim, all of whom represent more problematic relationships to capitalist values. And *The Plague* illustrates the way even characters with the same basic sense of human responsibility express their commitment in different and evolving ways as a result of the idiosyncratic material and ideological pressures by which they are informed. In these and instances to follow, moral consciousness is shown to be the product of temporal contingencies, in response to which the reader's own moral consciousness evolves in the material world. Moral dialogue is thus literary narrative's structural analogue for ethical criticism, for it provides a locus of tension from which moral instruction may be gleaned in the act of reading. Following the aesthetic structure of moral dialogue in literary narrative, responsible ethical readings do not attempt to reduce the ideological conflicts among pedagogic voices, since these conflicts may be assimilated and refined into a methodological principle for producing contingent ethical truth claims in the material world.

Rather, responsible ethical readings investigate the aesthetic dynamics through which specific ethical questions, resolutions, and further techniques for moral instruction may be shown to emerge. Put another way, responsible ethical criticism can use the example of moral dialogue among pedagogic voices for instruction, not so much on what to think is right and/or wrong, but on how to foreground the historical and methodological contingencies that contribute to all knowledge production, including that which pertains to morality. So when we see Myshkin's pedagogic voice hover on the fringe of *The Idiot*'s moral dialogue, we might be as much impressed by his inability to convey his ethic conclusively as we are by the skill with which other characters in Dostoevsky's novel participate in moral debate.

As an exceptionally monologic voice in a textual world that is unable to perform such a voice's power, Myshkin could be read as a representative of reductive ethical criticism. Fundamentally incapable of adjusting his ethical voice to historical demands, taking *his* values as *the* values, his mode of moral signification appears in stark contrast to that of his interlocutors, who understand that the validity of truth claims depends on material circumstances. Since circumstances can always change, so can what interpretive communities perceive as the truth. This is neither good nor bad; it is simply a basic premise underwriting the production of knowledge in any consciousness that concedes its status as a being in time. Subsequently, it becomes crucial that the processes whereby interpretive communities solidify their truths are as thoroughly understood as possible.

For literary theorists, critics, and exegetes, the instructive potential of an aesthetics of morality might immediately be realized if the dialogue among competing pedagogic voices comes to stand as a model for the theoretical and interpretive dialogue among those engaged with the study of literary narratives. An ethical reading of pedagogic voice and moral dialogue could, to recall Bialostosky, responsibly place its own voice into dialogue with other methodological voices to introduce a narrative of the manner in which context informs the history of interpretation of literary texts. Such a process would thus effectively make concrete my theoretical considerations on an aesthetics of morality designed to elaborate a method of ethical critique that answers the most vehement objections of the tradition's detractors.

2

History and Pedagogic Voice in *The Magic Mountain*

■

The important thing for me, then, is not the "work," but my life.
Life is not the means for the achievement of an esthetic ideal of
perfection; on the contrary, the work is an ethical symbol of life.
Thomas Mann, *Reflections of a Non-Political Man*

On August 3, 1915, Thomas Mann wrote a letter to Paul Amann in which he explained his conception of the narrative that would eventually become *The Magic Mountain*. Part of that letter reads as follows: "Before the war I had begun a longish story whose scene was a sanatorium for tuberculosis in the high mountains—a story with pedagogic and political overtones, in which a young man comes up against the most seductive of powers, death, and runs the gauntlet, in a comic-gruesome manner, of the intellectual polarities of Humanism and Romanticism, progress and reaction, health and disease; but not so much that he may be forced to decide, as for the sake of orientation and general enlightenment."[1] On the same day, Mann expressed his intention to put aside his work on the fiction and begin composing a political treatise that would defend Germany's conservative ideology against its wartime opponents.[2] He began this treatise in November 1915, and by March 1918 it had swelled into *Reflections of a Non-Political Man,* a monograph of more than four hundred pages.

In the eighth of twelve chapters, entitled "On Virtue," Mann again referred to his temporarily postponed sanatorium tale: "Before the war I had begun to write a little novel, a type of pedagogical story, in which a young person, landed in a morally dangerous locale, found himself between two equally quaint educators, between an Italian literary man, humanist, rhetorician and man of progress, and a somewhat disreputable mystic, reactionary, and advocate of antireason—he had the choice, the good youngster, between the powers of virtue and of seduction, between duty and service to life and the fascination of decay, for which he was not unreceptive."[3]

In the two and a half years it took to compose *Reflections,* Mann's attitude toward his sanatorium story underwent significant changes. What he once described as a "longish tale," he now directly called a novel. The hero of the tale had evolved from a passive receptor of others' ideas into a character expected to choose among them. Most tellingly, a moral dimension had emerged into the foreground of Mann's perception of the text. By 1918, Mann clearly maintained the plan for a pedagogic novel in which a target character would be exposed to the dialogue among a number of ethical positions that he would, of his own volition, assimilate to greater or lesser degree.

Not simply for its reference to *The Magic Mountain*'s genesis is *Reflections* valuable to a study of literary narrative's expression of pedagogic voice and moral dialogue. The relationship between the two texts might be synopsized thus: the moral tenor of *Reflections* informed *The Magic Mountain*'s moral dialogue as much as the events of the war determined the moral tenor of *Reflections.* Both stand as material inscriptions of Mann's interior dialogue regarding the moral repercussions of the historical events prior to the First World War: much of Mann's overt moralizing in *Reflections* becomes woven into the ideological fabric of the novel.[4]

The dispersal of ideas, from treatise to a record of competing ethical voices to which Hans Castorp's moral consciousness is exposed,[5] helps forestall the charge, frequently brought against novels with a predominantly philosophical content, that *The Magic Mountain* is a "failed" piece of fiction because it is too pedantic, too preachy, too dogmatic. Such charges are usually made possible when the pedagogic novel as a literary form is defined so as to be confused with the philosophical novel. For example, Hermann Wiegand writes, rather symptomatically, that the pedagogic genre "is always concerned with a very specific sort of education—an education that sets out to mould the plastic personality of a child along lines determined by its educators; and the process of education is pronounced complete when the youthful personality has come to conform dependably to the moral pattern that represents the educator's ideal."[6]

Critics of both the philosophical and the pedagogic novel underscore the final phrase of this definition, with its emphasis on "the" moral pattern, to dismiss the entire genre for using a convenient, familiar literary form to proselytize an audience with an inviolable moral lesson. While this may in fact be the case with some fiction—Sartre's *Nausea* and Rand's *The Fountainhead* come immediately to mind—*The Magic Mountain* stands outside the purview of this kind of dismissal precisely by virtue of its not being *Reflections*. In *Reflections*, Mann may, as his English translator suggests, grow into knowledge as his monograph progresses; but when the text concludes, it is fairly certain which educator's ideal moral pattern is expected to serve as the standard for a Europe that has lost its way.

"The" ideal moral pattern does not exist at all in *The Magic Mountain*. There is no exclusive ethical position to be represented in a target character. Least of all is Mann's own authorial voice easily isolated from the other characters' voices and brought forth as the ideal, even though *The Magic Mountain*'s moral dialogue is intimately informed by the moral speculations elaborated in *Reflections*. The fact that Mann's moral position in *Reflections* is not simply inserted into *The Magic Mountain* as an authoritative narrative voice prompts several important questions: How is Mann's discussion of ethics in *Reflections* redacted in *The Magic Mountain*? If we grant that Mann is speaking in his political monograph, where is his voice in the novel? Moreover, how does the actual dialogue—so crucial to the ethical dynamics of literary narrative—between *Reflections* and *The Magic Mountain* inform the ethically pedagogic voices of characters like Settembrini and Naphta? Finally, how can pursuing answers to these questions assist in the development of a nonreductive ethical criticism?

The moral climate of *The Magic Mountain* develops in the dialogue between competing ethical voices and, as such, is not guilty of bald, monologic sermonizing. The inflection of Mann's ethical voice from *Reflections* must therefore be supplemented in some way by additional voices that originate somewhere other than in the wartime monograph; we can expect these supplementary voices to have some influence over Hans Castorp. Furthermore, when Hans Castorp finally leaves the sanatorium, he acts on an ethical imperative that has ineluctably emerged from the array of values to which he has been exposed. How is the reader to describe this imperative? Is it finally the same lesson that Mann preached in *Reflections*? If so, is the reader to share Hans Castorp's final ethical conviction, as Mann would have wanted his readers of *Reflections* to share his own ethical principles? If it is not the same lesson that Mann preached in *Reflections*, then it must be some combination of the novel's different ethical ideals. It must be *a* moral pattern generated by the novel's pedagogic dialogue, not *the* moral pattern foisted authorially by Mann as ideal educator. In this case, what clues does the text offer to suggest that Hans Castorp's moral development is progressing in a particular way? Put simply, what are the aesthetics of *The Magic Mountain*'s morality, and how do they illustrate pedagogic voice as an ethically loaded textual structure?

Mann's attitudes toward both the moral dimension and the morally instructive capacity of aesthetics are most directly expressed in *Reflections*. These attitudes, which empower much of the pedagogy of, and dialogue between, both Settembrini and Naphta, never clearly theorize either the moral or the aesthetic obligations of the artist or the work of art. In *The Magic Mountain,* they also undergo transformation in the growing surrender of form to formlessness,[7] of the Absolute to the particular and contingent, of an aestheticized to an ethically charged conception of the world. The pedagogic dimension of *The Magic Mountain* is moreover informed by an overarching logic of historical urgency, a logic that Mann tries to repress until the very last chapters of *Reflections*. A sense of the inevitability of history itself becomes a formidable ethically pedagogic voice in the novel's moral dialogue. A knowledge of history's implacable reality exists in Hans Castorp's moral unconscious, for a time lies dormant in the interstices of Settembrini and Naphta's polemics, is aroused by Clavdia Chauchat, and emerges in full voice with the late arrival on the mountain of Mynheer Peeperkorn. It also gains strength in the narrator's persistent reflections on time that form a consistent intertext in *The Magic Mountain*'s moral dialogue.

Early in the "Prologue" of his *Reflections*, Thomas Mann calls "conscientiousness" the common denominator of his wartime writings (*RNM*, 5). As he defines it, conscientiousness is a "moral-artistic" quality that borders on the pedantic (*RNM*, 5). Of pedantry as an artistic quality, Mann is by turns disapproving and tolerant.[8] In his stance against the European literary man—or *Zivilisationsliterat*—whom he will severely criticize as the enemy of German culture, Mann is willing to bring out many of the polemical guns in his considerable rhetorical arsenal. Yet his distaste for the *Zivilisationsliterat*'s revolutionary program for art, a pedantic blurring of the distinction between artistic and political expression to serve an ethical agenda, stands to balance his tolerance for his own tendentious position in *Reflections*. This is a deep contradiction in the wartime writings, one whose

material determinants Georg Lukács traces to Mann's ethically contradictory role as critic and defender of Prussian culture (*RNM*, 26). This contradiction is also a product of Mann's inability to articulate a conclusive
conception of the artist that is finally distinct from the *Zivilisationsliterat* at
the same time that it accounts for both the aesthetic and the ethical obligations attending the role of creator. Contributing to Mann's ambivalence
toward the revolutionary potential of art was Mann's identification of his
own brother, Heinrich, with the figure of the *Zivilisationsliterat*.[9]

One might reasonably suspect that Thomas had a difficult time reconciling himself to what he perceived as Heinrich's betrayal of conservative
Prussian values; and yet, to renounce his own brother on the basis of
ideological disagreement could itself be interpreted as merely a different
manifestation of the same kind of betrayal. Throughout *Reflections*, Heinrich is therefore present as an absent interlocutor, in dialogue with whom
Thomas elaborates the character of the *Zivilisationsliterat* who will subsequently inform the moral dialogue of *The Magic Mountain*.

Recalling one of his articles that had been published in *März,* Mann
writes of the *Zivilisationsliterat*:

> Nothing, I said, was more indicative of the literary disposition than
> the twofold and basically only uniform activity of those humanitarian
> journalists of the time of the Enlightenment, who, in criminological-
> political writings, summoned society to the forum of humanity, who
> educated their contemporaries to despise the barbarisms in the adminis-
> tration of justice, to be against torture and capital punishment, and who
> paved the way for milder laws—and who characteristically made names
> for themselves at the same time by pedagogical writings on language and
> style and by treatises on the art of writing. Love of mankind and the art
> of writing as the dominant passions of one soul: this meant something;
> not by chance were these two passions found together. To write beauti-
> fully meant almost to think beautifully, and from there it was not far to
> beautiful deeds. All the moral improvement of the human race—this
> could be demonstrated—came from the spirit of literature, and even the
> popular teachers of antiquity considered the beautiful word to be the
> father of good deeds. What a sermon! (*RNM*, 69)

In *The Magic Mountain,* the European *Zivilisationsliterat* will come to
serve as the ideological model for Ludovico Settembrini, who often repeats
word for word the kind of Enlightenment humanism that Mann summarizes

above. But Mann's characterization of the *Zivilisationsliterat* is also the point of departure for his own self–characterization, which, as might be expected, he holds as the ethical standard for the aesthete as artist. Mann essentially objects to the *Zivilisationsliterat*'s ideology on moral grounds. His anger is directed against "the shamelessness with which the intellectual politician decrees the identity of politics and morality, against the arrogance with which he denies and slanders every morality that seeks to answer the question of human nature in another, more psychological way than that of politics—that uncultivated, I mean: un–Germanly cultivated arrogance that reviles everything that is not politics as estheticism" (*RNM*, 417–18).

Among these intellectual politicians, he particularly counts artists like his brother, who were broadsiding German culture with accusations of inhumanity and were trying to make art a propagandistic instrument of social change. For Mann, this was the gravest sin of all; it vitiated the aesthetic integrity of art in the name of an historical, political cause: "An artist who misunderstood his special and ironic type of leadership in such a way that he understood it to be directly political and began to act accordingly would fall victim to self-righteousness and moral security, to an insufferable pose of virtue—the result would be the emergence of a philistinism of respectability and a schoolmasterly attitude toward the people that would doubtlessly be followed directly by artistic ruin" (*RNM*, 425).

For several hundred pages in *Reflections*, Mann labors to differentiate between the political aesthete, who is synonymous with the *Zivilisationsliterat*, and what might be called the moral aesthete, who stands as the former's foil. Elaborating the moral aesthete, Mann adopts Lukács as "his" critic[10] and praises Lukács's paradigm for the burgherly artistic nature: "'Burgherly calling as a life form,' Lukács writes, 'means first of all the primacy of ethics in life.' . . . That primacy of ethics in life of which the critic speaks—does it not signify the predominance of ethics over *esthetics*? . . . An artist is burgherly when he transfers the ethical characteristics of the burgherly way of life . . . to the exercise of art" (*RNM*, 72–73). Mann identifies an ethical dimension in art that determines the form of the art itself, and he calls "this mixture of artistry and burgherly nature . . . the actual German variation of European estheticism, the German *l'art pour l'art*" (*RNM*, 72).

By way of demonstrating that aesthetic purity is the foremost standard of moral discipline for the artist, Mann even calls down his scorn, more often reserved for Zola in *Reflections,* on Beethoven and Wagner, for whom he generally has the deepest admiration both as composers and as German men of genius. As representatives of the nineteenth century, each was guilty at some point in his career of "rais[ing] his artistical-democratic massiveness to political self–consciousness, and beg[inning] to interpret it in a virtuous-agitative way" (*RNM*, 375). In Mann's view, the nineteenth century was a time of unparalleled artistic indiscretion: "One should not confuse desire with imagination, political with artistic imagination, just to flatter the spirit of the times—that spirit of the times that announces in the revues that the esthetic epoch is at an end and that belief is the order of the day. . . . I do not say that unbelief makes the artist. But when one says to me that belief makes him, then I reject this as *ideological impudence*" (*RNM*, 376). Concluding this characterization of the *Zivilisationsliterat,* Mann asserts: "There you have him, the politicized esthete, the poetic seducer of the people, the blasphemer of the people, the libertine of rhetorical enthusiasm, the belles-lettres-politician, the dago of the intellect, the miles gloriosus of democratic 'humanity'" (*RNM*, 426).

One cannot help but approach the character of Settembrini as a locus of moral dialogue after reading some of these phrases in their context, not because Mann was so hostile toward the figure of the literary humanist in wartime Europe, but because Mann was so close to reproducing the same kind of moral transgression of aesthetics for which he indicted the *Zivilisationsliterat*. What else is *Reflections* but a document of the deepest moral engagement with world sociohistoric forces? What else is it but a passionate plea designed to inspire a solidification of national-political consciousness? If Mann could label the *Zivilisationsliterat*'s philosophy of artistic production as ideologically impudent, one might not be wrong in labeling Mann's philosophy of artistic production as ideologically ambiguous, for in *Reflections* he wavers in choosing whether art is to have a greater political or moral function.

The project Mann espouses for his moral aesthete is nothing less than an ethics of art. But pedagogic momentum inheres in the art of the moral aesthete as much as in the art of the political aesthete. The principles used to determine artistic form, whatever those principles may be, must be chosen according to some standard of adequacy or correctness. Erich Heller describes Mann's standard as "the lived belief that aesthetic sensations which are not 'contained' by life as its organic refinements are ethically

utterly dubious and a debasement of life and art alike."[11] To fulfill this standard is always to say, "given this context, this is right." Only if an artist
were to succeed, as Flaubert professed to have tried, in creating a work
that "said" nothing, could that "right" be measured solely in aesthetic
terms. But if a purely aesthetic litmus for the success or failure of a work
of art is not forthcoming, then might one not unreasonably ask how the
political and the moral aesthete differ? How is Mann different from the
Zivilisationsliterat of whom he is so dismissive?

The difference is fundamentally a matter of the manner in which the
artist conscientiously tries to impress a moral idea by means of an aesthetic
medium: Mann's moral aesthete is the *Zivilisationsliterat* without the dogmatic, propagandistic edge. Acutely sensitive to criticism portraying him
as a "ruthless, parasitic esthete" (*RNM*, 397), Mann is careful to indicate
that what he has always sought throughout his literary career, whether in
his own or others' work, "was ethics, was morality; and it was art that had
a moral emphasis, that was bound up with morality, that I looked up to,
that I perceived as *my* sphere, as what was proper for me, as what had
always been familiar to me" (*RNM*, 396).

Whereas the political aesthete makes art the vehicle for monologic
rhetoric aimed at instructing an audience in what it *should* know, Mann
explains the moral aesthete's goal as the presentation of material in such a
way as to make the audience more active in the production of textual
meaning. As Heller puts it, "The morality of what Thomas Mann calls aestheticism lies in the conscientious contemplation of what is, not of what
might be enjoyed or might be done. . . . His ethics, therefore, are the ethics
of 'being,' not the morals of 'doing.'"[12] In such a technique, "ethics is pre-
dominant over esthetics, or more correctly: a mixture and equation of
these concepts appears that honors, loves, and cares for *the ugly*. For ugli-
ness, sickness, and decadence *are ethics*" (*RNM*, 74).

Stressing the ugly as that which would be ignored by the *Zivilisationsliterat,* Mann's account of the morality of art is tantamount to the accurate
and fair representation of the widest possible spectrum of human experience.[13] When the artist accomplishes his task correctly, a moral engagement with the text is compelled by the text itself, not by the artist.[14] To
press his point, Mann cites Goethe's dictum that "a good work of art can
and will have moral consequences, but to demand moral intentions from
the artist is to ruin his work" (*RNM*, 229). In this way, art can be faithful

to its aesthetic demands and still reflect a moral dimension that is not necessarily politically loaded; the political and the moral aesthete can remain distinct entities, and Mann need not fear being numbered among the former.

Until the final two chapters of *Reflections,* Mann seems satisfied with his image of a literary figure who manipulates moral and aesthetic responsibility into a balance that is not ideologically self-serving. Then comes the peremptory announcement:

> In these pages, I seem to have accepted and adopted as my own the antithesis of political or politicized art, and the art of estheticism. But that was a game; for seriously, I know better what the nature of this antithesis is, I know that it rests on a desired, nobly desired, self-deception that has gradually become all too successful for the one who decrees it, that it is wrong, that it does not exist, that one need not be an esthete *when one does not believe in politics,* but that one can, as a "serving" social-moralist and herald of resolute love of mankind, remain an arch-esthete. (*RNM,* 401, emphasis added)

On this disclaimer, it becomes easy to speculate on what has happened to Mann's complex position on art and ideology over the long course of writing the *Reflections.* The ideological ambiguity of his earlier condemnation of the *Zivilisationsliterat* is in part dispelled by the realization that many of the values to which he holds fast are belied by the way *Reflections* is taking shape as a response to the moment's historical exigencies.[15] For example, when Mann "perceives in the strangely organic, unforced and poetic word combination, *deutsches Volk,* something not only national, but also essentially different, better, higher, purer, yes, holier than in the expression, 'English people,' or 'French people'" (*RNM,* 267), his rhetoric is unabashedly propagandistic.

Aware that he is propounding an aesthetic that cannot quite transcend its material coordinates, Mann never ceases to imply that he does not believe in politics; however, with the nearly completed *Reflections* lying before him, he concedes that not believing in politics is not the same as not being political. The immediate material conditions of the war have evoked this document from Mann when he presumably would rather have been working on his sanatorium story. Mann, the moral aesthete, bears the imprint of Mann the political aesthete; *Reflections* corroborates both personae. Mann's summary conclusion that "the assertion that politicized art is the exact opposite of estheticized art must accordingly be considered by us as finally refuted" (*RNM*, 415) acknowledges the pressures of history with an appropriate transformation of consciousness.

In *Reflections,* Mann is concerned with establishing a morality of artistic creation whereby he appears as an artist who is politically disinterested in the presentation of lived experience. As he comprehends that history and politics are inextricable and ethically charged, he retreats from his position of hermetic aestheticism and confesses to the political complicity inherent in his vocation. In an unusual arrangement, Mann thus becomes the purveyor of, target for, and respondent to, his own pedagogic voice in *Reflections*: intending to convince his readers of one thing, he ends up convincing himself of something entirely different. On the model of ethical criticism presented in the first chapter, Mann's reflections on the relationship between aesthetics and morality thus do nothing if not maintain the kind of structural dialogue that makes ethical literary criticism a viable and responsible textual practice. This internal dialogue is then dispersed among *The Magic Mountain*'s pedagogic characters and, in the case of Settembrini, informs the Italian humanist's somewhat self-contradictory ethical voice.

One of the underlying themes of *Reflections* is Mann's gradual acknowledgment that moral thinking must accommodate temporal pressures; thus, the theme is the expression of a structural principle, and this principle subsequently becomes the source for a compelling pedagogic voice in *The Magic Mountain.* I have called this the voice of history, the record of conflicting social forces outside of which no lived human existence is ever possible. However, the sanatorium Haus Berghof is an environment whose function is to convince all but the most critical that such an atemporal life is possible. This is why, for most of the mountain's denizens, morality is a rather empty term. An ethics has no real value unless it is lived, that is, used to justify choice. The idea of choice is a consequence of the pressure to negotiate change in experience. Time is the record of change. And it is precisely time, as the record of change, that is all but absent on the mountain, whose surface spirit is aestheticism run amuck.

Because he gradually recognizes the reality of historical pressure in *Reflections,* Mann also stands as a model for Hans Castorp, who is for a time seduced by the spirit of the mountain, only to return to the "flatland" below when the war erupts. The reasons for Hans Castorp's departure from the Berghof are never conclusively clarified at the end of the novel, but they are the product of the many ethically pedagogic voices that act on his consciousness, stripping away the illusion of the mountain's place outside time and intensifying his historically contingent moral sensibility.[16] Among *The Magic Mountain*'s four major pedagogic characters, each espouses a different degree of ethical investment in historical circumstances,[17] but they can be grouped, by way of an introduction to the novel's pedagogic dynamics, quite expediently as follows: Settembrini, with his rhetorical *bello stile,* and Leo Naphta, with his acute, shrill discourse both maintain a moral posture that is freighted with formal accoutrement but that never really demonstrates an active connection with historical conditions away from the mountain. Both men are supremely gifted speakers, and they are more concerned with sounding persuasive than with acting in a morally instructive manner. Even when they do act, it is more to protect the formal conventions that empower rhetorical brilliance than to defend a lived ethical principle. Theirs, albeit in individual configurations, is a highly stylized moral consciousness analogous to Mann's, the moral aesthete of the early chapters of *Reflections,* who eventually aligns the moral with the political.

Opposite the primarily spoken values of Settembrini and Naphta is the pedagogic example of Clavdia Chauchat and her companion, Mynheer Peeperkorn. Chauchat and Peeperkorn approach the tension between morality and aesthetics by making life the first premise of existence, even at the expense of life's finer formal trappings. Chauchat's egregious "slackness," her concession to the life-giving power of "sin," and Peeperkorn's drunken unwieldiness express the formlessness that serves to answer Settembrini's and Naphta's aestheticized conception of morality. Theirs is the passion for life fulfilled through demonstrations of love and human solidarity. Their pedagogic voices are least effective if effectiveness is measured as rhetorical competence. Chauchat's speech is quirky and distracted, and Mann removes her entirely from the arena of generally accessible dialogue when he has her speak nearly entirely in French during her climactic scene with Hans Castorp. For his part, Peeperkorn can barely finish a sentence in any language. One characteristic that they do share with their more cerebral "inmates" is that they are both from the "'non-German' sphere."[18] The ethical positions that they represent thus differ from Settembrini's and Naphta's not only in theme, but also in structure and historical foundation.

Hans Castorp's own ethical ideology at the beginning of the novel is described in an extended authorial meditation on the reciprocity between history and consciousness:

> A man lives not only his personal life, as an individual, but also, consciously or unconsciously, the life of his epoch and his contemporaries. He may regard the general, impersonal foundations of his existence as definitely settled and taken for granted, and be as far from assuming a critical attitude toward them as our good Hans Castorp really was; yet it is quite conceivable that he may none the less be vaguely conscious of the deficiencies of his epoch and find them prejudicial to his own moral well-being. All sorts of personal aims, ends, hopes, prospects, hover before the eyes of the individual, and out of these he derives the impulse to ambition and achievement. Now, if the life about him, if his own time seem, however outwardly stimulating, to be at bottom empty of such food for his aspirations; if he privately recognize it to be hopeless, viewless, helpless, opposing only a hollow silence to all the questions man puts, consciously or unconsciously, yet somehow puts, as to the final, absolute, and abstract meaning in all his efforts and activities; then, in such a case, a certain laming of the personality is bound to occur, the more inevitably the more upright the character in question; a sort of palsy, as it were, which may even extend from his spiritual and moral over into his physical and organic part. In an age that affords no satisfying answer to the eternal question of "Why?" "To what end?" a man who is capable of achievement over and above the average and expected modicum must be equipped either with a moral remoteness and single-mindedness which is rare indeed and of heroic mould, or else with an exceptionally robust vitality. Hans Castorp had neither the one nor the other of these; and thus he must be considered mediocre, though in an entirely honourable sense.[19]

This passage is important for several reasons. First, it consolidates the connection between ethical ideology and social relations, since even the most exceptional personalities must distinguish themselves against the historically common by remaining connected to it. Second, Hans Castorp's being stamped as incredibly average by the narrator is a contextual designation, as indicated by his eventual moral education on the mountain, where he is surrounded by a host of other mediocre personalities who remain ideologically static. That Hans Castorp can change his moral perspective strongly suggests that values are contingent upon circumstance: sensing prewar tensions while in the sanatorium, Hans Castorp modifies his thinking and supersedes his flatland mediocrity. Third, Hans Castorp's life in the flatland is not intellectually stimulating. In short, before he departs for the Haus Berghof, he is not an entirely untroubled member of the technical bourgeoisie.

The narrator goes to great lengths to demonstrate that Hans Castorp "comfortably, not without dignity . . . carrie[s] the weight of culture with which the governing upper class of the commercial city endowed its children" (*MM*, 31). When he studies away from home and regularly sends his shirts back to be cleaned, he justifies this expenditure with the obligatory shibboleth that "outside Hamburg nobody in the kingdom [knows] how to iron" (*MM*, 31). He is always meticulously groomed; his comportment is "beyond cavil," (*MM*, 31); and he is sensitive to certain little things that a member of the petite bourgeoisie might not find offensive. For example, "it [goes] against his grain to eat butter served in the piece instead of in little fluted balls" (*MM*, 31). It is expected that he will, like his forebears, mature into a political rôle charged with protecting Germany's conservative values.

Occupying the space of conservative ideology would seem to insulate Hans Castorp from social and economic instability. He appears to be the kind of moral aesthete Mann described in *Reflections* who is outside of political responsibility and, therefore, of historical engagement. But Hans Castorp is lacking the one prerequisite for a truly sensualized life of bourgeois comfort: since his parents died when he was very young and he was placed in the care of his Uncle James Tienapple, whose biological children will inherit his wealth, Hans Castorp's financial security is hardly guaranteed. Tienapple tells him, "If you want to be somebody here in this town and live as you have been brought up to, you'll have to earn a good bit more to put with [your interest]" (*MM*, 33). His need to work establishes one of the contradictions of his class status before he departs for the mountain.[20] Hans Castorp approaches the prospect of work with the greatest aesthetic respect: "Work was for him, in the nature of things, the most estimable attribute of life. . . . It was the principle by which one stood or fell, the Absolute of the time; it was, so to speak, its own justification" (*MM*, 34). Yet it does not agree with him: "He liked better to have his time free, not weighted with the leaden load of effort; lying spacious before him, not divided up by obstacles one had to grit one's teeth and conquer, one after the other" (*MM*, 34).

Hans Castorp's inchoate tendency toward reducing ideological tension in his life through the carefully choreographed reproduction of bourgeois manners clashes head-on with his need to make vocational decisions that will carry him, however reluctantly, into the realm of the political and ethical. Hence the emphasis on Hans Castorp's ethical and aesthetic baggage—he is not a morally neutral tabula rasa waiting to be shaped into the protégé of the first clever philosophical charlatan to come along— when he arrives on the mountain to visit his cousin, Joachim Ziemssen. Hans Castorp's bourgeois ideology is so carefully detailed at the beginning of the novel because his education on the mountain is the record of a progress of consciousness, and such progress is best measured when a point of departure is available.

Moreover, Mann conscientiously constructs *The Magic Mountain* in such a way that the reader of the novel ideally participates in the moral climate on the mountain through his identification with Hans Castorp. Mann enables the reader's identification with Hans Castorp by employing the literary structure he referred to as the *Leitmotiv*. In the essay "The Making of the Magic Mountain" appended to the Lowe-Porter edition, Mann describes the *Leitmotiv* as "the magic formula that works both ways, and links the past with the future, the future with the past. The *Leitmotiv* is the technique employed to preserve the inward unity and abiding presentness of the whole at each moment" (*MM*, 720). Weigand elaborates the *Leitmotiv* as "a focal point from which lines extend in a multitude of directions, linking a great variety of elements in a complex network of relations" before reiterating Mann's observation that it creates the illusion of narrative simultaneity: "Each time such a *Leitmotiv* is sounded, all its associated content stirs in the reader's mind and plays about the immediate theme like a series of overtones."[21] The *Leitmotiv* can seriously compromise the experience of narrative telos; it can make it seem as though there is no diegetic time in the sense of a nice, neatly ordered sequence of events on the "once upon a time . . . the end" paradigm. It can persuade the reader that he or she is temporally suspended, just as Hans Castorp feels suspended during much of his time at the cure. Sharing the same hermetic starting point, the reader and Hans Castorp can theoretically experience

the novel's moral dialogue together.[22] To read *The Magic Mountain* in this
way necessitates the performance of ethical criticism in the construction
of the text's meaning.

One of the first things Hans Castorp remarks, when he reaches the
sanatorium, is that the mountain's "air" has "no content," holds "no associ-
ations" for him (*MM*, 6). His cousin warns him that acclimatization may
take some time. Down below, Hans Castorp has been forced to accommodate historical pressures in which he would prefer to take no part. On
the mountain, these pressures do not appear to exist. It is natural that
Ziemssen would find a hermetic environment threatening; his desire to
serve his country in the infantry makes him an unapologetic participant in
social relations. But Hans Castorp would just as soon forget the imposition
that vocational responsibility will make on his energies once his holiday is
at an end. Since the mountain pretends to elide historical considerations,
Hans Castorp can suppress his deeply ambivalent feelings toward his class
position. Since he "incline[s] to believe in the permanence of the particular state or circumstances in which he for the moment [finds] himself,"
(*MM*, 122), he can indulge without anxiety the proclivities of his flatland
manners.

He is most concerned with balancing his impeccable bourgeois manners with the "peculiar social standards" (*MM*, 115) of the cure so as not to
offend anybody. He is surprised that his cousin does not wear a hat to tip
politely when acknowledging passers-by and ladies. He is shocked to learn
that Hofrat Behrens, the head medical physician at the sanatorium, is abrupt
with his dying patients. He condemns the persistent door-slamming of
Clavdia Chauchat's entrance into the main dining room as "a piece of ill
breeding" (*MM*, 77). He is absolutely appalled by the obtrusive, spontaneous lovemaking of his married Russian neighbors: "Good Lord! . . . Well,
at least they are married, as far as that goes. . . . But in broad daylight—it's a
bit thick! And last night too, I'm sure" (*MM*, 40).

Observing all manners of courtesy, he tries to vindicate their tactless
behavior: "But of course they are ill, or at least one of them, or they wouldn't
be here—that may be some excuse" (*MM*, 40). After a brief comment on the
aesthetic inadequacies of the architecture—"The scandalous part of it is,
the walls are so thin one can't help hearing everything. Simply intolerable.
The place is shamefully jerry-built, of course" (*MM*, 40)— he conjures
a social scenario in which their dubious behavior might compel him to

betray his own sense of proper etiquette: "What if I should see them, or even be introduced? I simply couldn't endure it!" (*MM*, 40). And, at least for his first three weeks on the mountain, he refuses to participate routinely in the rest period: "I shan't lie out on the balcony at night. . . . I can tell you that at once. It would seem perfectly weird to me. Everything has its limits. I must draw the line somewhere" (*MM*, 88).

While adhering to the precepts of bourgeois manners, Hans Castorp first meets Settembrini. He is so impressed by the humanist's rhetorical skill that, in their first conversation, he "unconsciously . . . make[s] an effort to reply with eloquence" (*MM*, 60). After their meeting, he feels an impulse to philosophize, even though he is unaccustomed to doing so. The impact of Settembrini's formal mastery on Hans Castorp's own speech is characteristic of the foundation of the pedagogic relationship that instantly develops between the two men. Hans Castorp finds Settembrini interesting, if not exemplary, particularly in the form of his rhetoric: "What a pedagogue it is!. . . . But after all, it is worth listening to, he talks so well; the words come jumping out of his mouth so round and appetizing. . . . I get the impression that it is not simply and solely for the sake of edifying us that he talks; perhaps that's only a secondary motive. The important one, I feel sure, is the talk itself, the way he makes his words roll out, so resilient. . . . He is very pleased when you notice the effect" (*MM*, 101).

Ziemssen shrewdly perceives that Settembrini would be offended by the designation of aesthete. Indeed, the humanist's first dressing-down of Hans Castorp, "You should judge—to that end you have been given your eyes and your understanding" (*MM*, 64), ostensibly privileges an engagement with history over cant and political quietism. But his subsequent explanation of humanist pedagogy—"We humanists have all of us a pedagogic itch . . . the office of schoolmaster should not—cannot—be taken from the humanist, for the tradition of the beauty and dignity of man rests in his hands" (*MM*, 64)—provides the antithesis for the contradiction in Settembrini's axiological ideology. On the one hand, Settembrini voices the need for an ethically responsible pedagogy that will help to bring forth the liberty, fraternity, and equality of any revolutionary humanism worthy of the name. That goal, however, seems nothing more than the reproduction of bourgeois privilege. Settembrini desires a beautiful word before a socially, politically, or economically just world. In making a fetish of the form of morality at the expense of a lived ethical example, Settembrini seems to maintain his own internal moral dialogue—following Mann's internal dialogue in *Reflections*—while concomitantly protecting the bourgeois status quo.[23] This contradiction within Settembrini is never fully resolved. One of its more significant pedagogic consequences is that the harder Settembrini appeals to Hans Castorp's traditional proclivity for perceiving the world aesthetically, the further Hans Castorp drifts from his traditional aesthetics. The ambiguities in Settembrini's moral consciousness inflect the morally instructive force of his voice.

Hans Castorp does not detect Settembrini's ideological contradiction at once, partly because Mann does not order the narrative in such a way that the full force of Settembrini's aestheticism is articulated at once but also because the new arrival quickly finds himself distracted by the first and greatest real threat, besides the job he will have to take when he descends, to his sense of beautifully mannered bourgeois comfort. His profound and immediate love for Clavdia Chauchat shatters his bourgeois sense of aesthetic equanimity by catalyzing the unconscious expression of repressed historical and moral material in a recurrent dream in which he kisses her hand: "At that there swept over him anew, from head to foot, the feeling of reckless sweetness he had felt for the first time when he tried to imagine himself free of the burden of a good name, and tasted the boundless joys of shame" (*MM*, 92). However, in the early days of his acquaintance with Clavdia, Hans Castorp has no equivalent conscious mode of declaring a love that threatens flatland mores; he must resort, with some chagrin, to a "tender ditty altogether tasteless, wishy–washy, and sentimental," that a bourgeois youth might sing for some "healthy little goose in the flatland" (*MM*, 140). By the third day of his holiday, a pedagogic dialogue is therefore in place: Hans Castorp's moral instruction proceeds in the dialogue between Settembrini's aesthetically beautiful, ethically dubious revolutionary humanism and the demand for sensitivity to the pressures of historical contingency, of which Hans Castorp's love for the undisciplined, informal Clavdia Chauchat is the symptom. At stake, to put it simply, are Hans Castorp's bourgeois manners, which are designed to diminish his reflection on the moral implications of the flatland's social arrangement.

Settembrini and Hans Castorp spend hours in (most often one-sided) conversation. In the course of these hours, Settembrini's conception of history and morality is greatly elaborated. When Hans Castorp proclaims

his surprise that very ill people should also be stupid, Settembrini aggres-
sively demurs: "I take issue where you regard the combination of disease
with dullness as a sort of aesthetic inconsistency. . . . Disease has nothing
refined about it, nothing dignified" (*MM*, 98). According to the ethic that
Settembrini voices, true human dignity lies in "work, earthly labour,
labour for the earth, for the honour and the interests of mankind"
(*MM*, 98). That is why he belongs to the International League for the
Organization of Progress, which "envisages the founding of universities for
the people, the resolution of the class conflict by means of all the social
ameliorations which recommend themselves for the purpose, and finally
the doing away with national conflicts, the abolition of war through the
development of international law" (*MM*, 244).

These are noble goals, indeed. But his dossier on the International
League lacks certain important clarifications: For whom will the aforementioned universities be founded? What are, and who will be the judge
of, the social ameliorations designed to resolve class struggle? How will
national conflict be identified and eliminated? Who will write the proposed International, and on what standard will these writers be selected?
Settembrini elides all of these specifics in favor of an abstract rhetorical
flourish that could be used to rally virtually any social movement calling
itself progressive around even the most dubious political program: "The
powers of reason and enlightenment will in the end set humanity wholly
free and lead it in the path of progress and civilization toward an even
brighter, milder, and purer light" (*MM*, 98). His disavowal of Hans
Castorp's meditations on disease does, however, produce one significant
pedagogic consequence: Hans Castorp adopts Settembrini's motto "*placet
experiri*," which enables him, with Settembrini's sanction, to listen both
"keenly and critically" (*MM*, 149) to what the humanist has to say.

Keen and critical he is. Joachim realizes that Settembrini's rhetoric is
having an effect on his cousin's consciousness. "Funny. . . .You were saying
something quite like that just yesterday" (*MM*, 100), he mentions to Hans
Castorp upon hearing Settembrini explain something that had recently
been a topic of the cousins' conversation. But as he listens to Settembrini
recount his patrilineage, Hans Castorp demonstrates that he is no impassive
sycophant content to ape Settembrini's morally inconsistent humanism:[24]

> Grandfather Giuseppe, to the day of his death, wore black—in token,
> he said, of his mourning for the state of the fatherland, languishing in

misery and servitude. Hans Castorp, at this piece of information, thought of his own grandfather. . . . He too, for as long as his grandson had known him, wore black clothes. But for how different a reason! Hans Lorenz Castorp had worn the quaint old fashion to indicate his oneness with a bygone time and his essential lack of sympathy with the present. . . . Grandfather Settembrini had fought to obtain political rights; whereas the other grandfather—or his ancestors—had originally had all the rights, and the scoundrels had taken them away from him. . . . So both grandfathers had worn mourning . . . in the same idea; namely, to put a great gulf between them and the evil present. . . . Yes, these were two different worlds. (*MM*, 153–54)

Hans Castorp is shrewd enough to comprehend that two different sets of social conditions can produce the same aesthetic values. This insight further threatens the truth claims of Settembrini's idealized moral pronouncements, since conflicting social relations can evidently be discerned at the base of purportedly transcendent aesthetic symbols and Enlightenment principles.

When Settembrini does speak directly of ethical and historical progress, his rhapsodic rhetoric fails to conceal his ideological inconsistency. He "bring[s] together in a single breath categories which in [Hans Castorp's] mind had heretofore been as the poles asunder—for example, technology and morals!" (*MM*, 155–56). He praises the "brilliant course" of human progress, which snatches up more and more people in its imperialist conquest of presumably barbaric cultures (*MM*, 157). He avows that the "republic of the world . . . the dawn of universal brotherhood" will replace the aristocratic thrones of the Holy Alliance "if not on the wings of doves, then on the pinions of eagles" (*MM*, 157). As might be expected, Settembrini reserves a special place for literature in his utopian dream: "For writing well was almost the same as thinking well, and thinking well was the next thing to acting well. All moral discipline, all moral perfection derived from the soul of literature, from the soul of human dignity, which was the moving spirit of both humanity and politics. Yes, they were all one, one and the same force, one and the same idea, and all of them could be comprehended in one single word. . . . The word was—civilization! (*MM*, 159–60)

Even though Settembrini tries to anticipate the criticism that his humanism is too idealistic—"but what, after all, was humanism if not love of human kind, and by what token also political activity, rebellion against all that tended to defile or degrade our conception of humanity? He had been accused of exaggerating the importance of form. But he who cherished beauty of form did so because it enhanced human dignity" (*MM*, 158) —he does not demonstrate how simply voicing political activism is tantamount to living it. Still, Hans Castorp judges the sum of these pronouncements "worth listening to" and "test[s] by it his own inner experiences" (*MM*, 160). At this point in his moral education, he is comfortable enough in his flatland mores not to reject all aestheticism entirely on the basis of some minor philosophical quibbles between different aesthetic values.

It would seem that, in the early juxtaposition of teachers and student, Settembrini's pedagogic voice thoroughly dominates everyone and everything around him, especially the antibourgeois ethic of Clavdia Chauchat, which finds no equivalent articulation in Hans Castorp's presence until the *Walpurgis Nacht*. However, Clavdia's physical propinquity exerts a steady sway on Hans Castorp's moral and aesthetic sensibilities:

> This door-slamming, finger-gnawing, bread-pill-making foreigner— who carried herself so badly, who lived apart from her husband, and without a ring on her finger careered from one resort to another . . . this foreigner was indubitably not a person for him to cultivate. . . . A deep gulf divided their two existences; he felt, he knew, that he was not up to defending her in the face of any recognized social authority. Hans Castorp was, for his own person, quite without arrogance; yet a larger arrogance, the pride of caste and tradition, stood written on his brow and in his sleepy-looking eyes, and voiced itself in the conviction of his own superiority, which came over him when he measured Frau Chauchat for what she was. It was this which he neither could, nor wished to, shake off. (*MM*, 143, 144)

The result of her physical pedagogic example is Hans Castorp's mounting ambivalence toward his social status down below. He still knows "what [is] due to himself and his upbringing" (*MM*, 167–68) as he purchases his first thermometer; but the very act of purchasing, like his growing facility for "making a proper bundle, a sort of mummy, of himself" (*MM*, 148) with his rugs during the cure, indicates his acclimatization to the sanatorium's lifestyle. He politely asks Joachim, "May I?" (*MM*, 217) when invited by the Hofrat to view his cousin's thoracic cavity through the x-ray; but the sight of Joachim's heart suddenly smacks Hans Castorp with a vision of death far less abstract and aestheticized than his past experience at his grandfather's funeral. He reminds Joachim of his (unauthorized) excursion into the forest, where he heard peasants speaking, and reflects, "What a stately and solemn way the people hereabout have of talking. . . . I mean the common people; almost like poetry. 'Then thank ye kindly and God be with ye,'. . . . I heard that up in the woods, and I shall remember it all my life" (*MM*, 187).

Growing more and more cognizant of the discrepancy between flatland and sanatorium, between bourgeois manners and the alternatives voiced on the mountain, Hans Castorp experiences a recurring "uneasy sensation of groping for support" (*MM*, 148) until he finally conveys to Settembrini his sense of oppression down below when the humanist asks if he is rich:

> One is rich—or else one isn't. And if not, so much the worse. I myself am no millionaire, but what I have is secured to me, I have enough to live on and be independent. . . . if you had said one must be rich, I should have agreed with you. If you aren't rich, or if you leave off being, then woe be unto you. "Oh, *he?*" they will say about this or that person. "He hasn't any money, has he?" Literally that, and making just such a face. . . . No, I don't think you, for instance, as *homo humanus,* would feel very comfortable down there; it often struck me that it was pretty strong, as I can see now, though I am a native of the place and for myself have never had to suffer from it. If a man does not serve the best and dearest wines at his dinners, people don't go, and his daughters are left on his hands. That is what they are like. Lying here and looking at it from this distance, I find it pretty gross. . . . It is a cruel atmosphere down there, cruel and ruthless. When you lie here and look at it, from a distance, it makes you shudder. (*MM*, 198)

There is not a single pronominal reference to the first person plural in this sequence. There is no evidence of Hans Castorp's voluntary complicity in the flatland's ethics or aesthetics. It would be an exaggeration to say that at this moment Hans Castorp has relinquished his bourgeois values. Yet he sees these values as unnatural, vulgar, "gross."

Once a social sign is no longer naturalized in an individual's consciousness, ideological stability may quickly be lost. Settembrini presumably recognizes Hans Castorp's severe ideological crisis; he offers, most respectfully, to be beside his pupil in order to "exercise a corrective influence when there appears to be danger of [his] taking up a destructive position" (*MM*, 201). Settembrini knows that Hans Castorp naturally leans towards an aesthetic conception of life. He now knows that the young man feels detached from the aesthetics inhering in his upbringing. What better time to impress his own humanistic aesthetics on his pupil?

But on my understanding of the direction in which Hans Castorp's moral education is progressing, Settembrini fails to perceive that his pupil's ideological crisis is not prompted by the desire to replace bourgeois manners with another set of hermetic mores; rather, it is provoked by an intensifying desire to replace an aestheticized view of historical conditions with a more ethically responsible commitment to human life. If this is the case, then Settembrini misreads his pupil. In short, he miscalculates the influence of Clavdia Chauchat's pedagogic voice on Hans Castorp. Since Settembrini invests so much faith in the educative and ennobling capacity of the word, he does not suspect that Clavdia, who exchanges nothing more than the pleasantries with Hans Castorp, could have such an instructive effect on him.

The breakdown of Settembrini's monopoly on Hans Castorp's consciousness can be plotted through several scenes. When Settembrini and Hans Castorp first discuss Clavdia's egregious aesthetic offensiveness, the latter accepts his mentor's judgment that "her illness was in good part, if not entirely, a moral one . . . neither the ground nor the consequence of her 'slackness,' but precisely one and the same thing" (*MM*, 228). Clavdia's "immorality," if it may be construed as such, lies in the way she felicitously transgresses form. As Hans Castorp's self-criticism becomes more incisive and he falls more deeply in love with Clavdia, he relaxes his criticism of her: "One begins by being angry and disgusted, and then all at once 'something quite different enters in,' that has 'nothing to do with moral judgment,' and it is all up with your severity; you are simply not at home to pedagogic influences, however republican, however eloquent" (*MM*, 229). With a laconic observation, "when one is in love, the aesthetic judgment counts for as little as the moral" (*MM*, 240), the narrator suggests that Hans Castorp is floundering between the competing pedagogic influences of Settembrini and Clavdia Chauchat.

The most formidable challenge to Settembrini's pedagogic example comes when, for the second time, he advises Hans Castorp to return to the flatland. The scene is presented as a duel, Settembrini's political aestheticism versus Clavdia Chauchat's slack morality. Hans Castorp accuses Settembrini of being "more prudent for [himself] than for others" (*MM*, 248) since Settembrini, for all his humanistic talk about historical commitment, never leaves the sanatorium.[25] When Settembrini explains his impotence as a manifestation of the "evil propensities" of the body, whose satisfaction should never be the primary goal of ethical choice, the gauntlet is thrown down, and Hans Castorp giddily defends his passion for Clavdia: "But you are a humanist, are you not? What can you have to say against the body?" (*MM*, 249).

This is Settembrini's opportunity, as a clever pedagogue with fore-sight, to be aesthetically flexible, to avoid constraining Hans Castorp into an either/or axiological decision in which Settembrini stands to lose far more than his pupil. Yet, although there may be a certain integrity in Settembrini's rejoinder to Hans Castorp's provocation—"We are to hon-our and uphold the body when it is a question of emancipation, of beauty, of freedom of thought, of joy, of desire. We must despise it in so far as it sets itself up as the principle of gravity and inertia, when it obstructs the movement toward light; we must despise it in so far as it represents the principle of disease and death, in so far as its specific essence is the essence of perversity, of decay, sensuality, and shame" (*MM*, 250–51)—it tenaciously reiterates his hatred of any material condition that exposes his aesthetic sensibility to modification. Furthermore, on the same logic of the either/or, it signals a dangerous refusal to take Clavdia's pedagogic voice seriously.

At the *Walpurgis Nacht* carnival, Hans Castorp for the first time openly rejects Settembrini's humanistic rhetoric in favor of Clavdia's pedagogic example. He is not without preparation for this commitment, having devoted many hours toward easing the suffering of the moribundi, those patients whose condition is terminal. Settembrini is displeased by Hans Castorp's physical engagement with the dying, but the latter is not willing, for the sake of Settembrini's mere words, to relinquish actions that he finds "somehow helpful and significant" (*MM*, 309). During *Walpurgis Nacht*, the humanist sees his pupil under the sway of alcohol and desire. He offers his warning against a "belle dame sans merci" (*MM*, 327). Using the "du" form of address, Hans Castorp characterizes Settembrini's admonition as self-indulgence, and a conversation ensues that confirms Hans Castorp's assimi-lation of the pedagogic voice represented by Clavdia in that it reveals his comprehension that meaning is contingent on context, not forever frozen in time:

"Hark ye, Engineer—and take heed what I say. . . . You will kindly address me with the accepted form employed in the educated countries of the West, the third person *pluralis*, if I may make bold to suggest it."

"Why? Isn't this carnival? The other is the accepted form everywhere to-night."

"Yes, it is—and its charm lies in its very abandon. When strangers, who would regularly use the third person, speak to each other in the second, it is an objectionable freedom, it is wantonly playing with the roots of things, and I despise and condemn it, because at the bottom the usage is audaciously and shamelessly levelled against our civilization and our enlightened humanity"

. . . "I don't say I find it perfectly natural and easy to say thou to you. . . . But I do so freely, gladly . . . I simply address you as though we were old and close friends, without further ceremony, and you must excuse me, because I don't know any other way." (*MM*, 328–29)

It is symptomatic of his blind aestheticism that Settembrini is far less insulted by what Hans Castorp has said than by how he has said it. For Settembrini, form is atemporal, ahistorical, absolute. Having acclimated himself to the mountain's mores and routines, Hans Castorp has learned that different social relations may compel different expressions of form. Carnival is different from normal evenings. And his relationship with Settembrini is not what it was when they first met and the polite address was obligatory. Heeding the demands of mutable historical context, Hans Castorp's behavior would appear irreproachable. His statement, that he "doesn't know any other way," is the hardest hit of all at Settembrini's pedagogic example; it further threatens any hope that Hans Castorp will replace his own former, aesthetically conceived morality with Settembrini's. Instead, Hans Castorp inclines towards Clavdia's ethical position, whose import is articulated for the first and only time in the novel:

The moral? That also interests you? Good, it seems to us that one shouldn't search for the moral in virtue, that is to say, in reason, discipline, the accepted standards, decency, but rather in the opposites, I want to say in sin, in abandoning oneself to danger, to what is harmful, to what can devour us. It appears to us that it is more moral to lose one's way, even to let oneself waste away, than to protect oneself. The great moralists did not hold to points of virtue, but rather they were adventurers in evil, in the dissolute, great sinners who teach us to bow in a Christian manner before misery. All this is terribly unpleasant to you, isn't it? (*MM*, 340)[26]

On this occasion, Clavdia speaks French, further distancing herself from the linguistic form—particularly the classical Latin—of Settembrini's rhetoric. For Clavdia, sin, hence life, implies deviation from an absolute behavioral standard, from some kind of ideological Ten Commandments, empowered by a pretense to static, natural Truth; it constitutes concession to the discordant pressures of human desire, to the need to act in the name of passion, to serve the body instead of the intellect, even if the result is something less than beautiful. It is thus essentially the antithesis of Settembrini's highly stylized ethic, which need only be perfectly thought, not imperfectly acted. As Hans Castorp consummates his love for Clavdia and enjoys his single evening of sexual intimacy with her before she leaves the sanatorium the following morning, the first half of Mann's text draws to a close with the tension between Settembrini's and Clavdia's pedagogic voices in a firmly plotted moral dialogue within Hans Castorp's consciousness.

Structurally, the pedagogic dynamic between Settembrini and Clavdia Chauchat is repeated in the second half of the novel with the arrival of Leo Naphta and Mynheer Peeperkorn. While it would be fair to characterize Mynheer Peeperkorn as espousing a greatly exaggerated form of Clavdia's antibourgeois ideology, the relationship between Settembrini and Naphta is more complex: ethically, the two are at almost complete odds, but both subordinate the need for a historically conceived morality to a highly stylized version of political aestheticism.[27] Whereas Settembrini always sought his pupil's audience, Hans Castorp brings himself to Naphta after Naphta confesses that he is "perhaps not entirely without pedagogic tradition" and wishes to provide an ideological alternative to Settembrini's "bourgeois humanism" (*MM*, 384). However, at bottom Naphta's pedagogic voice contains as great a self-contradiction as Settembrini's. Naphta's irreconcilable belief in both an absolute and a contingent conception of truth makes him an instructive force no more or less potentially effective than Settembrini; hence, their dialogue remains spirited.

Naphta asserts the rudimentary principles of his morality in an early debate with Settembrini, at which Hans Castorp is primarily a listener. Settembrini inquires whether Naphta believes "in truth, in objective, scientific truth, to strive after the attainment of which is the highest law of all morality," and he receives the proclamation that "whatever profits man, that is the truth. . . . He is the measure of all things, and his welfare is the sole and single criterion of truth" (*MM*, 398).[28] Further on in the same conversation, Naphta links human welfare to its material conditions: "The question of freedom—the question of cities, to put it more concretely—has always been a highly ethical question, and is historically bound up with the inhuman degeneration of commercial morality, with all the horrors of modern industrialism and speculation, and with the devilish domination of money and finance" (*MM*, 405). Naphta deplores Settembrini's rhetorical manipulation of historical fact, wondering if the Italian can "conceive of liberty less as a beautiful gesture and more as a serious problem" (*MM*, 405). With such pronouncements, Naphta appears to be far more interested in the content than the form of human existence.

This tendency toward emphasizing historical commitment notwithstanding, Naphta eventually factors the need for a lived ethics completely out of his teaching. Abjuring Settembrini's bourgeois humanism, Naphta asks, "Is your Manchester liberalism unaware of the existence of a school of economic thought which means the triumph of man over the economic, and whose principles and aims precisely coincide with those of the kingdom of God?" (*MM*, 403). Naphta thus maintains a transcendent, wildly utopian version of Marxism that is dedicated to changing historical conditions, not in order to improve the quality of existential social relations, but to ensure eternal perfection in the afterlife. He views existence "not as a conflict between the ego and society, but as a conflict between the ego and God" (*MM*, 404).

To the end of resolving this conflict, Naphta recognizes "what must be the ultimate and significant principle of pedagogy: namely the absolute mandate, the iron bond, discipline, sacrifice, the renunciation of the ego, the curbing of the personality" (*MM*, 400). His goal is to see the proletariat "strike terror into the world for the healing of the world, that man may finally achieve salvation and deliverance, and win back at length to freedom from law and from distinction of classes, to his original status as child of God" (*MM*, 404). As might be expected from such a suprahistorical program for changing social relations, Naphta's moral philosophy disproportionately depends on an atemporal, abstract authority for its empowerment. As such, it represents precisely the kind of critical voice that the opponents of ethical textual practice find so disturbing. It pretends toward a monologic authority that is impossible in a being who understands his complicity in historical contingency, where knowledge is a site of dialogue and contestation, not an ideal given.

Naphta equates ethics with "ultra-bourgeoisiedom" (*MM*, 463). Since he is the self-proclaimed enemy of the bourgeois, he must in the last instance reject ethics, lest he rearticulate the Settembrinian morality whose "end and aim was to make men grow old and happy, rich and comfortable" (*MM*, 464). Naphta is forthright about the final uselessness of morality in his paradigm for human salvation: "Life is based on conditions and built up on foundations which are partly the result of experience, and partly belong to the domain of ethics. We call the first kind time, space, and causality; the second, morality and reason. But one and all of these are not only foreign to, utterly a matter of indifference to the nature of religion; they are even hostile to it" (*MM*, 463). Accurately disclosing the contradiction that underpins Settembrini's "revolutionary bourgeois humanism," Naphta completely misses the contradiction in his own ethical position. He cannot adequately reconcile his imperative of historical commitment with his religiosity. If human beings have an afterlife dangling before them like a carrot, what is the impetus to become engaged in class struggle on earth? Why not simply defer personal responsibility for brutal social relations to someone else and rest in the knowledge that, if one be contrite at the threshold of death, the kingdom of heaven is nigh? Through his pedagogy, Naphta is a model of irresponsible ethical criticism, since irresponsible ethical criticism, regardless of whether its object is a literary text or an intellectual tradition, refuses to open itself to response or to admit its internal contradictions, imperfections, and methodological limitations.

The rhetorical brilliance of the two pedagogues, whose voices speak immeasurably louder than their actions, does not impel Hans Castorp to a recrudescence of his earlier aestheticized view of morality. Two brief but crucial episodes amplify Hans Castorp's maturing conviction that, regardless of its particular thematic significance, morality has a lived, material dimension neglected only at one's peril. The first is Ziemssen's apostasy from the sanatorium in order to serve in his infantry regiment down below. At their leave–taking on the train platform, Joachim "call[s] his cousin by his first name. Not with the thou, not 'old fellow,' or 'man,' by which forms they had addressed each other their lives long. No, in defiance of all reserve, almost gushingly, he called his cousin by his first name" (*MM*, 425). The moment is one of the most powerful and evocative in the narrative, not least for its pedagogic import.

Ziemssen is perhaps the most consistently sympathetic character in the novel. Referred to frequently as "good cousin Joachim," he is a model of flatland manners, modesty, and virtue. The honorable patriot, he wants only to serve his country as something larger and more worthy than himself, and he refuses the path of voluptuousness and sensualization offered by the mountain. Yet Ziemssen rarely speaks. He is not interested in pedagogic things, though he is absolutely respectful when around those who are. He and Hans Castorp are genuinely fond of one another, though they are never physically demonstrative or emotionally effusive. All the more reason why Ziemssen's sudden use of the first name is an anvil out of the sky. Hans Castorp's presumption throughout his stay is that Ziemssen wishes to be well in order to defend their country's conservative values. Ziemssen's discipline in the cure seemed to evidence an unbending loyalty to an absolute standard of social behavior. Thus, Ziemssen's use of the first name is a pedagogic articulation of tremendous consequence. In one word, Hans Castorp hears the impact and the scope of social conditions on human consciousness.

The second event is Tienapple's visit to the mountain, which does not evince any repressed desire for the flatland's bourgeois mores in Hans Castorp's moral consciousness. Hans Castorp's only reaction to his Uncle James's precipitate return to Hamburg is that "the total failure of this embassy marked a crisis in the relations between himself and the world below. It meant that he gave it up. . . . the thought of which had gradually ceased to make him shudder" (*MM*, 440). Uncle James can do or say nothing to reclaim his lost nephew because they no longer share a social context that makes persuasive communication possible. Long inured to the comforts of his native city, Hans Castorp has grown deaf to the voice of bourgeois form. The incident with Tienapple thus exemplifies the premise that, without dialogue, there can be no pedagogy.

Possessing only the x-ray image of Clavdia Chauchat's chest to remind him of the morally instructive voice representing the surrender to life and passion, Hans Castorp grows restless for new experience and takes up skiing. The famous episode in which he finds himself near death during a sudden, ferocious storm culminates in an elaborate revelation that delineates his pedagogic progress thus far:

> [I will not hold] with Naphta, neither with Settembrini. They are both talkers; the one luxurious and spiteful, the other for ever blowing on his penny pipe of reason. . . . Disease, health! Spirit, nature! Are those contradictions? I ask, are they problems? No, they are no problems. . . . The recklessness of death is in life, it would not be life without it. . . . There is both rhyme and reason in what I say, I have made a dream poem of humanity. I will cling to it. I will be good. . . . Death and love—no, I cannot make a poem of them, they don't go together. Love stands opposed to death. It is love, not reason, that is stronger than death. Only love, not reason, gives sweet thoughts. And from love and sweetness alone can form come: form and civilization, friendly, enlightened, beautiful human intercourse. . . . I have taken stock. I will remember. . . . *For the sake of goodness and love, man shall let death have no sovereignty over his thoughts.* (MM, 496–97)

Hans Castorp's active confrontation with the natural sublime—an experience inimical to Settembrini's aestheticized image of Nature—engenders a moral affirmation of life as the expression of active love and human solidarity.[29] Implicit in this affirmation is the recognition that moral knowledge issues from ideological conflict and that any attempt to eliminate ideological tension from one's consciousness precludes moral education. Thus, the insight is as much structural, a comment on the production of moral knowledge, as it is thematic.

Only a few hours after Hans Castorp experiences his revelation, he forgets nearly all of it. Does this suggest that the revelation is in any way wrong or insufficient? Is his forgetting an ironic structural device to suggest that such a revelation, with its endorsement of the material and contingent determinants of consciousness, might be expected to fade when the material circumstances that evoked it are themselves changed? If so, then the remainder of the novel can be read as Hans Castorp's continued struggle to distill and stabilize an ethical position from the still-competing pedagogic voices on the mountain. His acquaintance with Mynheer Peeperkorn, the last of the novel's four main pedagogic characters, inserts another voice into the text's morally instructive dialogue. Peeperkorn's sway over the young man's moral consciousness can be measured in Hans Castorp's gradual turn from speech to gesture, from experiment to action.

Attended by Clavdia Chauchat, Mynheer Peeperkorn arrives on the mountain just after Ziemssen, who having returned from his excursion mortally ill, dies. In a gesture of brotherhood and love, Hans Castorp lays aside "traditional reserve" (*MM*, 540) and kisses his cousin on the forehead. Entirely susceptible to an ethical voice that promises to foster active human solidarity and love, Hans Castorp is immediately receptive to Peeperkorn's ethical position. Peeperkorn's most distinguishing character-istic is his outrageous elliptical speech, which is counterposed to the pol-ished rhetoric of Naphta and Settembrini. Physically, Peeperkorn is a massive presence. There is nothing ascetic about him. His movements are awkward, abrupt, peremptory. He is chronically drunk, in contempt of all bourgeois manners. He is a conspicuous being-in-time who indulges his historical condition. Naphta and Settembrini are dwarfed beside him. As Hans Castorp puts it, "He can stick us all in his pocket" (*MM*, 584). Peeperkorn's moral sensibility takes Hans Castorp's "placet experiri" and pushes it to the breaking point: "Life, young man, is a female. A sprawling female, with swelling breasts close to each other, great soft belly between her haunches, slender arms, bulging thighs, half-closed eyes. She mocks us. She challenges us to expend our manhood to its uttermost span, to stand or fall before her" (*MM*, 566). Hans Castorp views him as synthesiz-ing body and spirit without discarding either for the sake of glorifying a lopsided abstract ideal.[30]

Settembrini, who has seen his pedagogic voice all but silenced by Peeperkorn, defends the "logic, precision, discrimination" (*MM*, 584) of his, and perhaps even Naphta's, speech against Peeperkorn's formless dis-course. Characteristically, he is most offended by the Dutchman's aesthetic sloppiness. Hans Castorp, who would occasionally sprinkle little Latin and Italian Settembrinisms into his conversations, now responds, first with an elliptically phrased answer, then with a more epigrammatic sentiment that nonetheless challenges Settembrini's *bello stile*: "I'd rather go rambling on, and partly expressing something I find it difficult to express, than to keep on transmitting faultless platitudes" (*MM*, 585). He continues occasionally to speak in incomplete, fragmented sentences, most notably when Clavdia accuses him of living "for sake of experience" rather than "for the sake of living" (*MM*, 594). Clavdia instructs him in the meaning of authentic pas-sion, which is neither reflective nor narcissistic, through which a truly self-less human solidarity may be constructed.

Peeperkorn reiterates his ethic as a consecration of the "sacred duty to feel. . . . For feeling . . . is godlike. Man is godlike, in that he feels. He is the feeling of God. God created him in order to feel through him. Man is nothing but the organ through which God consummates his marriage with roused and intoxicated life" (*MM*, 603). The combination of Peeperkorn's elliptical speech and ethic of feeling suggests that love and passion are ineffable: to speak them would be to try to capture their lived, dynamic quality in a formal semantic vessel. Following Peeperkorn's ethic, Hans Castorp refuses to discuss his previous relationship with Clavdia. Despite the insult implied in this refusal, Hans Castorp and Peeperkorn reach an accord regarding Clavdia.

Prior to Peeperkorn's appearance at the cure, neither of Hans Castorp's rhetorical pedagogues ever reached agreement on anything, either with themselves or their pupil. Accord becomes solidarity when Peeperkorn, in the name of a "brotherly alliance" (*MM*, 611), offers the second-person singular to Hans Castorp. But how different is this third breach of formal address from the first two! Hans Castorp no longer labors to justify the breach of bourgeois etiquette; he does not stammer to explain that history moves forward and that with it contexts change. He simply imagines Settembrini as a dinosaur who cannot adjust to the times and risks extinction, "coming in suddenly and turning on the light, to let reason and convention reign" (*MM*, 612). For Settembrini, form determines the expression of history. For Peeperkorn, history determines the expression of form.

Peeperkorn's alliance with Hans Castorp ensures that the Dutchman's pedagogic voice will not be undermined *as* time passes because its verbal seal is the reminder *that* time passes. But the Dutchman's suicide, in capitulation to his incurable impotence, is his greatest pedagogic act. When Mynheer Peeperkorn can no longer live his moral, he does not aestheticize it into an ideal image to be glorified theoretically in the manner of a Settembrini or a Naphta. Rather, he kills himself. Hans Castorp's response to the suicide is to retreat further into silence and gesture. He begins to bow to his colloquists rather than produce spoken dialogue. And the text more and more describes his discourse rather than narrates it.[31]

Hans Castorp's emerging predilection for silence, for rhetorical formlessness, is part of a more emphatic symptom of change in the Berghof: an inescapable feeling of lethargy begins to infect even the most cheerful patients of the cure. The recollection of Peeperkorn's voice enables Hans Castorp to identify the root of the malaise as "life without time, life without care or hope, life as depravity, assiduous stagnation; life as dead" (*MM*, 627). At this juncture, Hans Castorp has rejected enough of Naphta and Settembrini's political aestheticism, and has assimilated enough of Clavdia and Peeperkorn's ethic of commitment to life, to believe that moral consciousness is predicated upon dialogue, which reflects the impact of historical contingency on the process of moral signification. However, although he is no longer content to reproduce bourgeois values and social relations, he has neither the physical dynamism of Peeperkorn nor an extended contact with the dynamics of class struggle needed to jump-start the mountain into a sense of the urgency of temporal change. Paradoxically, he is aware of his status as a being in history, but he has no idea where else to find ideological tension in the sanatorium besides in the Berghof's moral dialogue, and he has no impetus to return below to the bourgeois lifestyle he has forsaken.

Additional evidence of the record of temporal change comes to him. Its first two manifestations are symbolic. In an effort to dispel the prevailing lassitude, Behrens imports a state-of-the-art gramophone for the patients' general use and enjoyment. Hans Castorp is astounded by the instrument's fidelity; he cannot believe technology has advanced so far beyond the "antediluvian" sound machines with which he was familiar. Presiding over the device, he can, for the interval it takes a selection to run its course, guarantee that time itself is given voice. The reader is expected to recall Joachim's observation, with which Hans Castorp tacitly agreed, that "an unpretentious concert-number lasts perhaps seven minutes, and those seven minutes amount to something; they have a beginning and an end, they stand out, they don't so easily slip into the regular humdrum round and get lost. . . . there is always something going on, and every moment has a certain meaning, something you can take hold of " (*MM*, 114).

The seance is the context for another stark reminder of the force of temporal change. Hans Castorp participates in the event knowing that the medium has promised to make contact with the departed spirit of one's choosing. Hans Castorp requests that she conjure Ziemssen, who appears not in his dress colors, but looking "quite properly warlike" (*MM*, 681). The insinuation of historical conflict is powerfully conveyed. Furthermore, Hans Castorp instantly judges his desire to bring back

Ziemssen as a violation both of his pact with life and of his solidarity with his cousin. What began as a gesture of love ends with his whispered "Forgive me!" (*MM*, 681). He is deeply ashamed of his complicity in the little bourgeois parlor game. He is the one who ends it by tripping the light switch.

Historical pressures from the flatland obtrude once more onto the mountain in the form of growing tensions in the Berghof's social relations, which reflect in microcosm the mounting hostilities among the European nations down below. All polite manner and form are sacked when Hans Castorp witnesses an actual fist fight between an anti-Semitic patient and the object of his hatred. But the death knell for bourgeois manners certainly seems to sound most stridently when Settembrini is lured into a duel by Naphta. Hans Castorp tries desperately to dissuade Settembrini from satisfying Naphta, correctly observing that Naphta merely "threw the categories to the wind . . . and robbed conceptions of their academic dignity," and that the insult "was a matter of abstractions, an intellectual disagreement" (*MM*, 699). Settembrini's aesthetic sensibility has been offended. Yet he, the quintessential celebrant of Enlightenment humanism and beautiful life, willingly implicates himself in an arrangement designed to terminate in injury or death. His first real action in the novel signifies a physically horrifying shift of ethical locus from political aestheticism to the implacable demands of historical pressure. He cannot answer Naphta with quietism any more than Mann, in *Reflections*, could answer the *Zivilisationsliterat* with quietism. The voice of history proves too pedagogically compelling to allow either. Hans Castorp knows there can be no other way, since "at the end of everything only the physical remained, only the teeth and the nails" (*MM*, 700). Naphta's suicide is also instructive; combined with Settembrini's very appearance on the field of honor, it illustrates the pedagogic limits—even among its espousers—of an exclusively rhetorical engagement with life.

Following Naphta's suicide, Hans Castorp recalls his "abiding everlasting, his walk by the ocean of time, the hermetic enchantment to which he had proved so extraordinarily susceptible" (*MM*, 708). Lukács's claim that, at this point in the text, "Hans Castorp . . . sinks into the mean, mindless, repellent everyday life of the Magic Mountain" because he is "exhausted by his efforts to reach clarity in his political and philosophical thinking"[32] offers one possible contribution to the dialogue regarding the status of Hans Castorp's moral consciousness on the eve of the First World War. Its supplement might be the interpretation that Hans Castorp spends seven years coming to learn, as Mann learned while writing his wartime essay, that ethics and aesthetics are inextricably tied to historical conditions and thus remain in an irrepressible dialogue with one another.[33] That is, he too has learned to concede the contingency of moral values.

As long as the ethical positions of complacency and commitment continue to inform Hans Castorp's reaction to the growing anxiety in the Berghof, the ethical critic of Mann's text cannot univocally determine either the reason why the engineer descends from the mountain or the possible moral component of that reason.[34] The narrator provides little insight to these questions, relating only that Hans Castorp is pulled from the mountain by "the operation of exterior powers" (*MM*, 711). Although the pressures of historical contingency gradually gain instructive primacy over highly stylized moral principles, the "exterior forces" of which the narrator speaks are left sufficiently vague to keep the pedagogic dialogue among the mountain's ethical voices open in Hans Castorp's moral consciousness.

For example, nothing in the narrator's description of Hans Castorp in the trenches indicates conclusively why he is fighting. And though the narrator recounts Hans Castorp's singing: "And loving words I've carven / Upon its branches fair . . . Its waving branches whi-ispered / A mess-age in my ear-" (*MM*, 715), it is impossible to ascertain what the import of the message of that love is. Is it personal, a reflection of the love he felt for her whose flesh he once madly tasted? Is it an expression of sincere brotherhood, inspired by his love for Ziemssen and Peeperkorn? Does it represent a broader, more inclusive impulse, commensurable with the vision of human solidarity propounded by Settembrini? Or is it a radical *communitas*, the product of Naphta's violent historicism? The novel's famous concluding interrogative—"Out of this universal feast of death, out of this extremity of fever, kindling the rain-washed evening sky to a fiery glow, may it be that Love one day shall mount?" (*MM*, 716)— only emphasizes, despite Lowe-Porter's tendentious capitalization of "love," the text's lack of a final moral signature.

Hans Castorp's fate is left open at the end of the text. The reader is never told whether he lives or dies on the battlefield, only that his "prospects are poor" (*MM*, 716). Should one conclude from this observation that Hans Castorp would have been better off taking his chances on the mountain? If so, does this conclusion authorize Settembrini's pedagogic voice, which remains similarly insulated? Again, there is nothing in the text's moral dialogue to vindicate such an interpretation to the exclusion of others. There is no unitary, authoritative, authorial voice to impress determinate closure on the narrative; the pedagogic tension among competing moral voices remains intact. Since the ideological tension that dominates *Reflections* remains an informing structural principle on which *The Magic Mountain* concludes, attempts to demonstrate the pedagogic supremacy of one character over the others are made against the narrative's structural logic.[35] The novel does not offer its reader a thematic moral lesson.

This is not to say that *The Magic Mountain* fails to yield any stable knowledge on an ethical reading; but it is, first and foremost, a knowledge of signifying and interpretive method. Rather than reading for some kind of totalizing ethical lesson that can only be extracted from the text through violence to the text's aesthetic dimension, the text's ethical themes can serve as a conduit to a more developed understanding of how ethically charged voices express ideological information. The persistent pressure of the "voice of history," the constant reminder that ethical claims are temporal events, ensures that the conflict between referential and constitutive voices is sustained despite the monologic pretenses of some of Hans Castorp's interlocutors. The reader may then reinvestigate the ethical import of specific voices and attempt to gauge the morally instructive capacity of the text without being seduced into conclusions made at the expense of the text's moral dialogue.

After attending to the way textual voices signify, a reader may incorporate the ethical import of moral dialogue into his or her way of thinking about moral values. These values thereafter become options, none of which is absolute, any of which may come to inform a particular moral choice at a particular historical juncture. To recall Rorty: the more we read, the greater our options. In providing a model on which to expand these options, responsible ethical criticism affirms its value as a vital textual practice.

3

Time and Ethics
in *The Plague*

■

It is because there are two kinds of reason, the one ethical and the
other aesthetic.
                    Albert Camus, *Notebooks, 1935–1942*

The Plague is a tract.
                    Albert Camus, *Notebooks, 1942–1951*

Traditional ethical readings of Albert Camus's *The Plague* are likely to reflect
the criticism brought against the novel by leftist critics following Roland
Barthes and Jean-Paul Sartre that Camus's text fails to represent a moral
dimension because it fails to represent history. While Barthes's and Sartre's
evaluations are certainly strong voices of ethical criticism in the corpus of
textual interpretation of *The Plague*, they are expressions of a specific historical moment in that corpus; hence, they cannot be taken as the last word
on *The Plague*'s moral dimension. Their assessments of Camus's text compete with a more contemporary interpretive trend that affirms *The Plague*'s
moral component. Moreover, they exist in tension with Camus's own sense
of morally instructive fiction in general. This complex intertextual critical
dialogue, on both the moral affects of literature in general and those of *The
Plague* in particular, provides a fertile object of consideration on the aesthetic structures of moral pedagogy.

    Camus's thoughts on the potential function and responsibility of the
novel as a morally instructive instrument developed out of his sense of
"truth." On the one hand, Camus asserted the historicity of truth in a 1939
essay entitled "Nuptials": "Truth must decay, and what is more exalting?
Even if I long for it, what have I in common with a truth that is not des-
tined to decay? It is not on my scale. And to love it would be pretense."[1]
However, Camus's basic philosophical relativism never squared very well
with the first premise of his humanism, which claimed an absolute value

for "man, because he is the only creature to insist on having one."[2] Neither was his relativism convincing in the position, recorded in the fourth letter to a German friend, that "we have a right to think that truth with a capital letter is relative. But facts are facts. And whoever says that the sky is blue when it is gray is prostituting words and preparing the way for tyranny" (*RRD*, 168).

On some critics' account, Camus's entire philosophical career can be seen as an attempt to reconcile this apparently contradictory metaphysic, in which the same relativism that makes his theory of the absurd possible makes his theory of the indisputable value of human life highly disputable.[3] But Camus's comments on the rôle of the writer and of ethical fiction were invigorated by this internal dialogue. Emerging in these comments is a recurrent mistrust of any literature that pretends to monologic moral authority. Anticipating such contemporary writers as Booth, Rorty, and MacIntyre by half a century, Camus called for ethical fiction to foreground the foundations for its truth claims, which are contingent on temporal pressures and the indeterminacy of language. However, instances can also be adduced in which Camus's consideration of the novel inadvertently belies his official stance on the need for sensitivity to historical pressures in the creation and evaluation of ethical fiction.

Before his famous debate with Sartre, before the two men had even met, Camus began a review of *La Nausée* with remarks that reveal more about Camus than about Sartre: "A novel is never anything but a philosophy expressed in images. And in a good novel the philosophy has disappeared into the images. But the philosophy need only spill over into the characters and action for it to stick out like a sore thumb, the plot to lose its authenticity, and the novel its life" (*LCE*, 199). In summing up his criticism of Sartre's text—"The book itself seems less a novel than a monologue" (*LCE*, 200)—Camus established a criterion for evaluating literature that he would corroborate as late as 1957: "Art cannot be a monologue" (*RRD*, 257). Monologic art is merely a "pretension to the eternal . . . in which illusion offers itself automatically, in which conclusion is almost inevitable."[4] Camus warns the artist against "judg[ing] absolutely," lest he "arbitrarily divide reality into good and evil and thus indulge in melodrama" (*RRD*, 266). He chastens Dostoevsky, to whom he acknowledged an enormous intellectual and creative debt, for engaging in dialogue with his own fictional characters and making ethical judgments on their behavior

(*MoS*, 83). With peremptory if unconvincing authority, he asserts that his examples of absurd men "do not propose moral codes and involve no judgments: they are sketches" (*MoS*, 67).

Even after the war, when the impulse toward moral judgment of historical events was not uncommon on the Continent, Camus continued to abjure monologic practice in metaphysical speculation, telling an audience of Dominican monks at the Latour-Mauberg Monastery "that the world needs real dialogue, that falsehood is just as much the opposite of dialogue as is silence, and that the only possible dialogue is the kind between people who remain what they are and speak their minds."[5] Camus was not trying to provoke an audience whose ethics were obviously different from his own; he was simply reexpressing his lifelong suspicion of anything that might be interpreted as a static model of moral thought or action. Camus makes very clear that the consequences of a monologic text can take any number of forms, among which he most conspicuously counts formalism and realism. These he indicts as follows:

> The lie of art for art's sake pretended to know nothing of evil and consequently assumed responsibility for it. But the realistic lie, even though managing to admit mankind's present unhappiness, betrays that unhappiness just as seriously by making use of it to glorify a future state of happiness, about which no one knows anything, so that the future authorizes every kind of humbug.
>
> The two aesthetics that have long stood opposed to each other, the one that recommends a complete rejection of real life and the one that claims to reject anything that is not real life, end up, however, by coming to agreement, far from reality, in a single lie and in the suppression of art. The academicism of the Right does not even acknowledge a misery that the academicism of the Left utilizes for ulterior reasons. But in both cases the misery is only strengthened at the same time that art is negated. (*RRD*, 263)

Realism and formalism aestheticize their object by distracting attention from the historical conditions that determine any work of art. As a result of the repression of their historical determinants, the moral dimension of realist and formalist works is either entirely concealed or is expressed as dogma, which prohibits the potential for dialogue and choice that is necessary for moral thinking and education. As an egregious example of dogmatic literature, Camus cites socialist realism.

Socialist realism neither represents nor inspires moral dialogue; it merely expounds a univocal position and unscrupulously serves a bald political agenda. It is a "propaganda art with its heroes and its villains— an edifying literature" in which "art is reduced to nothing. It serves and, by serving, becomes a slave" (*RRD*, 260–61).[6] Dogmatic fiction becomes the amanuensis of any teleological conception of human development that implements an ethical code on the basis of some far-off, perhaps untenable, social ideal. Camus essentially repeats Mann's argument in *Reflections* that art must not be produced with the sole aim of impressing upon its audience an absolutely conclusive standard for behavior. Again following Mann, he subsequently translates this imperative into fiction in the form of an array of possible ethical contingencies among whose dialogue a moral climate evolves in response to a specific ideological moment. Put another way, for the novel to retain a responsible, that is to say historically contingent, moral component, it must remain "on the human scale" (*MoS*, 72). Translated into an aesthetic principle, the novel must attain to a balance "between the ideas in the work and the images that express them" (*LCE*, 201).[7] The work's ethical and aesthetic dimensions must not exceed one another; rather, they must mask one another so that what appears to the reader is a series of tensions among characters from which the structural mechanism of moral education may be elucidated. Such a tension foregrounds dialogue as both a narrative and a pedagogic textual device.

Accordingly, it follows that Camus conceives of nondogmatic art, especially the novel, as the aesthetic expression of an ethic of rebellion against anything that sacrifices the representation of reality to the representation of an ideal.[8] Stephen Kellman reiterates this commonplace of Camusian criticism when he cites Camus's distinction between "philosophical writing— which is provisional, suggestive, open—and thesis–mongering, which is absolutist and constrictive. . . . For Camus, great writers, by immersing us in history and particularity, free us to imagine human possibilities. They do not reject the concrete, the specific, and the contingent in pursuit of the abstract, the general, and the eternal."[9]

But Camus's language in defense of the distinction between philosophical writing and thesis-mongering occasionally reverberates with a tone that conveys its own sense of teleological purpose:

> Art thus leads us back to the origins of rebellion, to the extent that it tries to give its form to an elusive value which the future perpetually

promises, but of which the artist has a presentiment and wishes to snatch from the grasp of history. We shall understand this better in considering the art form whose precise aim is to become part of the process of evolution in order to give it the style that it lacks; in other words, the novel . . .

What, in fact, is a novel but a universe in which action is endowed with form, where final words are pronounced, where people possess one another completely, and where life assumes the aspect of destiny? The world of the novel is only the rectification of the world we live in, in pursuance of man's deepest wishes.[10]

Camus describes the novel as a kind of secondary elaboration of historical experience, filling in gaps between historical episodes in order to produce a highly stylized narrative that appears to be seamless. The authentic novel of rebellion also boasts an "evolutionary" aspiration toward an existential unity that is yet unfulfilled. Even if the "final words" inscribed in the novel are final only in the context of the narrative, it is difficult to understand the notion of "rectification in pursuance of man's deepest wishes" as without a programmatic element. What, then, is the difference between Camus's image of a destiny snatched from the grasp of history and a historicist image of the same, since both would underpin a literature that does not attempt to reproduce historical conditions faithfully? Does the same inconsistency that underpins Camus's definitions of truth underpin his theory of nondogmatic fiction?

It is tempting to answer yes, especially when one considers Camusian speculation that ostensibly conflates historicist thinking with thought that merely acknowledges the contingent status of all ethical truth claims. In a notebook entry written while he was composing *The Plague*, Camus laments, "Something in me tells me, convinces me that I cannot detach myself from my era without cowardice, without accepting slavery, without denying my mother and my truth. I could not do so . . . unless I were a Christian. Not a Christian, I must go on to the end. But going on to the end means choosing history absolutely, and with it the murder of man if the murder of man is necessary to history."[11] The last sentence of this entry could be read as endorsing either contingency or historicism, depending on how one reads the phrase "necessary to history."

On a historicist reading, Camus seems to equate a commitment to historical rather than metaphysical consciousness with a specific, almost proleptic vision of history. This should sound familiar enough: it is against precisely this kind of equation that Camus argues in his critique of socialist realism. If this reading can be proven correct, then the Left's critique of *The Plague*—that it fails to represent the moral implications of human complicity in historical circumstances—is given greater credence: what better way to undermine an opponent than to prove that he does not even realize that he agrees with you? However, it is also possible to read "necessary to history" as the expression of an absolute commitment, albeit a deeply ambivalent one, to the exigencies impelled by historical conditions; no historicist vision need inhere in the phrase. That either interpretation of the phrase can be substantiated confirms my contention that ethical interpretations of texts are directed by human interests that are themselves context specific.

Camus does not have a single protocol for the form of ethical fiction. He does, however, have a series of protocols that, though perhaps inconsistent with one another, are indeed consistent with a broader philosophical method that holds contingency as the basic premise of philosophical speculation. Camus may have a purposive agenda for fiction, but it is purposive only insofar as the novel must perpetuate some image of narrative unity whose terminus is the result of an artist's desire to find the best possible end to the story. The best possible ending to a fictional narrative need not, and in Camus's mind should not, try to sell itself as the best possible ending for the historical narrative of the fate of humankind. A novel may be said to rectify life when a reader is sympathetic toward the way the characters in the novel resolve whatever tension generated the narrative. Whereas socialist realism tries to convey *the* ideal image of a post-ideological future to all people, nonmonologic art may perhaps try to convey *an* ideal image of the future to some. On this account of Camus's attitude toward the morally instructive potential and responsibility of literature, the ethical value of the novel exists in the dialogue both among the novel's pedagogic voices and between the novel and its critics.

Thus, Camus's claim that "if it is not indeed the task of intelligence to modify history, its real task will nevertheless be to act upon man, for it is man who makes history" (*LCE*, 196) reveals a generous estimation of human volition. Subsequently, it provoked the ire of those Marxist intellectuals with a less-than-sanguine view of a person's or a people's ability to penetrate ideological opacity. But to position human beings as the target of intellectual labor is to abet the moral dialogue that Camus insists should ideally precede the modification of social relations. Nothing in Camus's writing signifies an irreparable break with socialist values; he simply wants to preserve the individual's right to choose these values as lucidly and as freely as possible, partly because he is certain that, given the freedom, the individual will choose an ethic founded in solidarity.

As for the didactic rôle of the artist in the creation of a morally instructive text, Camus is coy. In a 1959 interview, he first confesses his early desire to be a teacher, but then demurs when told he is considered an "intellectual master" by a large body of his readers: "As to being an 'intellectual leader,' it simply makes me laugh. To teach, you need to know. To guide other people, you must know how to guide yourself" (*LCE*, 359). The latter statement reiterates his response to a similar question posed to him in 1951: "A master already! But I don't claim to teach anybody! Whoever thinks this is mistaken. The problems confronting young people today are the same ones confronting me, that is all. And I am far from having solved them. I therefore do not think that I have any right to play the role you mention" (*LCE*, 352).

Camus cannot sincerely evade complicity in the morally instructive dimension of his work; he has written his texts. The very possibility of an investigation into the moral dynamics of *The Plague* presupposes the text's moral dimension, so the real question of an ethical reading is not "What ethics?" but "How ethics?" To allow himself the signature of master would probably put Camus too close for comfort to the historicist demagogues he most distrusted. Again, the subtext of these disavowals is the need for moral dialogue: Camus will admit to broadcasting common human experiences, judging them according to his standards, and then challenging his readers to develop a critical moral consciousness in response to their own social conditions.

The Plague was published by Librairie Gallimard in 1947. Thereafter, for a period of about twenty-five years, the text received considerable critical attention. Between the early 1970s and the early 1980s, with several notable exceptions, critical interest both in the novel and in Camus in general, waned measurably. The last ten years have seen a resurgence in Camus scholarship and interpretation, with several "series" studies even appearing exclusively on *The Plague*. Textual criticism of the first twenty-five years very often simply judged the legitimacy and inclusiveness of the narrative's historical and moral import, whereas recent criticism has been more scrupulous about evaluating the political assumptions on which earlier evaluations of the text's historical and moral import were based.

Early criticism of *The Plague*'s moral content frequently fell into one of two camps. On the one hand were the critics who either praised or condemned what they perceived as the novel's subordination of aesthetic concerns for the sake of the narrative's message. Stephen Spender represented the former position in his review article for the *New York Times Book Review:* "*The Plague* is parable and sermon, and should be considered as such. To criticize it by standards which apply to most fiction would be to risk condemning it for moralizing, which is exactly where it is strongest. *The Plague* stands or falls by its message."[12] Orville Prescott's evaluation in the *Yale Review* condemned the novel for the same moralizing signature: "Instead of writing about particular people [Camus] has written about people who are abstract symbols of various political and moral attitudes."[13]

An entirely different type of criticism brought against *The Plague* found its most persuasive spokesmen in Sartre and Barthes. Defending Francis Jeanson, a colleague who had written a review of Camus's philosophical treatise *The Rebel*, to which Camus himself responded harshly, Sartre wrote: "In 1940, political choice confronted our fellow Frenchmen . . . [Jeanson] did not claim that the Resistance could have been easy, and, although he had not yet had the benefit of your lectures, he had just happened to have heard about the tortures, firing squads and deportations, about the reprisals which followed attacks, and the excruciating decisions they involved for the individual conscience. . . . But these problems arose from the action itself, and to understand them, one had to be already engaged in it."[14] Sartre was making a distinction between Camus's theoretical dedication to the principle of revolt against whatever might threaten the value of human life, which Camus believed to be inviolable, and the material consequences of defending that principle. To enforce this distinction, Sartre made direct reference to *The Plague*:

> You were fortunate in that the common fight against the Germans symbolized, in your eyes and ours, the union of all men against inhuman fatalities. By choosing injustice, the German, of his own accord, allied himself with the blind forces of nature, and in *La Peste* you were able to have his role played by microbes, without anyone getting the joke. . . . Thus, a concurrence of circumstances . . . allowed you to conceal from

yourself the fact that man's struggle against Nature is, at the same time the cause and effect of another struggle, equally old and pitiless, man's struggle against man. You revolted against death, but in the iron belts which surround cities, other men revolted again [*sic*] social conditions which raised the toll of mortality.[15]

Sartre's commentary introduced an evaluative vocabulary on which Barthes would draw several years later in his 1955 review, "*La Peste:* Annales d'une epidemie ou roman de la solitude?" With its depiction of solidarity in the struggle against death as a metaphor for the Resistance, Camus's novel was obviously intended as an allegory of the German Occupation. But, contended Barthes, and later Sartre, because Camus chose to pit the citizens of Oran against a biological disease, a force of nature, he evaded the profound and immediate moral dilemma facing the Resistance against the Nazis. Put another way, "by inferring that human nature is inherently evil, and that the true sickness of society is not solely the result of historical influences, Camus was ignoring the role of social injustice and inequality as well as the specific historical events that spawned Fascism."[16] One would not unreasonably expect a clear-minded individual to want to protect his or her community from the threat of a deadly virus that could not exact calculated reprisals in response to the effort against it. It was, however, well known that the Nazis had no compunction about slaughtering "innocent" (the word is admittedly problematic, in that it implies the guilt of those not included in this substratum of victims) people when the Resistance successfully plotted against the German forces. The only consequences of fighting a plague was that it might continue to spread arbitrarily or return to a state of dormancy. Plague could not be vindictive. The same could not be said of the Nazis.

Barthes's critique was powerful for another, intimately related reason: it inaugurated the now notorious charge that Camus's novel, by virtue of its naturalizing evil, signifies a refusal to depict human existence as part of an historical equation. By bringing this additional indictment, a vicious critical cycle was put in place to direct the novel's readership. On Barthes's account, refusing to represent contemporary historical pressures intensified Camus's moral dodge, since there can be no ethics without historical time. Camus's allegory, with its pretense toward corroborating the absolute value of human life, thereby betrayed its morally instructive potential. Not only was it an attempt to validate a transcendental category,

but it was a failed attempt at that. At least socialist realism effectively transmitted its agenda, if too much so. Barthes's review essentially judged
Camus's text worthless, both ethically and aesthetically.

Camus rejoined Barthes's evaluation of *The Plague*'s antihistoricism and
ethos of political quietism in an open letter of January 11, 1955. The substance of his defense is worth reproducing:

> The question you ask: "What would the fighters against the plague do
> confronted with the all-too-human face of the scourge," is unjust in this
> respect: it ought to have been asked in the past tense, and then it would
> have received the answer, a positive one. What these fighters, whose
> experience I have to some extent translated, did do, they did in fact
> against men, and you know at what cost. They will do it again, no doubt,
> when any terror confronts them, whatever face it may assume, for terror
> has several faces. Still another justification for my not having named any
> particular one, in order better to strike at them all. Doubtless this is what
> I'm reproached with, the fact that *The Plague* can apply to any resistance
> against any tyranny. But it is not legitimate to reproach me or, above all,
> to accuse me of rejecting history—unless it is proclaimed that the only
> way of taking part in history is to make tyranny legitimate. (*LCE*, 340)

Camus's case that the Resistance made its choices and lived with the
consequences is weak; it does not significantly undermine Barthes's judgment that in the novel the plague's resisters are still fighting against a disease, not against other human beings. Camus does not fare much better in
trying to dismiss the general criticism that the novel thereby elides serious
issues regarding historical and ethical responsibility. He intimates an interpretive matrix in which *The Plague* either endorses some form of historicism, which it most assuredly does not, or it in hindsight records historical
conditions only thereafter allegorized as disease. The adequacy of Camus's
reply to Barthes thus hinges on whether one permits the either/or matrix
to govern an estimation of *The Plague*'s historical and moral dimensions.
Since the majority of the novel's first-generation critics flatly rejected the
either/or matrix, it followed that Camus's attempt to defend *The Plague*
was also judged a failure.

The second wave of *The Plague*'s critics also problematized the oversimplified either/or matrix that Camus offered to vindicate his decision to
allegorize human barbarity as a natural disease; the result of this theoretically informed critical work has been to assist in replenishing historical and

moral tension to the text.[17] An interesting characteristic about these critical revisions is that, because they are based on various theoretical discourses and practices that have dominated literary studies for only the last thirty years, they could not likely have been produced as the first critical response to Camus's novel. Furthermore, they suggest that responsible ethical criticism must know its place; that is, it must comprehend the historically contingent validity of its readings. But since the Left's virulent attack on *The Plague* has so overdetermined contemporary reception of Camus's text, the most recent exegetical work on the text's moral component has had to prove its credibility against considerable prejudice.

Barthes's most damaging hit to *The Plague* was advanced on the claim that Camus had allegorized evil, thereby diminishing the text's representation of history and morality. But it was just a matter of time before someone hit back on the grounds that contemporary ideas about allegory had rather diminished Barthes's argument. At least since Paul de Man's *Allegories of Reading*, most of which was composed between 1972 and 1973, it has been impossible to think of allegory as a systematic, one-to-one correspondence between a comprehensive series of phenomenal signs and a transcendent meaning. Basing his evaluation on Camus's deromanticization of historicism, Laurence M. Porter was one of the first to make a stab at rethinking the consequences of the novel's allegorical structure, explaining that the plague and history both lack "a discernible meaning for Camus."[18] In contrast to Porter, Serge Doubrovsky alleges that allegory "does not negate history, but extracts an ultimate meaning from it."[19]

Colin Davis has recently challenged the traditional bias, after Barthes, regarding allegory and exegesis: "What is at stake here is not whether or not *La Peste* can be called an allegory, but whether this designation succeeds in controlling possible interpretations of the novel. . . . the Defoe epigraph and auto-exegetical passages in *La Peste* can be seen to serve as signals of allegorical intention and to authorize allegorical interpretation; but the expedient of describing the text as allegory does not guarantee the exclusive truth of any particular reading." As an example of allegory's inability to govern univocal interpretation, Davis suggests that Rieux, by virtue of his sending infected citizens to the quarantine camps, could be read as being complicit with the "disease" and not in struggle against it; in this case, the traditionally disparaged allegorical reading "backfires on itself as Rieux's activities seem in conflict with what is taken to be the moral stance of the novel."[20] Once it is no longer possible to make the novel's pieces fit into a neat allegorical framework, an element of moral dynamism can be restored to the text's dialogue.

Disabling the traditional reading of allegory contributes to a reanalysis of *The Plague*'s historical and moral dimensions in a second way. Traditionally, allegory enabled a more referential model of signification than is usually acknowledged in the present theoretical climate. If the plague need no longer be understood as unsatisfactorily "representing" the Occupation, what may it more adequately signify?[21] In a study the more significant for its 1965 date of publication, Emmett Parker made the distinction between the plague's representing the "Nazi forces of oppression" and the "abstractions in the name of which the Nazis had waged their war."[22] This is no quibble. Barthes's dissatisfaction with the novel depended on solidifying the allegory wherein biological disease is tantamount to Nazi barbarism. The more opaque this equation, the more suspect Barthes's judgment. Furthermore, refiguring the plague metaphor as abstraction rather than human brutality effectively protects the disease's opponents from reprisals, thus challenging the opinion that *The Plague*'s depiction of ethical crisis is naive and oversimplified.

Shoshana Felman's scrutiny of *The Plague* as authentic chronicle of historical events (Nazi brutality and the Holocaust) might be a persuasive way to conclude this rather abridged survey of the dialogue among contemporary critics who have evaluated the historical and moral import of Camus's text. Drawing on seminal deconstructive and structuralist Marxist theoretical principles, Felman elides the simplicity of Barthes's allegorical reading; rather, she affirms, "What is striking in Camus' choice of metaphor in lieu of the historic referent, is that the Plague designates not simply a metaphorically substitutive event, but an event that is *historically impossible: an event without a referent*. . . . The Plague (the Holocaust) is disbelieved because it does not enter, and cannot be framed by, any existing frame of reference." Felman could certainly be appropriating Althusser's explanation of ideology as something a bit more complex and compelling than mere "false consciousness" when she observes that

> the event historically occurs through its disappearance as an historic actuality and as a referential possibility. It is as though the vanishing point of its literality . . . is what constitutes, precisely, the historical particularity of the event before and after its occurrence. The event . . . occurs,

in other words, as what is not provided for by the conceptual framework that we call "History." . . . Since we can literally witness only that which is within the reach of the conceptual frame of reference we inhabit, the Holocaust is testified to by *The Plague* as an event whose specificity resides, precisely, in the fact that it cannot, historically, be witnessed.[23]

On Felman's interpretation, Barthes's dismissal of *The Plague* as eliding historical commitment is predicated on an empiricist view of historical knowledge that is, at the least, debatable. Considering the historical moment in which he reviewed *The Plague*, Barthes might be forgiven his critical naïveté for having relied on a Lukácsian model of the temporary character of ideology and the relative accessibility of the historical. However, anyone writing in a post-Althusserian theoretical milieu would have a more formidable time demonstrating the absence of history solely on the basis of the absence of a transparent historical referent.[24] Ironically, Felman's own asseveration regarding the impossibility of an event without a referent seems to me to draw as much on the Lukácsian perspective on ideology as on the Althusserian; thus, her reading of *The Plague* provides an intriguing site where the exegetical dialogue between first- and second-generation critics is most alive.

Since the nature of any ethics is to inform choice in time, a novel's moral dynamic is supported by the narrative structures that manufacture and underscore the text's sense of temporality. Concurrent with the experience of temporality is some kind of ideological tension. In *The Plague,* ideological tension is assured when a city's populace is compelled to confront a phenomenon that tears it from its habitual lifestyle and forces it to negotiate hostile temporal conditions. In so doing, a moral dialogue is set in place that is informed by competing pedagogic voices. These voices reflect a range of ethical agendas, from those that seek to validate an absolute ethical standard for behavior to those that affirm the contingency and historical specificity of ethical value. The dynamic of this dialogue offers a site where the structural component of ethical claims may be investigated.

Camus's novel contains at least two theoretical benchmarks to help the reader determine whether a specific ethical voice supports an absolute or a contingent ethical position. First, a character's sensitivity to ethical contingency is revealed in the character's willingness or desire, once the plague appears, to renounce the routine of daily habit and persevere in the fight against disease.[25] Second, a character's acknowledgment of moral contingency is coterminous with a diminished faith in the referentiality of language. This latter textual principle at work in *The Plague* is a rather obvious effect of Camus's definition, cited above, of truth as being mutable.[26] Both a commitment to some kind of struggle and an awareness of language's limits silently confirm temporality and underwrite a propensity toward moral thinking.

The Plague's narrator is first of all concerned with assuring his readers that the story they are about to hear is true. This is important. Camus does not come right out and say in his notebooks that he wants his readers to identify with the fighters against plague, but the notion of fighting against something that seeks to injure us is a condition with which most of us can presumably empathize. On a first reading, before Rieux reveals himself to be the narrator, one has no reason to doubt that the text's ethical positions are being represented fairly and accurately.[27] The threat of didacticism or proselytizing is reduced because the narrator scrupulously labors to avoid disclosing his own agenda. If the reader does not precisely grant the narrator a privileged view from nowhere, he or she certainly has a difficult time defining the ethical stakes of the narrator's choice of material. The overall diegetic effect is the illusion that the narrator's choices masquerade as the product of autonomous forces.[28] In the absence of a clearly subjective narrative voice, ethical tension is subsequently easier to maintain: no single ethical position is permitted to dominate the others.

The Plague's first chapter begins with a characterization of Oran, a town where the seasons are "cried in the marketplaces" (*P*, 3). The sum of the narrator's observations may be encapsulated in the picture of a citizenry that is, with extremely few exceptions, entirely reified:[29]

> The truth is, everyone is bored, and devotes himself to cultivating habits. Our citizens work hard, but solely with the object of getting rich. Their chief interest is in commerce, and their chief aim in life is, as they call it, "doing business". . . . You can get through the days there without trouble, once you have formed habits. . . . Viewed from this angle, its life is not particularly exciting; that must be admitted. But, at least, social unrest is quite unknown among us. . . . Treeless, glamourless, soulless, the town of Oran ends by seeming restful and, after a while, you go complacently to sleep there. (*P*, 4–6)

Day to day, nothing changes in Oran. Prior to the plague, there does not appear to be any significant tension between individuals or between social and economic classes. There is no time where there is no measure of change. There is no need for morality where there is no time. There is only an aestheticized facsimile of life. Before the outbreak of the epidemic, Oran is a city of the dead. In the course of this description, the narrator either recounts or implies the relationship of each of the central characters to an ideology of comfort through commercial success, an ideology I will hereafter refer to as bourgeois.[30] The narrator also provides a sense of the length to which certain central characters acknowledge the contingency of language. The first chapter thereby yields a vigorous sense of the predisposition of each of the main characters toward moral pedagogy before the disease appears and the pedagogic dynamic proper begins to shape the text's moral dialogue.

For example Rieux, whose financial security as a prominent physician would ostensibly qualify him as bourgeois, indicates a sensitivity to social injustice when Rambert solicits the doctor's opinion about the sanitary conditions of the virtually unrepresented Arab population. When Rambert confesses that he will not be permitted to report a condemnation of the conditions, Rieux withholds his judgment in the name of truth. He is unwilling to put a corrective spin on the contradictions he perceives in bourgeois ideology. An instance is also recounted in which Rieux does not charge a poor patient who is gravely ill.[31] Correlating action to circumstance, Rieux is not uncritically trapped in the capitalist relations of production that determine the behavior of the majority of the Oranais. After Rieux does not cooperate with Rambert's inquiry, the journalist observes, "You talk the language of Saint-Just" (*P*, 12). This is more than a reference to the kind of derisive epithets directed at Camus himself by the 1940s. It intimates that Rieux's refusal to compromise truth is merely an idiosyncratic version of moral absolutism.

But Rieux is far from propounding the correspondent theory of language on which moral absolutisms would traditionally depend. In the controversy over naming the disease once it erupts (*P*, 48–50), most of the town officials and doctors demur when the word *plague* is mentioned. On their view of linguistic reference, to utter the *word* plague is to incarnate the *thing* plague; by controlling the use of the word, they may control the growth of the epidemic.[32] Rieux postpones using the word until he is fairly certain that it accurately denotes a commonly understood syndrome. When he is convinced of the identity of the disease, he then suggests that the disease be denoted through signifiers that have entered the lexicon with some stability (*P*, 42). He wants to use language responsibly. He knows that there will be social consequences if the disease is not called by a name that will set the bureaucratic ball rolling to stop it.

More important, this knowledge is predicated on his understanding that language has no *natural* connection to what it signifies. When asked by another doctor, "Please answer me quite frankly, Are you absolutely convinced it's plague?" Rieux answers, "You're stating the problem wrongly. It's not a question of the term I use; it's a question of time" (*P*, 51). Contrary to most of his colleagues—staunch defenders of their materially comfortable lifestyles—Rieux never for a moment imagines that by *not* using the word, the disease will disappear: "It has small importance whether you call it plague or some rare kind of fever. The important thing is to prevent its killing off half the population of this town" (*P*, 49). Rieux's problematized relationship toward his social class, in addition to his attention to language's historicity, stabilizes his pedagogic voice when the plague overcomes Oran.[33]

Of the novel's protagonists, Grand also does not participate uncritically in the Oranais' proclivity toward acquiring wealth and comfort. Unlike Rieux, he is a "menial" (*P*, 23), but a menial who avoids vocational promotion from fear of losing his free time. Like Rieux, he is not attracted to the routinized lifestyle so glorified by the overwhelming majority of Oranais:

> All he desired was the prospect of a life suitably insured on the material side by honest work. . . . He was one of those rare people, rare in our town as elsewhere, who have the courage of their good feelings. What little he told of his personal life vouched for acts of kindness and a capacity for affection that no one in our times dares own to. . . . He confessed to dearly loving his nephews and sister. . . . He admitted that the thought of his parents, whom he lost when he was very young, often gave him a pang. He did not conceal the fact that he had a special affection for a church bell in his part of the town which started pealing very melodiously at about five every afternoon. (*P*, 44, 46)

The narrator is most impressed by Grand's reason for aiding the attempted suicide Cottard: "One's got to help a neighbor, hasn't one?" (*P*, 20). Committed to dynamics of an interpersonal nature, sharing

Rieux's inclination toward solidarity, acutely sensitive to temporal pressure, Grand is not so easily implicated in the Oranais's ethos of ideological stasis.

His self-criticism and satisfaction with his social status notwithstanding, one of Grand's most significant characteristics is his linguistic impotence: he can never "find his words" (*P*, 45). As a result, he magnifies their importance to the point of compulsion, spending his free time over several years rewriting the first sentence of a planned novel; he wants his words to refer perfectly to some imaginary referent so that his ideas can be incarnated aesthetically. As a consequence, the morally instructive potential of his ethical voice is somewhat vague; it hinges on an internal tension between moral and aesthetic pressures.

Both the ideological coordinates and the pedagogic capacity of Tarrou's ethical voice are also hazy. Tarrou has "private means" but is not engaged in business. A man of leisure, there is nothing to suggest that he wishes to multiply his fortune. Tarrou's only evident discipline is the journal he assiduously keeps. The journal provides insight into Tarrou's potential as a morally instructive voice. If Grand is overly sensitive to the aesthetic presentation of words, Tarrou is arguably not sensitive enough.[34] A collection of fragments and episodes, the journal becomes ordered through the narrator's principle of selection so that it seems more cohesive than it actually is. The journal's lack of a seamless, authoritative narrative also helps to preclude the idea that Tarrou might have complete knowledge of the town's activities during the epidemic.[35]

Tarrou's ethical position is one among many. What distinguishes his contribution to *The Plague*'s moral dialogue is a lucid perception of time's effects on the development of moral consciousness. Tarrou notes in his journal: "'*Query:* How contrive not to waste one's time? *Answer:* By being fully aware of it all the while. *Ways in which this can be done*: By spending one's days on an uneasy chair in a dentist's waiting room; by remaining on one's balcony all of a Sunday afternoon; by listening to lectures in a language one doesn't know; by traveling by the longest and least-convenient train routes, and of course standing all the way; by lining up at the box-office of theatres and then not buying a seat; and so forth'" (*P*, 26).

Cottard and Paneloux complete the cast of characters whose ethical voices considerably color the moral dialogue of Camus's text. Cottard has "private means in a small way" (*P*, 32). He welcomes the plague as an opportunity to exploit black market conditions and amass a small fortune. Cottard simply seeks wealth for its own sake, not particularly for the sake of the comfort it brings. For him, language is merely a means to establish the conditions for reproducing capital. His expression of an ethical position occurs almost by default in that he doesn't desire a return to the Oranais's habits prior to the plague; without plague, his financial scheming must come to an end.

Although he does not play a substantial rôle in the novel's first chapter, Father Paneloux's ethical presence before the plague can be synopsized with some accuracy. He has faith in the incarnationist power of the Word, and he believes it is the responsibility of all human beings to use language so as to approximate most closely the perfect form of God's will. This view toward language would be commensurate with a moral absolutism immune to the contingencies generated by time.

As the first Oranais—who are metonymically associated with the dying rats—succumb to the disease, the remainder of the townspeople deny that plague exists and conduct business as usual. They are neither accustomed to, nor enamored of, anything that disturbs their economic routine. Even public safety is motivated by preservation of the status quo.[36] Only when the bourgeoisie see their own fall ill are they possessed by "fear, and with fear serious reflection" (*P*, 23). But the majority of the townspeople are singularly unprepared for a situation requiring moral engagement with temporal exigency. Put simply, they do not have the ability to think morally. David Sprintzen explains why: "The moral values offered to justify and guide [bourgeois ideals] have been shown to be hypocritical formalisms, *simply used to cover the drive for power and wealth of that privileged minority*"; and he quotes Camus: "'The entirely formal morality by which bourgeois society lives had been emptied of its substance by the gaping holes our elites have opened in it for their profit.'"[37]

Habit and routine diminish both the experience of temporal change and the capacity for moral thought before the plague. When the epidemic occurs and the Oranais are forced from their sheltered, thoughtless lifestyle, the perception of time becomes foregrounded in the narrative, not least in the feeling of exile, of being sedimented in the moment without future hope.[38] This is one of the great ironies of Camus's text. When the town is bustling with economic activity, time can only be represented as habit, which, like ritual, is a way of mastering history and diminishing the effect of temporal change. However, when commerce dies in Oran (*P*, 77), and nothing seems to be moving, people are suddenly cognizant of their precarious position in the course of natural and social events. The Oranais better notice stasis than they do the action surrounding trade, but the very phenomenon of notice is compelling evidence of temporal consciousness.

While it is certainly true that many Oranais "mark time" during the plague (*P*, 184–85), it is less evident that, under this condition, "even the words at one's disposal lose their impact."[39] It is fairer to say that, under plague conditions, some people's words lose their impact, but even this assessment may not be accurate. Those characters who suffer total linguistic impotence are those who, uncritically reproducing the Oranais' economy, never entered public moral dialogue in the first place.[40] The words of these characters never had impact, and their general response to plague is either denial or capitulation. Indeed, these responses could imply an ethical position, but the active pedagogic dynamic of the text truly begins when those characters who already demonstrate a potential for moral thought—among whom are Rieux, Grand, Tarrou, Cottard, and Paneloux—react to the epidemic and enter into a moral dialogue regarding the best possible course of action to take against the plague. Moreover, the changes through which the respective ethical voices of these characters go provides yet another significant record of *The Plague*'s temporal dimension.

There is ample textual evidence to suggest that a temporal logic informs the Oranais' social conditions even as the majority of the Oranais themselves disclaim the plague: the epidemic accentuates the effect of context on semiotic meaning, a sure index of the presence of time. For example, the town's ordinary laws become better respected as the public's perception toward violent crime changes (*P*, 145–46). When town officials decide to award a military medal of honor to border guards who die at their post, controversy ensues. Some believe that the medal is warranted since, under the prevailing state of martial law, the guards qualify as military men; others believe that the award is too easily won and cheapens the honor of legitimate military distinction (*P*, 170).

As the plague drags on, people gradually forget things about the loved ones from whom they are separated; time implacably erodes their memories (*P*, 180). And, in what is perhaps the grimmest reminder of temporal exigency in the text, the routine for burial grows more mechanized and impersonal with every significant increase in the daily body count until the "last remnant of decorum [goes] by the board, and men and women [are] flung into the death-pits indiscriminately" (*P*, 175). The emergency burial procedures culminate in the transformation of an outlying section of the town into a huge crematorium. The working-class residents of this section, convinced that they are being poisoned by germ-laden ash, threaten to storm the center of the city if the smoke is not diverted, a demand to which the authorities immediately concede (*P*, 178). This is one of only two references to class struggle to be found in *The Plague*.[41] It is no coincidence that it occurs after time is supposed to have stopped.

After the plague is confirmed, Rieux and Rambert discuss the latter's separation from his lover. Finding Rieux unreceptive to his pleas to be released from the quarantine imposed on the town, Rambert indicts the doctor with living in a world of "abstractions" (*P*, 87). This is a serious charge, for the abstract is, on my understanding of it, something not firmly grounded in phenomenological time. Rieux's response to Rambert is narrated as an interior monologue: "Could that term 'abstraction' really apply to these days he spent in his hospital while the plague was battening on the town, raising its death-toll to five hundred victims a week? Yes, an element of abstraction, of a divorce from reality, entered into such calamities. Still, when abstraction sets to killing you, you've got to get busy with it" (*P*, 88–89).

Were the plague figured as a literary text to be read, Rieux would exemplify an exegetical method of the responsible ethical critic: his idea of what is needed to fight the epidemic is couched in language that, like his official diagnosis of the plague, is careful to avoid any kind of referential presumption. It doesn't matter how he identifies his stand on the epidemic; the epidemic, abstract or not, is real and must be addressed. Denial and escape, both of the plague and of moral engagement with temporal pressures, are unacceptable to the doctor.

The source of Rieux's ethical voice is his repudiation of anything that is not contingent. "Since the order of the world is shaped by death," he asks Tarrou, "mightn't it be better for God if we refuse to believe in Him and struggle with all our might against death, without raising our eyes toward the heaven where He sits in silence?" (*P*, 128). To press his point about the contingency of moral value, Rieux compares his commitment to alleviating human suffering to Paneloux's: "He hasn't come in contact with death; that's why he can speak with such assurance of the truth—with a capital T.

But every country priest who visits his parishioners and has heard a man gasping for breath on his deathbed thinks as I do. He'd try to relieve human suffering before trying to point out its excellence" (*P*, 126).

Rieux's ethical position is tested when he and Rambert consider whether it is better to fight or flee the plague. At first, Rambert remains convinced that Rieux represents an empty ethic devoted to serving an idea.[42] Rieux's disclaimer, "Man isn't an idea, Rambert" (*P*, 162), does not persuade. However, when Rambert learns from Tarrou that, like the journalist, Rieux is also separated from someone he loves, Rambert is converted to the struggle. Rieux's pedagogic voice therefore successfully promotes solidarity through an experience of shared, material conditions, and it serves as an ethical position that resonates in the text's moral dialogue.

Grand's commitment to fighting the plague closely resembles Rieux's; he merely wants to do what needs to be done to defeat the epidemic: "Plague is here and we've got to make a stand, that's obvious. Ah, I only wish everything were as simple" (*P*, 134). Grand conveys no overt desire to escape his moral responsibility to other human beings and return to the Oranais' daily, desensitizing routine. But his persistent devotion to his sentence, even while assisting the sanitation squads, continues to distract him far into aesthetic concerns. His uncompromising devotion to literary form while the plague rages on prompts the question of whether Grand can adequately articulate a sustained, responsible moral engagement with the contingencies generated by the disease. Tarrou also reiterates the ethic of solidarity predicated on an acknowledgment of temporal contingency. He summarizes his code of morals to Rieux in one word, "comprehension" (*P*, 130). He appears to want the greatest possible knowledge of the material conditions surrounding him in order to maximize the impact of his resistance.

Paneloux completes the inventory of characters who in some way commit to nullifying the plague. Although he delivers a sermon interpreting the plague as a symbol of God's dissatisfaction with humankind's moral conduct, Paneloux joins the sanitary squads. This dual engagement with the epidemic reflects a complex pedagogic motive; at this point in the plague's progress, it is impossible to determine whether his greatest commitment is to a human or a transcendent moral code. Only Cottard appears entirely self-interested, appears not to care about his contribution to the town's moral climate. But this indifference to specifically moral concerns is his ethical position. He revels in the circumstances induced by the plague, and his ethic of participation in the plague's disruption of the Oranais' previous lifestyle persists unchanged throughout the novel. He justifies his position to Tarrou by avowing the sterility of struggle: "The plague has the whip hand of you and there's nothing to be done about it" (*P*, 157). What compromises Cottard's ethical voice is that his stated premise for surrender—the plague has the whip hand over the town—does not contradict the belief of the other characters, who also appreciate the enormity of their task. The premise does not necessitate surrender.

With the exception of Cottard, *The Plague*'s pedagogic characters all espouse some expression of an ethic of struggle against plague in the name of solidarity. Comprising the novel's moral climate, the tension among these expressions is sustained by the respective faith that each character invests in language's ability to refer. The issue of the possibility of linguistic correspondence is thus a meeting point for both the content and the modality of *The Plague*'s moral dynamic. Camus is able to suggest that pedagogically effective ethical voices are sensitive to historical pressures and linguistic indeterminacy by structuring *The Plague* in such a way that those characters who maintain an absolute standard for moral behavior succumb to the disease. However, this is not to say that these characters' pedagogic voices are thereby completely eliminated from the text's moral tension. Rather, the physical absence of a deceased character can powerfully recall the character's ethical position in a moral dialogue. Paneloux is the first of the novel's pedagogic characters to succumb to plague. His death does not guarantee the removal of his position from the text's moral dynamic. Despite his active service in the sanitation squads, Paneloux never relinquishes the absolute foundation for his solidarity with the townspeople. His adherence to absolute Truth places his ethical voice at some odds with Rieux's, as illustrated by their respective reactions to a child's death:

> "That sort of thing is revolting because it passes our human understanding. But perhaps we should love what we cannot understand."
>
> . . . .
>
> "No, Father. I've a very different idea of love. And until my dying day I shall refuse to love a scheme of things in which children are put to torture."

A shade of disquietude crossed the priest's face. "Ah, Doctor," he
said sadly, "I've just realized what is meant by 'grace.'" (*P*, 218–19)

To love what we do not fully understand is to love abstraction, a possibility that Rieux rejects. What is not phenomenal and human does not concern Rieux. He does not fight the plague to fulfill the requirements of an
absolute faith; he fights because, under the circumstances, fighting is the
best contingency available. Rieux denies God's way of ordering the world;
so Paneloux, with the doctor's ethic obviously on his mind, recalls the
temptation of denial in his second sermon: "My brothers, a time of testing
has come for us all. We must believe everything or deny everything. And
who among you, I ask, would dare to deny everything?" (*P*, 224). Paneloux's ethic of "All or Nothing" (*P*, 225) for the sake of metaphysical
redemption challenges Rieux's moral relativism.[43] Such an ethic is essentially an ideological buffer between human beings and unhappiness, since
heaven awaits those who live justly even in misery. Heaven, the goal of
Paneloux's ethic, is the apotheosis of the aesthetic—a purely formal being-
present. Paneloux's "ethic" reproduces a desensitizing relation of production that is fundamentally hostile to the development of a contingent moral
consciousness.

The narrator's early observations about Tarrou suggest that his ethical
voice most closely overlaps with Rieux's. He seems satisfied to record in
his journal only limited information about the minutiae of daily life. He
preaches "sympathy" toward his fellow men in "plain, clear-cut language"
(*P*, 254). Pledging his energy to keep a prominent sense of historical contingency alive in peoples' minds, he voices a profound mistrust of any
social, political, religious, or economic movement that proclaims that a
"few deaths [are] inevitable for the building up of a new world in which
murder [will] cease to be" (*P*, 250). Tarrou thus possesses all the necessary
qualifications for a powerful pedagogic voice. Why, then, does he, like
Paneloux, succumb to the epidemic?

Tarrou's death can in part be attributed to the absolutism that gradually emerges in his ethical position. A strong hint of this absolutism occurs
in a conversation with Rieux, in which to the doctor's question, "Do you
really imagine you know everything about life?" Tarrou confidently answers,
"Yes" (*P*, 129–30). Tarrou arrogantly implies that, though he understands
his place in time, historical contingencies will never challenge or compromise his comprehension of his existential predicament. Rieux indirectly

intimates the danger of such arrogance when, discussing Rambert's decision to remain in the city to fight the plague even when his escape has been
arranged, the doctor remarks, "A man can't cure and know at the same
time" (*P*, 210). Not intentionally aimed at Tarrou, this judgment essentially
condemns Tarrou's self-confident estimation of his own knowledge as
incommensurable with the attitude needed to battle the plague authenti-
cally. When Tarrou instructs Rambert that if the journalist wishes to take
a share in other peoples' unhappiness, then he'll have no time left for his
own happiness—"the choice ha[s] to be made" (*P*, 209)—the extremism
attending this mandate is easy to overlook.

It is harder to miss the evident either/or logic—a logic that has
no place in responsible ethical criticism—in his comment on mankind's
experiments with various manifestations of historicism: "I resolved to have
no truck with anything which, directly or indirectly, for good reasons or
for bad, brings death to anyone or justifies others' putting him to death"
(*P*, 253). Finally, he confides to Rieux that what he really desires is to be
"a saint without God" because, unlike the doctor, he is not "ambitious"
enough to be a man (*P*, 255).

When the first critics of *The Plague* accused Camus of dodging historical responsibility and failing to take a stand on the repercussions that could
conceivably follow direct acts of resistance, Tarrou's ethical position
on violence provided a convenient analogic target for their detraction.
However, to condemn the entire text, and Camus's ethical ideology along
with it, on the evidence of Tarrou's conviction seems egregious. Camus's
novel is not a monologic philosophical treatise. Hence, Tarrou simply cannot be taken as Camus's exclusive spokesperson.

The strength necessary to engage a temporal contingency like the
plague is ostensibly too great for Tarrou to bear. But the desire to escape
from historical pressures, which would effectively eliminate the need
for a self-critical moral consciousness, contradicts his earlier, more conditional dedication to solidarity. Like Grand, Tarrou tries to balance aesthetic
and moral proclivities in an internal dialogue that does not impede his
commitment to the suffering Oranais; but he fails. And yet, Tarrou's death
does not end his pedagogic contribution to the development of the text's
moral climate; indeed, the actual timing of Tarrou's death is itself a pedagogic event, for it helps the reader to evaluate Rieux's commitment to
temporal consciousness and provisional ethical foundations.

Before Tarrou dies, Grand suffers a near-fatal battle with the plague. Although Grand is committed to fighting the epidemic, his belief that he might one day produce his flawless, referential sentence is a potential distraction from moral thinking. Paneloux's death, predicated on his adherence to a perfect moral code of absolute faith, might cue the reader to one of the structural reasons for Grand's illness: his relentless pursuit of a perfect literary expression. Perhaps what saves Grand from death is his last-minute demand that Rieux destroy every trace of the notorious sentence. Grand's temporary renunciation of his literary endeavor is symbolic of his ability, consistent throughout the narrative, to rethink the relationship between ethical and aesthetic pressures in his moral consciousness from one temporal exigency to the next. Such critical resourcefulness underscores a formidable pedagogic voice, from which any responsible ethical criticism may learn to avoid essentializing even the most cherished ideological presumptions.

As he contemplated *The Plague*'s moral during his composition of the narrative, Camus wrote: "It was of no use to anything or anyone. Only those who were touched by death directly or in their families learned something. But the truth they have arrived at concerns only themselves. It has no future."[44] The fifth and final chapter of the text addresses this observation. In some ways, it became a self-fulfilling prophesy, as early critics including and after Barthes propounded the interpretation that the text was itself a formal ethical shell, containing no real comment on the unjust social relations of the time. Barthes's exegesis was based on passages such as this one, which describes the populace once the quarantine is lifted and everything has a chance to return to the status quo:

> Calmly they denied, in the teeth of the evidence, that we had ever known a crazy world in which men were killed off like flies, or that precise savagery, that calculated frenzy of the plague, which instilled an odious freedom as to all that was not the here and now; or those charnel-house stenches which stupefied whom they did not kill. In short, they denied that we had ever been that hag-ridden populace a part of which was daily fed into a furnace and went up in oily fumes, while the rest, in shackled impotence, waited their turn. (*P*, 297–98)

Barthes's estimation of *The Plague*'s inability to address real moral injustice is based primarily on the contention that Camus's novel fails to represent either temporality or moral themes in any but an allegorical manner.

But the dynamics of the novel's moral dialogue and the changes within each major character's distinct ethical voice indicate that Camus's novel quite adequately chronicles measurable temporal change and the moral reactions to it. Nevertheless, passages like the one just cited make it easy to understand why readers seeking a forthright, enthusiastic confirmation of an ethic of solidarity might be dissatisfied with Camus's narrative. Few who have survived the plague seem to have learned anything from it. The apparent dissolution of a morally instructive atmosphere preponderates among the Oranais after the epidemic is over, but to reject *The Plague*'s moral component solely on that evidence would be premature.

Despite Barthes's evaluation of its moral component, *The Plague* provides the aesthetic locus for a responsible ethical reading even after the epidemic ends. One need only position the townspeople's denial following the quarantine as simply one more ethically pedagogic voice, albeit a collective one, to be added to the novel's moral dialogue. Further prompting this suggestion is the reminder that the majority of townspeople begin the narrative ignoring moral considerations. From first to last, they want only to direct their attention to a routine whereby they might increase their wealth and comfort. It is the ethical position of the townspeople, so powerful in its absence, that serves to keep a vital moral tension alive in *The Plague* until the chronicle is over. Their collective voice throws into sharp relief the individual pedagogic voices of the novel's surviving major characters, whose respective ethical positions now reflect the consequences of the disease.[45]

Cottard, who stands to lose the most when the epidemic fizzles out, is leery of an absolute forgetting and an accompanying return to social organization prior to the plague. He is not interested in the development of moral consciousness and solidarity. Cottard remains concerned only with himself. He gambles on Tarrou's prediction that all sorts of bureaucratic problems will arise and require a revised public administration once the furor dies down. Moreover, Cottard ideally pictures the town, that is to say himself, "entering on a new lease of life, blotting out its past and starting again with a clean sheet" (*P*, 280). Cottard wants to substitute one manifestation of routinized, habitual social relations with another. Neither will necessitate a self-reflective moral consciousness. Is it likely that Cottard appreciates the irony of his fate? Dragged away by the police after shooting up a small section of town, Cottard ends up entangled in a system of justice whose function is to blot out the past and preserve the kind of static social order he so desires.

After his convalescence, Grand avidly resurrects his sentence. What does his returned attention to form signify for the pedagogic force of his ethical voice? On the one hand, the narrator intimates that Grand's renewed authorial vocation is not undiscerning: reviewing his sentence, Grand decides to "cut out all the adjectives" (P, 306), those linguistic units that are most likely to distract people's attention from his idea's primary meaning. Grand appears wary about perpetrating any linguistic act that might help to perpetuate aesthetic indulgence. And yet, he takes leave of Rieux with a courtly sweep of his hat, the same motion of appreciation he had earlier hoped to inspire in future readers of the bombastic version of his sentence. Grand thus appears able to sustain a lively tension between moral and aesthetic desires.

Rambert is reunited with his wife when the gates are opened: "For the moment he wished to behave like all those others around who believed, or made believe, that plague can come and go without changing anything in men's hearts" (P, 295). Much of the force of Rambert's ethical position hangs on the phrase "he wished." Does he fulfill this wish with full control over the duration of his indulgence? Or is the realization of this wish obstructed by his moral consciousness, which would instruct him that time does not come to an end just because the epidemic ostensibly has? How far does Rambert heed Rieux's injunction, uttered when the quarantine ends, that "it's up to you *now* to prove you're right" (P, 300)?

This gauntlet could almost be taken as the challenge of the entire narrative: moral development is predicated upon an acknowledgment of the way temporal pressures intrude upon consciousness to force constant revaluation of one's commitment to responsible moral thinking. Ethical positions may be adopted in response to temporal exigency, but different exigencies prompt different responses. As with responsible ethical criticism, the position is not more important than the commitment to foreground the aesthetic, structural component of ethical truth claims.

Rieux himself temporarily envisions a "fresh start" (P, 282) in life when his wife returns from the sanatorium for which she departed before quarantine was imposed. Does he thereby hope to exact a suspension of his previous sensitivity to the acute pressures of historical, linguistic, and moral contingency? Tarrou's death has served a pedagogic end, for it inspires Rieux's revelation that "no peace [is] possible to him henceforth" (*P*, 290). But is this revelation, like Hans Castorp's in the snow, conclusive, particularly when silhouetted against Rieux's subsequent consideration: "These people were 'just the same as ever.' But this was at once their strength and their innocence, and it was on this level, beyond all grief, that Rieux could feel himself at one with them" (*P*, 308)? Rieux's identification with the majority of his fellow Oranais is interesting for its lack of precedent; he seems not to judge too harshly the fact that the old routines are so insidiously reemerging. Does he, who is in many respects the narrative's most exemplary rebel, capitulate to these routines and verify Barthes's critique of Camus's text? Or does he keep faith by his commitment to an ethic of rebellion?

What Rieux does do is assimilate the import of Tarrou's other pedagogic pronouncement just before his death—"All a man could win in the conflict between plague and life was knowledge and memories" (*P*, 291)—and bear witness to the epidemic. He writes. By writing the chronicle, Rieux remembers and reintegrates the past into the present. Thus, even though the last few pages of *The Plague* are without immediate moral dialogue between ethical voices, the auto-referential, analeptic structure of the chronicle creates the impression of the text's being in dialogue with itself. Put another way, Rieux assumes the rôle of ethical critic and has himself as his text. A more forthright answer to the question of whether Rieux betrays his ethic of rebellion in order to forget the past and its moral pressures is untenable.

The moral dialogue that Rieux creates in his account is the projection of an internal tension among the moral and aesthetic considerations that must be juggled during any ethical reading. The example of Rieux's literary enterprise—and of Grand's sentence, Tarrou's journal, Rambert's journalism, perhaps even Paneloux's sermons—is metonymically associated with Camus's authorship of *The Plague*: in all these instances, a writer is placed in an intimately self-critical relationship with his text. The construction of a diegetic timeline requires a sustained sensitivity to context, to the way meaning is signified in a less than determinate medium.

By writing moral dialogue about the process of writing moral dialogue, Camus, like Rieux, becomes the subject of his own ethical criticism. Moreover, once published, the novel and its author become the locus of further interpretive practice, part of whose history forms a dialogue that future critics may enter with their ethical readings. On mine, *The Plague* illustrates less a thematic moral lesson than a paradigm for the way moral consciousness may be developed and nourished aesthetically in the conflict between ethical voices. Certainly Rieux, Rambert, Grand—and, in a more absolute way, Paneloux and Tarrou—all voice an ethical position of solidarity. But this is secondary to a manner of creating solidarity— through an acknowledgment of ideological tension and the impact of time on signification—that underscores contingency as the fundamental premise of both moral thought and ethical textual practice. The premium placed on contingency ensures the structural tension among competing ethically pedagogic voices. At the same time, the contingency of ethical knowledge satisfies Camus's definition of the novel as a vehicle for moral dialogue. It is only after the structure of this dialogue is established that its content can be contested.

4

Marlow's Moral Education, from *Heart of Darkness* to *Lord Jim*

![▪]

> We looked on, waiting patiently—there was nothing else to do till
> the end of the flood; but it was only after a long silence, when he
> said in a hesitating voice, "I suppose you fellows remember I did
> once turn fresh-water sailor for a bit," that we knew we were fated,
> before the ebb began to run, to hear about one of Marlow's incon-
> clusive experiences.
>
> Joseph Conrad, *Heart of Darkness*

Few critical studies of Joseph Conrad's literary corpus fail to somehow
engage the texts' representations of moral conflict. Replete with inconclusive commentary on the connection between aesthetics and morality,
Conrad's nonfiction writing seems to encourage this interpretive dialogue.
He draws the connection that creative art is composed "for the edification
of mankind" without much ado.[1] However, this rather synoptic remark
hardly conveys the otherwise characteristically elaborate, and occasionally
ambivalent, tenor of Conrad's thoughts on the morally instructive component of literature.

Conrad's position on the manner in which literature produces moral
effects affords a suitable opening for an analysis of the intertextual
progress of Marlow's moral education from the moment he joins the
Company in *Heart of Darkness* to the moment he ends his letter to the
Privileged Man in *Lord Jim*. As his nonfiction writing suggests, Conrad is
unwilling to validate ethical truth claims that are not produced in a dialogue of interpretive voices. Analogously, what makes Marlow a compelling subject for ethical criticism is his sensitivity to historical pressures
and the structural tension among his and other ethically pedagogic voices.
Throughout *Heart of Darkness* and *Lord Jim*, Marlow keeps moral dialogue

alive in his consciousness, regardless of the manifold anxieties such dialogue may generate. He remains critical of moral codes that pretend toward naturalized, authoritative ethical claims. Marlow's moral education is thus the product of a methodological principle from which responsible ethical critics of literature may learn.

One of Conrad's earliest and perhaps most famous protracted statements regarding the relationship between morality and aesthetics is the preface to *The Nigger of the Narcissus* (1897), where he writes, "Fiction— if it at all aspires to be art—appeals to temperament. And in truth it must be, like painting, like music, like all art, the appeal of one temperament to all the other innumerable temperaments whose subtle and resistless power endows passing events with their true meaning, and creates the moral, the emotional atmosphere of the place and time."[2] The artist is the agent making the initial appeal to other temperaments, but it is apparently the agency of these other temperaments that subsequently impresses a specific moral meaning on the work of art. As Conrad notes in a letter written twenty years later, it is the affair of the critic to bring his honesty, sensibility, and intelligence to bear on estimating the "final effect" of art.[3] Interpretive tension, which takes the form of a dialogue between writer and reader, constructs a text's moral component.

Conrad maintains, in the preface, that art possesses some kind of morally instructive capacity. It is far less clear just how, and more important where, fiction is supposed to engender its moral effects. The pedagogic consequence of the reader's engagement with the text is ostensibly determined by where one locates "the place and time" indicated in Conrad's assertion. If the phrase refers to an atmospheric quality captured by the artist in the work and corroborated by the reader's interpretation, then the reader's experience of the text's moral component is confined to the text itself: the reader simply charges the work with a certain significance, "creates" the text's moral atmosphere, and can, I suppose, according to Conrad's standards, be said to have read well. On the other hand, the phrase can also be taken to say that, in a given exegetical engagement with the text, the reader creates the moral atmosphere of the specific social climate in which his or her reading has just taken place. This second interpretation implies that Conrad views art as a means of informing both individual and social consciousness. For him, the text is not a formal end in itself but a means to a qualitative end. As such, Marlow's moral education may be expected to affect not only Marlow himself, but those who read about him as well.

This said, the argument produced in the Preface cannot be taken as Conrad's authoritative position on the morally instructive potential of art. Put alongside this early view, the following confession from *A Personal Record* suggests that Conrad was occasionally as entangled as some of his characters in the complexities of mooring stable ethical claims:

> The ethical view of the universe involves us at last in so many cruel and absurd contradictions, where the last vestiges of faith, hope, charity, and even of reason itself, seem ready to perish, that I have come to suspect that the aim of creation cannot be ethical at all. I would fondly believe that its object is purely spectacular. . . . Those visions, delicious or poignant, are a moral end in themselves.[4]

Here the role of the reader in the construction of a text's moral import is severely diminished. Whatever moral effects the text produces seem almost gratuitous; the artist is not expected to offer a "creed,"[5] so it seems dubious to expect the reader to find one. Still, it remains possible to recuperate a reverberation of the Preface in this second passage. Though the conscious aim of creation may not be moral, the inadvertent consequences of creation may nevertheless take the shape of a particular moral effect generated by a reader called upon to evaluate the textual spectacle itself. This would explain Conrad's refusing the artist, in what would appear a blatant contradiction of his suspicion concerning art's morally instructive force, the "freedom of moral Nihilism" (*NLL*, 8). There is simply too much at stake in the reception of the literary work for the work to be produced irresponsibly.

Conrad's shifting attitude toward the morally instructive capacity of literature can be anchored in two general compositional principles that govern his literary texts: first, Conrad does not seek to bifurcate art and morality in his literary writing; and second, the reconciliation of art and morality must begin with art rather than with morality.[6] For Conrad, art renders truth; truth does not render art: "Fiction is history, human history, or it is nothing. But it is also more than that; it stands on firmer ground, being based on the reality of forms and the observation of social phenomena, whereas history is based on documents, and the reading of print and hand-writing on second hand impression. Thus fiction is nearer truth" (*NLL*, 17).

His assertion notwithstanding, I am not sure that Conrad satisfactorily demonstrates the distinction between fiction and history. Even if Conrad is claiming the immediacy of the fiction writer's experience as the ground for fiction's authority, to base the validity of a truth claim on the perception of social phenomena and the reality of forms is to offer an ideological base for legitimating truth claims. It is doubtful that Conrad was using the above passage to profess a Platonic faith in the ontological reality of forms—no form of representation could be less Platonic than the nonomniscient, modernist narrative technique with which he composed a considerable portion of his corpus—so whatever truth a form might have would need to be understood as idiosyncratic and ideological.

Nonetheless, by representing the perception of social phenomena, Conrad could be assured that he was, in fact, truthfully representing a very specific type of reality; that is, the reality of an individual human consciousness for whom ideological knowledge may well be assimilated as the real thing. With this in mind, fiction may be redescribed as the history of human consciousness, which is itself a real ideological phenomenon, if not a real material "thing." If Conrad's representation of consciousness may still be said to elicit a moral response from its readers, one could then say that those readers are responding to the moral force of ideology as it is expressed by fictional characters who are probably unable to detect the difference between ideological knowledge and knowledge of the source of that ideology. I say probably, because Marlow is an exception. His moral education is an ideological event that derives from a very specific socioeconomic relation. The history of Marlow's consciousness in *Heart of Darkness* and *Lord Jim* is the record of a consciousness that struggles to expose, comprehend, and perhaps even reject the ethical pretenses of European capitalist and imperialist values.

In both *Heart of Darkness* and *Lord Jim*, Marlow perceives that the moral code supporting both a capitalist culture and its mechanism of imperialism is arbitrary and flawed. He takes up his experience in *Heart of Darkness* with the knowledge that a contradiction exists between the ethics of the merchant seaman vocation, of which he is a representative, and the material acts of this vocation's members. Benita Parry aptly describes these ethics as supporting a "spiritually repressive culture demanding unreflective obedience to the laws of order and progress, misrepresenting social utilities in the service of class interests as moral axioms, and restricting the definition of knowledge to exclude meditations on alternative human conditions."[7] *Heart of Darkness* and *Lord Jim* are both structured in such a way

that, when the inconsistencies inhering in European capitalist and imperialist ethics begin to pressure Marlow to the point where he can no longer
successfully manage them, he encounters pedagogic characters who serve
either to magnify or to temporarily repair the contradiction. In his dialogue with these characters, Marlow refines a moral consciousness that is
tenaciously sensitive to the historical determinants of ethical claims. In so
doing, he exemplifies an important methodological principle of responsible
ethical criticism.

As Marlow is exposed to the fabric of the texts' competing pedagogic
voices, he judges some of these voices more authoritative than others. The
problem of judging the authority of truth claims is one of the most pressing subjects of inquiry for contemporary literary theory and criticism.
While the critical operation performed by Marlow when he reads Kurtz
is not exactly identical to the critical operation performed by the exegete
when he reads Marlow, the operations are similar enough to enable Vincent
Pecora's statement that *Heart of Darkness*—and, I would add, *Lord Jim*—
is "at the same time exemplary and diagnostic," that it is ultimately a story
about the limits of language to express "truth." Since there is no extratextual criterion against which to measure the validity of a given character's
voice, the truth of every voice that speaks in the narratives is questioned. The
text generates its climate of skepticism through both formal and thematic
effects: even the use of quotations marks around Marlow's recounting
undercuts the metaphysics of presence.[8]

It is important, however, to recognize that the text's self-referentiality
and critique of metaphysical presence do not preclude an ethical reading
of Marlow's education. As Eric Tretheway accurately and neatly comments, "The most pressing issue that language raises for Conrad, though
rooted in epistemological difficulties, is ultimately ethical and concerns
the relationship, judged by ethical criteria, implied in th[e] passage
between inward and outward, depth and surface, an impenetrable darkness and a voice."[9] Put another way: because there neither is, nor can be,
a single authoritative ethical voice in Conrad's texts, both the texts' moral
dimensions and the truth claims they propound are the result of dialogue
among competing ethical positions.

Possessing a firsthand knowledge of their limitations, Marlow desires
a more legitimate material referent for moral thought and behavior than
any that the socioeconomic relations of his European culture can provide.

Marlow's dissatisfaction with imperialist ethics prompts his initial attraction to what he perceives as the pedagogic potential of Kurtz and Jim. Knowing that his empirical knowledge of imperialism yields no satisfactory moral code, Marlow will at times invest the pedagogic voices of Kurtz and Jim with the burden of an almost incarnationist authority that they cannot possibly bear. Kurtz and Jim thus come to represent for Marlow a possible alternative to his culturally determined moral code, an alternative that, prior to his encounter with them, only exists as an absence, as a "something else" for which he longs but that he does not yet understand.[10]

As he constructs it in his consciousness, the content of this alternative is some form of natural, essential, almost nonideological system of morality with which he desires dialogue. This is not to say that Kurtz and Jim are intended to symbolize, or possess insight into, a natural referent for moral thought and behavior. It does not matter one way or another. The structural dynamics of Marlow's moral education in these texts would follow the same route regardless of whether a natural, material referent for moral consciousness could be demonstrated to exist ontologically.[11] The important factors for the texts' pedagogic dynamics are that Marlow *perceives* Kurtz and Jim as each bearing an ethical voice that is apparently an alternative to the ethical ideology that supports imperialism; moreover, Marlow desires a dialogue with this alternative so as to avoid blind capitulation to the behavior expected of him.

The extratextual consequence of using Marlow's consciousness as the locus of moral dialogue is that Conrad constructs a more interpretively flexible narrative than if he simply conveyed his tale through an omniscient third-person narrator. By avoiding ontological speculation and emphasizing the ideological effects of pedagogy, Conrad makes the observer a part of what he or she observes and interferes with the full closure of plot, the final effect of narrative order and lucidity, and the illusion of full authorial understanding.[12] The layering of vocal resonances, from which Conrad's texts are made up, denies the observer a single access to any one event.[13] Returning again to the similar exegetical operations performed by Marlow on his experiences and by the reader on Marlow, the definition of the "observer" with regard to Conrad's texts can be expanded via nonlinear perspectival technique to include more than just the figure of Marlow. To press the analogy a bit further, the reader's ability to process the material that has informed Marlow's moral consciousness by the end of *Lord Jim* will be predicated upon Marlow's own ability to process the same material. This is one of the consequences of Marlow's declaration, regarding Jim, that "he existed for me, and after all it is only through me that he exists for you."[14]

Technically and structurally, Conrad's narrative is meant to solder a moral dialogue between Marlow and the reader: "Marlow is much more than a device for circumventing the modern taboo on authorial moralising; he is also a means of allowing his author to express himself more completely than ever before; through Marlow Conrad discovered a new kind of relation to his audience, and one which enabled him to be more fully himself."[15] Ian Watt's account of Marlow juxtaposes the aesthetic and moral dimensions of Conrad's texts in such a way that neither abrogates the other. Using Marlow as a filter, Conrad's authorial presence can be felt but is kept very hazy; indeed, Marlow arguably permits the reader the same access to events as Conrad permits Marlow.[16]

But because of the obstacles to referential legitimacy that everywhere distinguish the text's narrative operation, the reader's ability to interpret Marlow's experiences in exactly the same manner as Marlow interprets them is compromised. Conrad ends up eating and having his cake. The indication of his authorial presence satisfies his pedagogic criteria for art that were cited earlier. Conrad's modernist rendition of Marlow's consciousness helps to prevent the possibility that he might exceed the boundaries of nonoppressive moralizing and reduce his narrative to propaganda. Instead of a univocally instructive document, Conrad's text offers a structure on which a reader may develop a particular ethical reading, depending upon his or her methodological predilections.

Marlow tenaciously pursues his connections with Kurtz and Jim despite the frequent inconveniences and anxieties in which such perseverance results. The tenacity of Marlow's desire allows *Heart of Darkness* and *Lord Jim* to be read as a single narrative whose central subject is Marlow's moral education. Between *Heart of Darkness* and *Lord Jim*, Marlow's moral consciousness is not wiped clean: many of Marlow's thoughts and actions in *Lord Jim* that resist interpretation when read exclusively in the isolated context of recounting Jim's biography are rendered more comprehensible when considered in the light of Marlow's earlier experiences in *Heart of Darkness*. Up until the moment that he meets Kurtz, Marlow straddles the fence between Company man and dissatisfied agent. His ideological oscillation, only briefly suspended during his confrontation with Kurtz, returns to inform his consciousness by the end of *Heart of Darkness* and becomes one of the fundamental determinants of his moral progress in *Lord Jim*. Marlow indeed acquires moral knowledge in these narratives, and certain scenes of pedagogy can be identified by the impression they leave on Marlow's moral thinking. But the final shape of Marlow's moral consciousness is never drawn. His geophysical relationship to European culture, from which he comes and to which he eventually returns, remains just stable enough always to challenge the ethical alternatives he encounters throughout his career in the persons of Kurtz and Jim. These alternatives subsequently keep the texts' various moral dialogues alive.

Heart of Darkness begins with a remarkable economy of third-person description. A mere nine paragraphs, broken only by the peremptory observation with which Marlow starts his recollection, introduce both the narrative's dominant ideological climate and Marlow's ambivalent relationship to it. Nearly everything about this climate is designed to deflect the process of moral speculation toward which Marlow inclines. In the symbol of the old river, which "rested unruffled at the decline of day after ages of good service done to the race that peopled its banks, spread out in the tranquil dignity of a waterway leading to the uttermost ends of the earth,"[17] two components of the text's dominant ethic are entwined. First, the stillness denotes an absence of the tension that compels moral dialogue, choice, and judgment. Second, the stillness is the river's reward for services rendered to an imperialist culture. Thus, in one sentence we are presented with Marlow's inchoate ideological climate, one that reproduces itself by appropriating nature to an artificial end whose moral status is so dispersed across the surface of the water that not a ripple of its import can be detected. In social relations under capitalism, surface appearance is crucial, for it perpetuates the illusion that no ideological conflict exists as far as the eye can see.

Excepting Marlow, the dynamism of whose moral consciousness is placed in conflict with the scene's stasis and prompts the text's moral tension, none of the characters occupying this aestheticized stage is named. The absence of the listeners' names allows for the interpretation, frequently offered by readers of the novel, that the Director, the Lawyer, the Accountant, and the third-person narrator are character types representing specific values whose sum helps empower the ethically evasive mechanism against which Marlow's desire for moral dialogue may be identified. The positions of these characters are capitalized not only because they represent types in a larger allegorical context but also because the very process by which such a semantic ascription occurs is endemic to the ethical ideology that underwrites imperialism: to validate its claims to ideological legitimacy, imperialism tries to naturalize its pretense to an ontological referent and represent it as an essential category. That Marlow is named with a proper, not an abstract, noun further distinguishes him from the uniform semantic field that the third-person narrator so carefully constructs to forestall moral thinking.

Any action that ruptures the introductory stasis established by the narrator would produce a palpable tension that might disclose ideological conflict and compel moral dialogue. Marlow inaugurates the text's moral ethos with his judgment that Europe, too, "has been one of the dark places of the earth" (HoD, 9). More important than what this judgment means so early in the text is how the narrator addresses it. The narrator avoids entering into a moral dialogue with Marlow, ostensibly because he is incapable of playing the disputant. His response does not address Marlow's statement; rather, it interprets Marlow: "The worst that could be said of him was that he did not represent his class. He was a seaman, but he was a wanderer too, while most seamen lead, if one may so express it, a sedentary life" (HoD, 9). Clearly indicating his ideological complicity with the other characters aboard the ship, the narrator's response just as clearly problematizes Marlow's relationship to those aspiring to a sedentary life of unreflective material comfort. Marlow is of a different "class." This difference will manifest itself in his ability to think morally, an ability that is allowed by an ambivalence towards imperialism. The specifically moral structure of Marlow's ambivalence lies in the deepest registers of his consciousness in the form of an internal pedagogic dialogue between European imperialist ethics and something else.[18]

Once Marlow assumes the rôle of narrator, he recalls the experiences preparatory to his traveling down-river toward the Inner Station. What emerges from Marlow's recollections is a much more elaborate index of Marlow's insight into the ethical pretenses of European culture and imperialism. In his parting conversation with the Aunt who secured him his position with the Company, Marlow reflects,

> In the course of these confidences it became quite plain to me I had been represented . . . as an exceptional and gifted creature—a piece of good fortune for the Company—a man you don't get hold of every day. Good Heavens! And I was going to take charge of a two-penny-half-penny river-steamboat with a penny whistle attached! It appears however I was also one of the Workers, with a capital—you know. Something like an emissary of light, something like a lower sort of apostle. There had been a lot of such rot let loose in print and talk just about that time, and the excellent woman living right in the rush of all that humbug got carried off her feet. She talked about "weaning those ignorant millions from their horrid ways," till, upon my word, she made me quite uncomfortable. I ventured to hint that the Company was run for profit. (*HoD*, 15–16)

The ethical fantasy of imperialism has done its job on the Aunt, but Marlow has moral misgivings about an economic enterprise that falsely represents itself as a socially beneficent force. Expressing these misgivings, Marlow forges the pedagogic voice that he will put into dialogue both with the ethics underpinning European imperialist values and with the characters he perceives as having challenged these values.

His misgivings about the legitimacy of imperialist ethics notwithstanding, Marlow nevertheless capitulates uncritically to some of the most formidable ideological strategies enforced by imperialism to naturalize injustice on his way down-river. For example, just moments after being somewhat startled to be taken as a proponent of imperialism by a guard of the Central Station, Marlow expresses his admiration of the chief accountant's ability to keep up his physical appearance despite the "great demoralization of the land" (*HoD*, 21). Shortly thereafter, he muses over the logic of acquisition characteristic of imperialism: "There is something after all in the world allowing one man to steal a horse while another man must not look at a halter. Steal a horse straight out. Very well. He has done it. Perhaps he can ride. But there is a way of looking at a halter that would provoke the most charitable of saints into a kick" (*HoD*, 27). Then he produces the following appraisal of work: "No. I don't like work. I had rather laze about and think of all the fine things that can be done. I don't like work—no man does—but I like what is in the work—the chance to find yourself. Your own reality—for yourself—not for others—what no other man can ever know. They can only see the mere show, and never can tell what it really means" (*HoD*, 31).

How is the reader to judge Marlow's perception of labor? Is it a state-ment of a profound naïveté, or an equally profound elision of reification, or both? On the one hand, Marlow makes a fetish of the vision of material comfort that appears as the promised end of imperialist and capitalist suc-cess. On the other, Marlow demonstrates both the ability and the need to see beyond the seduction and penetrate to the essence of labor. But that essence is not depicted in terms of brutality and violence, exploitation and alienation; rather, it is depicted as the greatest vehicle of consciousness raising, as an almost Nietzschean *principium individuationis,* whose moral value is the solipsistic satisfaction of self-mastery. Not even the context in which the original speculation on labor occurs offers help in distilling a single, clearly defined position in Marlow's early attitude toward the Company. This inchoate tension in his moral consciousness, stemming from his ambivalence toward capitalism and imperialism, is what drives him to expand his moral knowledge in the presence of alternative peda-gogic voices. Like the responsible ethical critic, Marlow is too cognizant of the historical pressures that inform moral speculation to validate the pre-tense of any one moral code toward absolute authority.

While conveying his moral ambivalence—toward the Company's "pro-gressive policies" and something else he can as yet only perceive as prob-lematizing his disposition toward such progress—Marlow appeals to his listeners' habitual reflex for endorsing truth through corroborating visual perception, a banal version of "seeing is believing." However, in the midst of reproducing this safe standard of referential validity, Marlow addresses his listeners on board the *Nellie* as follows:

> Of course in this you fellows see more than I could then. You see me, whom you know. . . . It had become so pitch dark that we listeners could hardly see one another. For a long time already he, sitting apart, had been no more to us than a voice. There was not a word from anybody. . . . I listened, I listened on the watch for the sentence, for the word that would give me the clue to the faint uneasiness inspired by this narrative that seemed to shape itself without human lips in the heavy night-air of the river. (*HoD,* 30)

Ironically, Marlow is authorizing the power of vision just as vision is being rendered most impotent. The impact of Marlow's editorial on his listeners suddenly prepares the reader for the potential primacy of vocal over visual signification that Marlow himself will gradually realize as he moves closer to Kurtz's pedagogic example. The scene introduces the question of Marlow's credibility, for if Marlow envisions his access to moral truth as a visual process that the text ostensibly invalidates, then what is Marlow's access to truth?

This question of credible access to a referent for truth, which is at first a consequence of Marlow's empirical perception of exterior space, becomes redescribed as a product of Marlow's insight into a series of interior spaces. The same signal physical event that will explode the ideological calm of *Lord Jim*—the bottom of a ship's striking something submerged below the water's surface—impels Marlow's observation that "when you have to attend . . . to the mere incidents of the surface, the reality—the reality I tell you—fades. The inner truth is hidden" (*HoD*, 36). Hidden, yes, but hidden where? Marlow's conception of truth as something not superficial, not visually accessible, directs the reader toward two of its possible loci: Marlow's own consciousness, and the natives' culture that surrounds Kurtz. Furthermore, Marlow comes to connect these two sites and to position them as the pedagogic alternative to European values as a foundation for moral thought.

Marlow cannot empirically see the value of the natives' culture; he cannot read their musical and vocal signs: "The prehistoric man was cursing us, praying to us, welcoming us—who could tell? . . . We could not understand because we were too far and could not remember because we were traveling in the night of first ages, of those ages that are gone, leaving hardly a sign—and no memories" (*HoD*, 37). Compelled by his ambivalence toward European values, Marlow consciously equates the impenetrability of the natives' culture with his sense of the impenetrability of truth. Thereafter, he arrives at the tentative conclusion that the voice of the jungle represents a more ontologically legitimate referent for truth than European economic and ethical ideology.

But the equation in turn prompts a number of questions. If, in fact, the jungle is the source of a truth Marlow seeks, how then can he so judge it if he cannot understand it? Marlow does characterize the voice of the jungle as "truth stripped of its cloak of time" (*HoD*, 38), so it is a truth incommensurable with capitalist ideology, whose simulation of a natural, essential, absolute paradigm for social relations Marlow views as a lie: "Principles? Principles won't do. Acquisitions, clothes, pretty rags—rags that would fly off at the first good shake. No" (*HoD*, 38). Or, as Marlow puts it, the jungle is of a time that has left "hardly a sign—and no memories" (*HoD*, 37), that is almost pre-ideological. If, for the sake of argument, such a pre-ideological category could be shown to exist, what could its moral value be for a mind already ostensibly informed by a very different series of ideological determinants?

It is important to note that, although Marlow himself does not and cannot answer this question by ascribing any consistently positive descriptive attributes to the natives' culture, he can and does grope toward some classification of the natives' culture by specifically suggesting that the voice of the jungle is not utterly foreign: "If you were man enough you would admit to yourself that there was in you just the faintest trace of a response to the terrible frankness of that noise, a dim suspicion of there being a meaning in it which you—you so remote from the night of first ages— could comprehend. And why not? The mind of man is capable of anything—because everything is in it, all the past as well as all the future" (*HoD*, 38). With this avowal, Marlow intimates that human consciousness possesses a deeply repressed, atavistic, universal dimension that ensures our moral complicity with one another; but the interpretation of this shared knowledge is a profoundly personal, idiosyncratic gesture. The pedagogic voice of the jungle is therefore both stable and ambiguous. Marlow perceives it as an ontologically real, nonideological referent for truth, whose meaning, as it is filtered through subjective consciousness, always remains in tension with European values.[19]

In the figure of Kurtz, the known and the impenetrable are conjoined in the text's most formidable manifestation of a referent whose materiality is taken for granted but whose moral value is highly questionable. Marlow's initial impression of Kurtz is the result of others' verbal depictions of him, depictions whose frequency has prompted notice that "if Marlow had never met Kurtz, he would nonetheless have reconstructed him from the descriptions passed on to him in a host of voices."[20] And, as the text gradually but deliberately emphasizes the signifying mechanism of voice over vision, Marlow finds himself most anticipating a dialogue with the Chief of the Inner Station: "That was exactly what I had been looking forward to—a talk with Kurtz. I made the strange discovery that I had never imagined him as doing, you know, but as discoursing. I didn't say to myself, 'Now I will never see him,' or 'Now I will never shake him by the hand,' but, 'Now I will never hear him.' The man presented himself as a voice. . . . Of all his gifts the one that stood out preeminently, that carried with it a sense of real presence, was his ability to talk, his words—the gift of expression" (*HoD*, 48).

When considering the various moral tensions in *Heart of Darkness*, it is crucial to distinguish between the referential credence Marlow bestows on Kurtz's voice as a phenomenon and that voice's actual denotative import. At times Marlow romanticizes the value of Kurtz's words to such an extent that he is transported by the "unbounded power" of the latter's manifesto for imperialist progress in the jungle, even though the document discloses no "practical hints to interrupt the magic current of phrases" (*HoD*, 50–51).[21] One way to read Marlow's seduction by form at the expense of content is to find him unconsciously capitulating to imperialism's most potent mechanism of ideological control and to let it go at that. But if Kurtz may be read as a representative of the voice of the jungle, which is Marlow's foil to imperialism, then Marlow is not expressing a proclivity for form over content as much as a proclivity for one form over another. So while Marlow may certainly unconsciously reproduce an ideological strategy that underpins imperialism, he is at the same time consciously rejecting imperialism in favor of what the voice of the natives signifies. What is consistent is his engagement with the morally instructive effects of a structure—the tension among competing pedagogic voices—instead of a preconceived thematic lesson.

Conrad persistently confronts the opportunity to codify the moral significance of the natives' voice with a steady stream of indeterminate words and phrases. This indeterminacy both confuses Marlow and enhances the text's overall impression of moral tension.[22] Who are the "brutes" (*HoD*, 51) whose extermination Kurtz demands in his manifesto? Who are the "rebels" (*HoD*, 58) whose heads line the entryway to Kurtz's chamber? What exactly are the unsound methods with which Kurtz "ruined the district" (*HoD*, 57), and for whom was the district ruined? The identity of the brutes is particularly germane to my attempt to categorize the pedagogic voice of the jungle in opposition to the culture of European imperialism. Traditional readings of Conrad's text interpret the brutes as those natives who did not voluntarily succumb to the various agendas of the European colonizers and who therefore needed to be corrected. But Frances Singh offers the less traditional exegesis that "given that Kurtz

became one with an African tribe and learned to understand the meaning
of their customs, his words *may* be taken to mean that the only way Africa
could develop would be if the real brutes or savages, the colonizers, were
removed."[23] Moreover, and perhaps more important for a discussion of
responsible ethical criticism, the tension between Singh's and more traditional readings of these signifiers exemplifies precisely the kind of exegetical dialogue that ethical criticism can profitably foreground in order to
avoid monologic, dogmatic interpretations of literature.

Singh's contention, that the brutes may be associated with European
imperialists, cannot be demonstrated by appeal to what actually happened
at the Inner Station before Marlow's arrival. The text works at every turn
to preserve the mystery of these activities. Rather, Kurtz's antipathy
toward the culture that originally dispatched him to perform its imperialist work is conveyed through Marlow's understanding of what Kurtz represented before entering the jungle. Michael Levenson intimates Kurtz's
ethical code by first delineating his "prelapsarian" relationship to "an ideology of enlightenment, a collective moral inheritance that, plainly enough,
arouses virtuous aspiration and then proves unequal to the passion it
excites," and then concluding that "the failure of principle does not mark
the demise of value in *Heart of Darkness,* only a change in its source. If value
cannot descend from social ideals, it must ascend from the psychic abyss."[24]
If one interprets the "psychic abyss" as a primordial repository of collective moral consciousness that is, according to Marlow's earlier conception,
pre-ideological, before culture, then Marlow's estimation of Kurtz's moral
significance remains consistent with Marlow's estimation of the ethical
voice of the natives: though represented as an absence, both are structural
alternatives to the ethics of European imperialism.

Having already perceived the manifold ideological and moral pretenses of imperialism, Marlow finally has occasion to experience the imagined referential authority of the voice he has heretofore romanticized
when he and Kurtz meet. Marlow's temporary but profound fear that
Kurtz will order an attack on the Company's steamer is an index of the
degree to which he has endowed Kurtz's voice with a potential to signify
that exceeds the various empirical illusions perpetrated by capitalism and
imperialism in the name of progress. Marlow has virtually no idea what
Kurtz is saying to the natives; but since Marlow has found no satisfactory
moral value in the European languages he comprehends, the very foreignness

of Kurtz's sounds has great pedagogic appeal. Moreover, Conrad orchestrates a series of technical and thematic moves that accelerate the momentum of the mystique with which Marlow invests Kurtz. He keeps the contact between Marlow and Kurtz inconclusive by virtue of the latter's frequent elliptical utterances and general omission of concrete vocabulary. When Kurtz does intelligibly respond to Marlow, the effect is only to magnify his pedagogic authority in Marlow's estimation. For example, to Marlow's question, "Do you understand this?" after hearing the cries of the native woman on the shore, Kurtz replies, with a smile of "indefinable meaning. . . . 'Do I not?'" (*HoD*, 66). Even the "moral platitudes" of European civilization that Kurtz mouths "like an automaton" in the moments preceding his death are unconnected with the realities that constitute his life in the natives' culture.[25]

In this context, one may read Marlow's assertion that Kurtz is "a remarkable man" (*HoD*, 61) as an acknowledgment that Kurtz has faced the moral contradictions in European culture and has chosen to renounce his long-sedimented Western ideological moorings despite the psychological chaos that inevitably attends such a decision. The possibility that Kurtz has disclaimed imperialist ideology may then well be the source of Marlow's "moral shock" (*HoD*, 63) upon finding that Kurtz has disappeared from aboard the steamer and returned to the jungle. On the other hand— in a revelation that seems to belie everything for which I have been arguing— Kurtz's disappearance strikes Marlow as "something altogether monstrous, intolerable to thought and odious to the soul," even though the sensation lasts "the merest fraction of a second" (*HoD*, 63). What happens in this fraction of a second? Does Marlow reflexively and unconsciously desire recourse to the safety of the European values he has up to now consciously scrutinized? Has Kurtz's pedagogic voice failed to have any formidable morally instructive effect on Marlow's moral consciousness?

The solution to these questions largely depends on the significance of Marlow's reflection, after he upsets Kurtz's escape plans, that Kurtz "had kicked himself loose of the earth . . . had kicked the very earth to pieces" (*HoD*, 65). Put in terms of the text's moral tension, the earth either connotes the positive morality that man has made for man (the gender reference is not an oversight), or it connotes the natural morality that Marlow sees residing in the jungle and expressed through Kurtz's pedagogic voice. It seems unlikely that Kurtz has divorced himself from the latter, since it is to the jungle that the Inner Station's Chief is desperately laboring to return. Kurtz is thus only loose of the earth as parceled out according to Western definitional parameters.

Marlow may well respond to the moral shock of Kurtz's leaving the ship by spontaneously silhouetting the import of Kurtz's action against Western ethical standards familiar to both men. After all, to this point, Kurtz has merely offered the very real possibility of an alternative moral code to Marlow; he has not conclusively eliminated the moral tension in Marlow's consciousness. How could he? Whether Kurtz has completely assimilated, and been assimilated by, the natives' culture is surely doubtful; he is still a man, of whom all of Europe went into the making. But watching Kurtz dragging himself on his belly through the brush, Marlow sees a man who has to some degree abandoned the principles of European capitalism and imperialism in favor of the natives' culture. The pedagogic example he presents to Marlow is of one who has confronted the moral contradictions in European culture, weighed these contradictions against the alternative represented by the natives, and pronounced judgment on the horror, which can now felicitously be read as referring to "the whole mess of European rapacity and brutality in Africa into which he is being taken back."[26]

Kurtz dies almost immediately after he pronounces upon the horror, a fairly clear compositional decision on Conrad's part both to focus the final burdens of the narrative's moral tension onto Marlow and to impel the reader to evaluate the impact of Kurtz's pedagogic example on Marlow's ambivalence toward the socioeconomic philosophy and ethics of European imperialism. Marlow's soliloquy on Kurtz's death elaborately informs the reader's evaluation of just how deeply Kurtz's voice has registered in Marlow's moral consciousness:

> Droll thing life is—that mysterious arrangement of merciless logic for a futile purpose. The most you can hope from it is some knowledge of yourself—that comes too late—a crop of unextinguishable regrets. I have wrestled with death. It is the most unexciting contest you can imagine. It takes place in an impalpable greyness with nothing underfoot, with nothing around, without spectators, without clamour, without glory, without the great desire of victory, without the great fear of defeat, in a sickly atmosphere of tepid scepticism, without much belief in your own right, and still less in that of your adversary. If such is the

form of ultimate wisdom then life is a greater riddle than some of us think it to be. I was within a hair's-breadth of the last opportunity for pronouncement, and I found with humiliation that probably I would have nothing to say. This is the reason why I affirm that Kurtz was a remarkable man. . . . He had summed up—he had judged. "The horror!" He was a remarkable man. After all, this was the expression of some sort of belief; it had candor, it had conviction, it had a vibrating note of revolt in its whisper, it had the appalling face of a glimpsed truth. . . . He had made that last stride, he had stepped over the edge, while I had been permitted to draw back my hesitating foot. And perhaps in this is the whole difference; perhaps all the wisdom, and all truth, and all sincerity, are just compressed into that inappreciable moment of time in which we step over the threshold of the invisible. (*HoD*, 69)

On the surface, Marlow's reaction is common, even predictable: death inspires an urgent need to take stock. But the subtext of Marlow's thoughts contains the language of a headlong critique of capitalist ideology. On Marx's diagnosis of capitalism, the merciless logic, the futile purpose, the inextinguishable regrets are all descriptive of the alienation of the worker from product, process, and especially from species life. It is not so easy to imagine such an isolated confrontation with death, as Marlow recalls having experienced, in a "primitive" culture whose communal rituals are designed precisely to underscore a sense of solidarity among its members. Once the facade of community erected by capitalism to empower alienating social relations is dismantled, the remaining historical dynamic provides no foundation for a sanguine judgment on the meaning of existence. Behind capitalist and imperialist ideology is a moral contradiction that has the appalling face of a glimpsed truth for Kurtz, a truth against which Kurtz has whispered his vibrating note of revolt.

The general tenor of Marlow's perception of Kurtz's moral knowledge is predicated on a line of demarcation between natural and positive morality. Marlow finishes his meditation on Kurtz's death by observing that truth may consist in crossing "the threshold *of* the invisible." Marlow's choice of prepositions identifies the direction of Kurtz's moral education in the jungle and, subsequently, of his pedagogic impression on Marlow. What direction of moral education does this preposition indicate? It has been argued that Kurtz's experience on the threshold of the invisible is evidence of his moving from the morally stable and natural into "the void of a complete and deracinating moral relativism . . . beyond moral values where the culturally sanctioned significance of certain imperatives appears to be no more than an illusion supported by the exigencies of power." On this view, "Kurtz learns that, like a god, he can manufacture value anew, that he can almost single–handedly establish his own moral order." This would make Kurtz's horror "a multidimensional product of this lesson . . . the terror of his weightless status in a morally unordered world, of the final absence he feels within."[27]

The opposite interpretation of the direction of Kurtz's moral progress is also feasible. It is a commonplace of historical criticism to assert that, under capitalism, ideology is designed to prevent critical access to the brutal material conditions that define capitalist relations of production. Put simply, since it is hidden by ideology, history is invisible. If Kurtz's insight to the truth is tantamount to his crossing the threshold *of* the invisible, a movement which I take to mean *away from*, rather than *into* some unknown category, then Marlow again comprehends the import of Kurtz's pedagogic voice as a departure from arbitrary moral codes toward something Marlow understands as more natural and legitimate.

It is Marlow himself who verifies the latter explanation of the moral significance of Kurtz's death by figuring Kurtz's hostile attitudes toward imperialist ideology as valid pedagogic examples of just moral behavior.[28] When he returns to Europe, Marlow expresses a now unmitigated contempt for a culture everywhere aspiring toward material comfort and complacency:

> I found myself back in the sepulchral city resenting the sight of people hurrying through the streets to filch a little money from each other, to devour their infamous cookery, to gulp their unwholesome beer, to dream their insignificant and silly dreams. They trespassed upon my thoughts. . . . Their bearing, which was simply the bearing of commonplace individuals going about their business in the assurance of perfect safety, was offensive to me like the outrageous flauntings of folly in the face of a danger it is impossible to comprehend. I had no particular desire to enlighten them, but I had some difficulty in restraining myself from laughing in their faces so full of stupid importance. (*HoD*, 70)

Marlow's forthright condemnation of mores that had earlier merely been the target of ambivalence intimates that he has heard Kurtz to espouse an antipathy toward the logic of European socioeconomic relations and their concomitant ethics. Marlow's moral consciousness has, in Levenson's appropriate formulation, moved "from an institutional to an instinctual domain" and has offered "the Impressionist temperament as itself a basis for individual moral autonomy."[29] Just as ideology can obstruct criticism of socioeconomic injustices, so institutional restraints can obstruct the self-conscious expression of deeply repressed natural desire. In both dynamics, what lies below the surface of appearance is ostensibly less vague and more real than not. By demonstrating the movement of consciousness that Levenson has outlined, Marlow has temporarily constructed for himself a moral insight that he has long desired as part of his romanticized image of Kurtz's referential authority.

While *Heart of Darkness* does reveal a fairly clear narrative structure presenting Marlow's perception of two dramatically different and basically incommensurable ethical codes, this structure is not designed to allow the reader conclusive evidence regarding which of the two codes Marlow ultimately endorses.[30] The ambiguity surrounding the final status of Marlow's moral consciousness as he ends his report can be traced to the indeterminate significance of his lie to Kurtz's Intended. Kurtz's pedagogic example has indeed accompanied Marlow back to Europe, and Marlow carries a "clear distinction between good and evil" into his meeting with the Intended.[31] Why, then, does he lie? More important, how is a reader concerned with Marlow's moral education to understand what the lie means in the larger context of Marlow's moral sensibility?

On one view of Marlow's conversation with the Intended, Marlow is thought not to have lied at all, since his experience in the jungle has compelled him to equate the horror with the Intended. As a sterling representative of bourgeois ideology, the betrothed lady in mourning, pining away in her drawing room, is part of a complex of social relations that both Kurtz and Marlow have judged morally dubious. As convenient as the correspondence between the Intended and the horror is for my account of Kurtz's morally instructive influence on Marlow, it does not sufficiently explain Marlow's behavior in the text's penultimate scene. The fact remains that Marlow *perceives himself* as having lied, and that perception cannot be dismissed.

Marlow emphasizes several times to his listeners that Kurtz's voice is in the room with him and Kurtz's fiancée: "The memory of what I had heard him say afar there . . . those broken phrases came back to me, were heard again in their ominous and terrifying simplicity" (*HoD*, 72). He even assures the Intended that, no matter what, "[Kurtz's] words will remain" (*HoD*, 75). It is not unreasonable to surmise that with Kurtz's voice comes the full pedagogic resonance of his pronouncement on, and of, the horror. This resonance would presumably guide Marlow's participation in his half of the conversation by showing him a solid criterion for right and wrong.

One might figure that, regardless of the pain it caused her, Marlow would tell the Intended the truth, as he perceived it, of what happened to Kurtz in the jungle; to misrepresent the facts would be tantamount to reproducing the kind of operation capitalism performs to misrepresent the materially real. Such an action would be unfaithful to Kurtz. Several critics have explained Marlow's lie as the action of a "practical moralist."[32] The disparity between a practical and an ideal morality is roughly analogous to the disparity between a positive and a natural morality. For Marlow to choose a positive over a natural morality is to diminish the influence of the natives' voice, and of Kurtz's pedagogic example, on his moral consciousness. Such a choice does, however, keep the text's moral tension intact.

All of Marlow's moral education, from the moment he leaves Europe on the steamship to the moment he confronts Kurtz's Intended, inclines him toward what he has all along desired and comprehended as an alternative to the moral contradictions of European culture. If he suddenly and (only somewhat) unexpectedly commits to relativistic ethical behavior, it is perhaps for no other reason than that the meeting with the Intended occurs back in Europe. The anxiety produced by former and familiar physical surroundings could predictably inspire former and familiar moral thoughts and actions. Marlow's listeners hear the first signs of his anxiety— which stands in marked contrast to the superiority and control he felt when earlier he waded through the crowded streets and called down his disgust on the somnambulant masses—when, while facing the Intended, he recalls Kurtz's voice: "I seemed to see his collected languid manner when he said one day 'This lot of ivory now is really mine. The Company did not pay for it. I collected it myself at a very great personal risk. I am afraid they will try to claim it as theirs though. H'm. It is a difficult case. What do you think I ought to do—resist? Eh? I want no more than justice'" (*HoD*, 72). Once again, Kurtz's pedagogic voice denotes an ambiguous moral example. What was the risk Kurtz braved to amass the ivory? Is his extreme possessiveness a true rebellion against, or just a magnification of, the Company's capitalist values? How does he conceive of justice? Once again, the text provides no conclusive answers to these questions.

Perhaps at the moment he recalls it in the drawing room, Marlow takes Kurtz's pedagogic voice to mean something other than what Kurtz intended in the jungle, for *something* has to actuate Marlow's recapitulation to European mores. Kurtz imagines his hoard of ivory to represent an illicit control over accumulated capital. To assume this control, he has positioned himself as an opponent of the socioeconomic forces that sent him to the jungle in the first place. There is no reason not to believe that, in the midst of the natives' culture, Marlow would have interpreted Kurtz's words as an example of his apostasy from the ethics that underpin imperialism. But ideology is not produced in a vacuum. Back in Europe, Marlow's perspective apparently changes. He lies. He submits to a deception that the text's moral dialogue positions as the product of European values. He wants to fulfill Kurtz's request for justice, yet he is unable to do so, because "it would have been too dark—too dark altogether" (*HoD*, 76). Marlow concedes to an ethical code now intimately associated with an aesthetic that confers a premium on maintaining the proper form of things. Nothing could be further from what he learned from Kurtz. Nor could anything provide greater evidence that Marlow continues to work through the tension of competing pedagogic positions in an internal moral dialogue.

Thus, the status of Marlow's moral consciousness at the end of *Heart of Darkness* cannot be neatly synopsized. He knows he has fallen short of what he perceives as the truth. When Marlow stops speaking, the narrator looks up-river "into the heart of an immense darkness" (*HoD*, 76). Ironically, the concluding phrase of Conrad's narrative can be taken to signify that Marlow's tale has had a morally instructive impact on his audience, who now seem to perceive London as morally suspect—or worse, without value. Marlow, who has challenged European imperialist ethics with a formidable alternative, is left straddling the same ideological fence that supported him when the narrative began. His investigation into moral contradiction and ambiguity resumes in *Lord Jim*. There is, however, a difference between Marlow's moral consciousness at the beginning of *Heart of Darkness* and his moral consciousness at the beginning of *Lord Jim*: both the residue of Kurtz's pedagogic voice and, just as important, the memory of his lie to the Intended exist in *Lord Jim* to inform the direction of Marlow's moral education.

Consider Marlow's inchoate fascination with Jim: "Why I longed to go grubbing into the deplorable details of an occurrence which, after all, concerned me no more than as a member of an obscure body of men held together by a community of inglorious toil and by fidelity to a certain standard of conduct, I can't explain. . . . I have a distinct notion I wished to find something. Perhaps, unconsciously, I hoped I would find that something, some profound and redeeming cause, some merciful explanation, some convincing shadow of an excuse" (*LJ*, 31). If Marlow's monologue is read as the speculations of a man who has traveled into the jungle, met Kurtz, assimilated his pedagogic voice, and then undermined its moral import at the first truly significant opportunity, then the absent referent that Marlow fails to identify as the object of the cause, explanation, and excuse he desires could feasibly be his lie to the Intended. Interpreting the moral legacy of this lie as a principal determinant of Marlow's perception of Jim's actions aboard the *Patna* provides a felicitous scene of tension on which *Heart of Darkness* and *Lord Jim* may be put into dialogue with one another.

The third-person voice that narrates the first four chapters of *Lord Jim* describes the ocean before the shipwreck as "still, without a stir, without a ripple, without a wrinkle—viscous, stagnant, dead" (*LJ*, 11), a scene reminiscent of the ideological stasis before the moral storm of *Heart of Darkness*. In this excessively aestheticized environment of business as usual, the shipwreck and its effects inaugurate the moral conflict of Conrad's text. On the one hand, Marlow wants to be able to vindicate Jim's actions because he sees the similarities between Jim's case and his own during the Kurtz episode. Marlow goes to such great lengths to protect Jim because the degree to which he can justify Jim's jumping is tantamount to the degree to which he can justify his own lie to the Intended, which, according to the dynamic of the competing ethical voices of *Heart of Darkness*, returned Marlow to a utilitarian ethical position. Put another way, Marlow cannot bear the thought that Jim's decision was a moral failure, since whatever judgment is conferred on Jim applies just as appropriately to himself.

On the other hand, Marlow also conveys the impression that he wants to convince himself that Jim has failed. If Jim is unable to satisfy the

romanticized demands of his consciousness, then Marlow is able to vindicate his decision to lie to the Intended, regardless of the morally "correct"
action underwritten by Kurtz's pedagogic voice. Marlow can simply blame
both ethical mistakes on hostile ideological pressures. As Marlow sums up
this dilemma, "What I could never make up my mind about was whether
his line of conduct amounted to shirking his ghost or to facing him out"
(*LJ*, 119). Marlow cannot make up his mind about Jim's behavior because
such a choice would require him to resolve the internal moral tension that
he carries from his pedagogically inconclusive experience with Kurtz.
Moral dialogue between capitalist ethics and some alternative becomes the
animating aesthetic structure that binds the texts together and allows them
to be read as variations on the same theme.

That Marlow can retain concurrent evaluations of Jim's behavior discloses the moral contradiction, contained in imperialist philosophies of
"humane progress," that recaptures Marlow's consciousness during and
after the lie. The simultaneous existence of both of these historically
inflected pressures on Marlow's moral consciousness could account for the
criticism that Marlow's narrative reliability is suspect, since it is impossible to determine precisely which of these two motivations is acting at any
given time to inform his estimation of Jim.[33] What makes Marlow such an
intriguing subject for ethical criticism is his exemplary reluctance to claim
authority for his ideological biases and moral predispositions, even though
such a gesture would ostensibly significantly reduce his moral anxiety.
Hence, for Marlow, Jim can represent "one of us" (*LJ*, 48)—when "we" are
the imperialist culture whose ethics Marlow finds not entirely tenable—
at the same time that he represents an alternative to capitalist ethics.
Marlow reads Jim with the same historically informed limitations with
which responsible ethical critics read Marlow or, for that matter, any text.

Marlow's reaction to Jim at the trial concretizes their relationship
and sets the stakes of Jim's reputation for Marlow's moral consciousness.
During the inquest, Jim's moral destiny is effectively aligned with
Marlow's. This is why, after the trial, Marlow makes himself "unreservedly
responsible" (*LJ*, 111) for Jim. But Marlow's solidarity with Jim is not limited to beneficent actions. Throughout the address to his listeners, Marlow
periodically becomes so transported by his own emotions in defense of
Jim that the boundary between Jim's words and Marlow's nearly vanishes.
Regarding Jim's decision to jump—the moral crux of the novel—Marlow

exclaims: "You must remember he believed, as any other man would have done in his place, that the ship would go down at any moment; the bulging, rust-eaten plates that kept back the ocean, fatally must give way, all at once like an undermined dam, and let in a sudden and overwhelming flood. He stood still looking at these recumbent bodies, a doomed man aware of his fate, surveying the silent company of the dead. They were dead! Nothing could save them! There were boats enough for half of them perhaps, but there was no time. No time! No time!" (*LJ*, 53).

The fervid entreaty with which this passage concludes could just as well be Jim's to Marlow as it is Marlow's to his audience. Magnifying Marlow's identification with Jim are the moments when Marlow specifically implicates himself in Jim's fate. He worries about the way Jim will be perceived by the socioeconomic standards of capitalism: "That, to tell you the truth, was the only danger I could see for him and for me" (*LJ*, 137). Just as important as Marlow's identification with Jim at and after the trial is the disparity he sees between the ethical code of the young man and the expectations of Jim's fellow seamen, the majority of whom the narrator characterizes thus: "In all they said—in their actions, in their looks, in their persons—could be detected the soft spot, the place of decay, the determination to lounge safely through existence" (*LJ*, 9). Granting the third-person narrator less motive for bias, the reader can still hear in this description echoes of the language with which Marlow denounced his countrymen after returning from the jungle and Kurtz.

In his essay on *Lord Jim*, Watt reproduces a passage of the Rosenbach typescript of Conrad's novel, subsequently excised, that could as easily apply to Marlow and Kurtz as it does to Marlow and Jim: "I don't know what was the matter with me that morning but . . . they all seemed to me strange, foreign, as if belonging to some order of beings I had no connection with. It was only when my eyes turned towards Jim that I had a sense of not being alone of my kind, as if we two had wandered in there from some distant regions, from a different world. I turned to him for fellowship. He alone seemed to look natural."[34] I assume Conrad cut this monologue out of the fear that it would make the text's moral tension too transparent—and worse, too neat. But all it really does, albeit brilliantly, is reemphasize the content of Marlow's moral consciousness and the lingering effects of Kurtz's pedagogic voice therein at the start of *Lord Jim*. Although it has been years since he has heard Kurtz's voice or been in the presence of what he believes might be a natural referent for morality, Marlow has never ceased desiring an alternative for the capitalist and imperialist moral codes that he has learned and lived in the West. To sum up quickly before proceeding: with Jim serving to represent the moral alternative in the immediate absence of Kurtz's pedagogic voice, Marlow is poised once again to oscillate between contending standards for moral thought and action. Moreover, his relationships to Kurtz and Jim are specular and serve to forge the narrative connection between *Heart of Darkness* and *Lord Jim*.

Like *Heart of Darkness*, *Lord Jim* is a modernist narrative. The diegesis of Jim's biography is frequently interrupted by an extradiegetic level representing Marlow's editorials, judgments, and self-reflections. The text's diegesis essentially conveys Marlow's perception of the moral conflict regenerated for him by the Jim episode. The extradiegetic moments are the loci wherein Marlow's recollections of Kurtz's pedagogic voice are most specifically intimated. Examples of the text's extradiegesis abound. Marlow seizes the first opportunity to tell his listeners that his complicity with Jim made him profoundly uncomfortable, since he had "enough confidential information about [himself] to harrow [his] own soul till the end of [his] appointed time" (*LJ*, 21); this could be a veiled reference to the lie and to his betrayal of Kurtz. Elsewhere, he notes "with momentary sadness" that "I have met so many men . . . met them, too, with a certain —certain—impact, let us say" (*LJ*, 58). Kurtz would certainly number among the men who have left a pedagogic impression on Marlow.

Of Jim's inability to proclaim the truth at the trial, Marlow remarks, "I didn't know what he was playing up to—if he was playing up to anything at all—and I suspect he did not know either; for it is my belief no man ever understands quite his own artful dodges to escape from the grim shadow of self-knowledge" (*LJ*, 49). Marlow's compulsive interest in Jim is implied testimony that he has done his fair share of dodging. When he sees Jim's elation over the prospect of shipping to Patusan, Marlow stammers, "I—even I, who had been no end kind to him—even I remembered—remembered—against him—what—what had happened. And what about others—the—the—world?" (*LJ*, 144). The source of these hesitations might be Marlow's recollection, never far from his consciousness, of his conversation with the Intended. And in a protracted meditation on Jim's moral anguish, he explains, "It seemed to me I was being

made to comprehend the Inconceivable—and I know of nothing to compare with the discomfort of such a sensation. I was made to look at the
convention that lurks in all truth and on the essential sincerity of falsehood. He appealed to all sides at once. . . . The mystery of his attitude
got hold of me as though he had been an individual in the forefront of his
kind, as if the obscure truth involved were momentous enough to affect
mankind's conception of itself" (*LJ*, 57). For Marlow, the figures of Kurtz
and Jim provide a site of ideological contestation, where arbitrary convention and naturalized falsehood conspire in the name of profit to hide a
potential source of moral knowledge whose release into Europe could
irreparably alter long-sedimented socioeconomic relations.

While trying to adjudicate Jim's case, Marlow is everywhere reminded
of this ideological conspiracy. Thus Brierly: "This is a disgrace. We've got
all kinds among us—some anointed scoundrels in the lot; but, hang it, we
must preserve professional decency or we become no better than so many
tinkers going about loose. We are trusted. Do you understand?—trusted!
. . . We aren't an organized body of men, and the only thing that holds us
together is just the name for that kind of decency. Such an affair destroys
one's confidence" (*LJ*, 42). The ethical ramifications of Jim's case are inci-
dental to Brierly's wider vision: for business to thrive, there must be a fundamental sense of faith among those participating in economic exchange.
At whatever cost, appearances must be preserved. Engström corroborates
Brierly's utilitarianism when he implies that moral principles count for
nothing in the world of trade. "And who the devil cares about that" (*LJ*,
119) is his response when Marlow discloses Jim's past actions. Chester
thinks Marlow an "incomprehensible fool" (*LJ*, 102) for refusing to sell
Jim on the guano idea; after the incident aboard the *Patna*, Jim's market
value is zero. Excepting Marlow, none of these characters is committed to
self-critical moral thought because none possesses either the ability or the
desire to scrutinize the pretense of European economic and ethical values
toward a nonideological, absolute ethical code. As a point of contrast,
Marlow's pragmatic interlocutors underscore his nonreductive critical
operation.

Marlow's ability to rebuff Chester's deal evidences his capacity to
speak the language of capital with considerable fluency without succumb-
ing to its dubious ethics, a talent he says Jim lacks: "It struck me that it is
from such as he that the great army of waifs and strays is recruited, the

army that marches down, down into all the gutters of the earth. As soon as he left my room, that 'bit of shelter,' he would take his place in the ranks, and begin the journey towards the bottomless pit" (*LJ*, 109). Although there is something frightening and pathetic about Jim's ideological purity as Marlow imagines it, Marlow has already indicated that he would not be willing to imagine Jim any other way. On Jim's comportment at the trial, he comments: "It was solemn, and a little ridiculous, too, as they always are, those struggles of an individual trying to save from the fire his idea of what his moral identity should be, this precious notion of a convention, only one of the rules of the game, nothing more, but all the same so ter-ribly effective by its assumption of unlimited power over natural instincts, by the awful penalties of its failure" (*LJ*, 50). Marlow's condescension toward Jim's attempt to meet the demands of maritime conduct shows him actively composing his picture of Jim as a potential foil to arbitrary, relativizing, utilitarian ethics. The burden of an ethical reading of *Lord Jim* thus remains squarely on Marlow's perception of Jim's value.

Marlow's attitude toward Chester is also a morally charged gesture intended to protect the ingenuous young man from the exploitative mech-anism of a corrupt economic relation with which Marlow has no little inti-macy.[35] Yet there is a passage in the text where Marlow anxiously debates whether it might not be best simply to sell Jim off somewhere where the young man's guilt will not follow him. This narrative sequence sharply focuses the conflict between Marlow's divided moral consciousness and Jim's uncompromising absolutism. While Marlow admits that "I don't defend my morality. There was no morality in the impulse which induced me to lay before [Jim] Brierly's plan of evasion" (*LJ*, 93), he recognizes the exigency of "the material aspect of [Jim's] position . . . the degradation, ruin, and despair that out there close so swiftly upon a friendless, home-less man" (*LJ*, 110). Hearing Jim's avowal that "I may have jumped, but I don't run away" (*LJ*, 94), Marlow also believes that Jim will never allow his redemption to be bought, because he views Jim as an anomaly within European capitalist and imperialist ethical economies.

As Jim's pedagogic example of a possible absolute standard for moral-ity comes to stand in for Kurtz's, so Marlow grants Jim's voice a commen-surable incarnationist, pedagogic authority: "You would have to paddle, pole, or track a long, weary way through the jungle before you passed beyond the reach of [Jim's fame's] voice. Its voice was not the trumpeting of the disreputable goddess we all know—not blatant—not brazen. It took its tone from the stillness and gloom of the land without a past, where his word was the one truth of every passing day" (*LJ*, 166). In Patusan, Marlow consistently silhouettes Jim's ethical voice against European values, where "three hundred miles beyond the end of telegraph cables and mail-boat lines, the haggard utilitarian lies of our civilization wither and die, to be replaced by pure exercises of imagination, that have the futility, often the charm, and sometimes the deep hidden truthfulness, of works of art" (*LJ*, 172).

Of the natives' respect for Jim, Marlow insists, "Those people had trusted him implicitly. Him alone! His bare word . . . decided everything" (*LJ*, 163–64). Perhaps this is the reason Marlow entrusts Jim to Stein rather than to Chester: Stein instantly recognizes Jim's romanticism, which Marlow believes has no place in the service of the imperialist goddess. Irrespective of the actual ideological disturbance Jim causes in Patusan during and after his ascendancy—and there is, of course, plenty of textual evidence to suggest that this disturbance is not inconsiderable[36]—Marlow views Jim on the island as he views Kurtz at the Station: "Romance had singled out Jim for its own—and that was the true part of the story, which otherwise was all wrong" (*LJ*, 172).

Stein may indeed be able to judge Jim, much as Kurtz judged the horror and Marlow once judged Kurtz. But Jim is "too much" (*LJ*, 82) for Marlow inasmuch as the unyielding demands of his moral consciousness evade Marlow's comprehension. Marlow never fully participates in Jim's moral insight as he once, for a tentative and precarious moment, shared in Kurtz's. If Marlow's lie to the Intended inspires his interest in Jim, it also sets the pattern for the moral tension that seems to impede his complete identification with Kurtz's and Jim's pedagogic examples of an alternative to capitalist ethics. Some twenty years separate Marlow's experiences in *Heart of Darkness* and *Lord Jim*. In that time, he has been more gradually and more thoroughly overdetermined by the ethical code of imperialism; hence, his desire to duplicate the act of referential correspondence to an exterior, objective truth is not consummated.[37] Nonetheless, the question subsequently arises: what is Marlow's affiliation with the incarnationist potential of language in *Lord Jim*?

At the trial, Marlow first envisions Jim's incarnationist capacity to express nonideological insight to moral truth at the moment when Jim "had come round to the view that only a meticulous precision of statement would bring out the true horror behind the appalling face of things" (*LJ*, 19). Jim tries to find the words to confess something of "the strength, the power, the horror, of human emotions" (*LJ*, 35). Following Marlow's view of him, Jim believes there are such words and such truth. Thus his— and Marlow's—frustration that the maritime bureaucracy conducting the trial asks purely superficial, epistemological questions of Jim, and nothing else: "The questions put to him necessarily led him away from what to me, for instance, would have been the only truth worth knowing. You can't expect the constituted authorities to inquire into the state of a man's soul" (*LJ*, 35). The institution that originally commissioned Jim deflects moral discussion at the legal forum, probably for fear of exposing its own crimes. Marlow already knows the crimes, has already seen the horror, and is only interested in the state of Jim's, and by extension his, soul.

Perhaps Marlow's faith that Jim's pedagogic voice can pronounce with the same authority as Kurtz's can be ascribed to his personal moral stake in the trial. However, such a conclusion may be a bit premature, especially since, commenting on the *Patna*'s officers implicated in the same trial, Marlow assures his listeners that "as a matter of fact, nobody lied. . . . Not consciously, at least. . . . They had seen no light of any sort though they were well within range, and they could only explain this in one way: the ship had gone down. It was obvious and comforting" (*LJ*, 83). Absolute values are rarely comforting, and it is fairly clear that Marlow's comments are a sincere editorial on the arbitrary moral standards of the marketplace. What, then, is the reader to make of Marlow's fear that, as a consequence of his vanishing from one job after another, Jim "would lose his name of an inoffensive, if aggravating, fool, and acquire that of a common loafer. . . . I could not help reflecting that in such cases from the name to the thing itself is but a step" (*LJ*, 121)? Is this the credo of an ontological foundation for reference and absolute moral truth? Or does it, with its emphasis on "such cases," corroborate the arbitrary ethics of capitalist and imperialist ideology? Given the traces of the various pedagogic voices in Marlow's moral consciousness, the answer is probably that it is both.

Marlow himself can provide little by way of an answer when, speculating on whether to sign Jim over to Chester, he considers that "there is a weird power in a spoken word" (*LJ*, 106). One assumes that this knowledge guides Marlow's behavior as he speaks with Jim about the young man's options: "I . . . who a moment ago was so sure of the power of words . . . now was afraid to speak, in the same way one dares not move for fear of losing a slippery hold. . . . It was the fear of losing him that kept me silent" (*LJ*, 109). Yet this apparent endorsement of correspondent linguistic expression is belied by the following assessment of Jim's moral consciousness: "I don't know how much Jim understood; but I know he felt . . . the demand of some such truth or some such illusion—I don't care how you call it, there is so little difference, and the difference means so little" (*LJ*, 136). Competing pedagogic voices have informed, but have not conclusively finalized, Marlow's attitude towards language's ability to refer.

In contrast to the ambiguity that characterizes his relationship to language in scenes with and about Jim, Marlow's own pedagogic voice pretends to refer with absolute authority in his conversations with Jewel. Responding to what Jewel understands as Jim's moral aloofness and infidelity, Marlow avows, "Nobody here . . . would dream of doubting his word—nobody would dare—except you" (*LJ*, 191). Like the Intended, Jewel is depicted as entirely lacking in insight to the production of moral knowledge. Marlow relates that "it was impossible to make her understand" (*LJ*, 192) the profundity of Jim's moral consciousness. The greatest hit to Jewel's value in the moral dialogue of *Lord Jim* comes in Marlow's appraisal of Jewel's capacity to signify: "To discover that she had a voice at all was enough to strike awe into the heart" (*LJ*, 192).

Recalling Marlow's interview with Kurtz's affianced, Jewel's rôle throughout her colloquy with Marlow is basically restricted to that of the hysterically inquiring wife. Marlow is once again provided the opportunity to speak with the same pedagogic command with which he invests Kurtz and Jim. Dwarfed beneath their moral knowledge, which he views as having challenged the boundaries of European ideological determinants, Marlow in turn assumes a formidable moral legitimacy with those characters who are least able to challenge these same ideological determinants.

Marlow's conversation with Jewel culminates in her contesting his pronouncement that nobody wants Jim on the Continent because the young man is not good enough. In disbelief, she says, somewhat predictably, "You lie!" (*LJ*, 194). Marlow has indeed lied, and his effort to vindicate his judgment might be taken to account, not for his behavior in the interview with Jewel, but for his prevarication years earlier. "Hear me out," Marlow entreats, "nobody, nobody is good enough" (*LJ*, 194). This admission prompts several questions. How can Marlow say that "nobody is good enough" when, for example, Brierly was considered the epitome of professional behavior, and Jim, according to Engström, was just as exemplary, regardless of the *Patna* episode? Having acknowledged the corrupt moral standards that support imperialism, which bases ethical truth claims on the outcome of economic enterprise, does Marlow number himself among its perpetrators or its victims? If his statement is meant to denote his complicity with European imperialist mores, does it subsequently signify his concession that he will never again be able to attain the ludic insight to natural morality that he once imagined himself possessing after hearing Kurtz? If, on the contrary, he means to align himself with Kurtz and Jim as misunderstood idealists in a brutal culture that shams moral responsibility in the service of profit margins, is there anything in the text besides his admission that confirms Marlow's place among such company?

Here, where *Lord Jim* would most urgently need to provide some kind of conclusive response to solidify the reader's interpretation of Marlow's moral consciousness, the text is not forthcoming. Yet there is neither a reason why the text should, nor a way that it can, be conclusive at such a moment. The very fact that a single textual event—like Marlow's attempt to account for Jim's behavior—can compel so many interpretive questions and so few authoritative answers helps to verify the claim that the moral lesson of a text is less significant for ethical textual practice than the aesthetic structure of that traditionally anticipated lesson. In *Heart of Darkness,* Kurtz, to whom Marlow had already ascribed a certain referential authority, judged the horror; his pedagogic voice carried to its target, who was temporarily able to confirm the deep contradiction between positive and natural morality and to align himself with the latter. In *Lord Jim*, the two characters best prepared to offer Marlow an ethical claim that he is likely to privilege above those propounded by the representatives of his merchant seaman vocation are rendered silent at the moment of speaking. On the verge of sending Marlow back to the Continent with a clue to what he has learned on Patusan, Jim's pedagogic voice breaks off: "Tell them. . . . No—nothing" (*LJ*, 204). Earlier, Stein is poised, with a pedagogic voice that seems "inspired by some whisper of knowledge" to initiate Marlow into the secret of "how to be," only to withhold this crucial disclosure (*LJ*, 130). Whatever ontological truth to which these characters have access, in the tradition of romanticism, it remains ineffable.

Instead, a judgment comes from Marlow, whose power to signify is considerably more dubious: "I had made up my mind that Jim, for whom alone I cared, had at last mastered his fate. He had told me he was satisfied . . . nearly. This is going further than most of us dare. I—who have the right to think myself good enough—dare not" (*LJ*, 197). Informed by the painful memory of his experiences in *Heart of Darkness*, Marlow offers a solipsistic judgment that no longer inclines toward universality or absolute knowledge; rather, it diagnoses a pervasive state of epistemological uncertainty that is closely linked to the problem of validating any moral knowledge that is contingent upon particular socioeconomic determinants.[38] The reader is thus returned to the conflict between economic pressure and ethical desire whose dynamic directs Marlow's moral education in both *Heart of Darkness* and *Lord Jim*.

Certain stable benchmarks of Marlow's moral instruction can be ascertained, at which the pedagogic effects of various voices on his moral consciousness can be measured. Marlow, in fact, comes closest to satisfying his desire for an alternative to the ethical ideology of European imperialism in *Heart of Darkness*, where he is young, is less fully interpolated by imperialism's utilitarian agenda, and has the fleeting opportunity to internalize Kurtz's pedagogic example. What cannot be authenticated is a final judgment on the "ultimate" status of Marlow's moral consciousness at the end of *Lord Jim*. One need not look very far for the source of the text's indeterminacy: Marlow retains the desire, diminished or no, for an alternative to the moral standards that empower imperialism; but he has continued to incubate this desire in Europe, where no alternative can ever take sufficient foothold to modify people's thoughts conclusively. Thus Marlow's challenge to his listeners:

> The last word is not said—probably shall never be said. . . . I have given up expecting those last words, whose ring, if they could only be pronounced, would shake both heaven and earth. There is never time to say our last word—the last word of our love, of our desire, faith, remorse, submission, revolt. . . . My last words about Jim shall be few. . . . Frankly, it is not my words that I mistrust, but your minds. I could be eloquent were I not afraid you fellows had starved your imaginations to feed your bodies. I do not mean to be offensive; it is respectable to have no illusions—and safe—and profitable—and dull. (*LJ*, 137–38)

I am not for a moment convinced that Marlow could have been any more eloquent a raconteur had he addressed a different crowd. The insinuation that he could say more were his audience better prepared to hear is very coy, as it momentarily distances Marlow from a culture that he knows has relentlessly conditioned his thoughts and actions. How else could he have forgotten the impression of Kurtz's last words, his final pronouncement on the horror, which once resonated so deeply in him, not only for *what* they signified, but for *how,* with precisely the degree of finality that Marlow now finds entirely wanting. In his letter to the Privileged Man, the one listener among his audience who Marlow believes can appreciate the truth of his relationship to Jim, Marlow confesses that he does not bear the means to complete the sentence with which Jim last took leave of him: "There will be nothing more; there will be no message, unless such as each of us can interpret for himself from the language of facts, that are so often more enigmatic than the craftiest arrangement of words" (*LJ*, 206). Still able to comprehend ideology's naturalization of the artificial, Marlow is nonetheless without the voice to silence the rhetoric of capitalism and imperialism and give *Lord Jim* a tidy ending.

Readers of *Lord Jim* should, I suspect, number themselves with the Privileged Man, since they also hear more of Jim's fate than Marlow's collected listeners. While this information does not resolve the moral tension that inspires Marlow's narrative, it does permit access to Marlow's final words regarding what Jim has signified for him: "There are days when the reality of his existence comes to me with an immense, with an overwhelming force; and yet upon my honor there are moments, too, when he passes from my eyes like a disembodied spirit astray amongst the passions of his earth, ready to surrender himself faithfully to the claim of his own world of shades" (*LJ*, 253). Inevitably, Marlow reiterates the inescapable contradictory pressures on his desire to locate an ethical code that does not complacently reproduce social and economic relations under capitalism. The critical operation that would enable Marlow to pronounce an absolute ethical position would simply be another version of an attempt to naturalize the historical so as to make it appear essential.

Instead of springing this trap, Marlow foregrounds the tension among competing ethical positions and the pedagogic voices through which they are made articulate from the beginning of *Heart of Darkness* to the final speculative moments of *Lord Jim*. Reading the process of Marlow's moral education, the ethical critic is thus exposed to a structural model of responsible ethical textual practice. This model sustains ideological conflicts among pedagogic voices that may then be assimilated and refined into ethical truth claims. While individual readers will assuredly answer the questions provoked by Marlow's inconclusive moral judgments according to their own theoretical and exegetical biases, it is the responsibility of specifically ethical readings to elaborate the aesthetic dynamics through which these moral questions can be shown to emerge.

5

Reading *The Idiot* as Ethical Criticism

■

> "I sent the prince a hedgehog to-day, and I want to know his opinion. Well, prince?"
>
> "What sort of opinion, Aglaia Ivanovna?"
>
> "Of the hedgehog."
>
> "That is, I suppose, Aglaia Ivanovna, you want to know how I took . . . the hedgehog . . . or, rather, how I regarded the . . . sending . . . of the hedgehog, that is . . . I imagine in such a case, that is, in fact . . . "
>
> He gasped and was silent.
>
> "Well, you've not said much," said Aglaia.
>
> Fyodor Dostoevsky, *The Idiot*

When Richard Posner, whose dismissal of ethical criticism I discussed in the first chapter of this study, suggests that, in order to be taken seriously as a potential conduit to moral instruction, ethical criticism must focus on "undeniably ambivalent works, works that seem to wobble around the moral center,"[1] he is absolutely correct. Ethical criticism that fixates on the moral of a story, that attempts to extract guiding thematic moral principles from literature, is vulnerable to the criticism that he and others have brought against it.

But what happens to Posner's dismissal if ethical criticism is somehow successfully applied to an ambivalent text? What happens if the standard for judging the success of an ethical reading is not whether it extracts some preconceived moral position from an ambivalent text, but if it contributes to a better understanding of the aesthetic structures whereby any literary text generates issues of ethical concern? Such an ethical reading would address, and moreover refute, two of Posner's primary objections to ethical literary study. First, it would escape the charge of making a fetish of, and unscrupulously reducing, the moral themes of a text. Second, it would offer a morally instructive structural model on how ethical claims, regardless of their content, might be successfully made and authorized.

The character of Prince Myshkin in Fyodor Dostoevsky's *The Idiot* provides precisely the kind of wobbly moral center that Posner asserts is a necessary precondition to a serious ethical reading. While Myshkin's ethical position is fairly clearly expressed throughout the text, it is not at all certain whether his ethical position dominates all others in the text's final moral climate. The ethical significance of *The Idiot* is not a matter of whether or not Myshkin's purportedly Christian ethic is worthy of primacy. Rather, the text is ethically instructive insofar as it investigates the morally pedagogic potential of two distinct modes of linguistic reference, the referential and the constitutive. Such a reading is less disclosive of a critic's interpretive biases about a specific ethical code than it is of the structural features of persuasive ethical discourse. Confronting Posner head–on, such a reading may thus serve both as a responsible way to practice ethical criticism and as a metacommentary on what ethical criticism may expect from itself as a method.

Opponents of ethical criticism commonly dismiss the practice for what they perceive to be its presumption of a referential evaluative authority that takes itself as the univocal word on a text's moral "lesson." Myshkin does not consciously manifest this presumption. Nevertheless, throughout Dostoevsky's text, Myshkin's pedagogic voice betrays an incarnationist, referentially authoritative proclivity that would seem to have as little place in the materially chaotic world of the novel as it does in the arena of ethical criticism. Thus, Myshkin's pedagogic example can be read on at least two levels. The first is in the closed context of Dostoevsky's literary product. Myshkin is responsible for imbuing the text's myriad social conflicts with a moral dimension. If, despite his uniquely referential method of signification, his instructive effect on his listeners can be corroborated, then Dostoevsky has taken a significant step toward indicating a possible arrangement between individual and social relations in which unconditional moral knowledge might be generated and transmitted. Second, an investigation into the pedagogic impact of Myshkin's incarnationist voice analogously serves as a commentary on the methodological limits governing all acts of responsible ethical evaluation in a historically contingent context.

It has become fairly common for studies of Myshkin's character to refer to the *Notebooks* for *The Idiot*, where Dostoevsky documents his painstaking and tortuous efforts to produce the final version of the Prince that has become known to the novel's audience. Not until the sixth plan does Dostoevsky grant the Prince his title, and the Christian image of Myshkin as a truly beautiful, humble, and compassionate figure does not appear until plan seven. Thereafter, the *Notebooks* are devoted more to delineating scenic and conversational dynamics than to character development. But in an entry dated April 10, 1868, Dostoevsky inscribes the following items: "The chief thing: *stories*. . . . N.B. Prince Christ. . . . Conversation with Ptitsyn about the King of the Jews."[2] There is no reason to think that the third of these entries reveals much more than Dostoevsky's desire to use his latest novel to reflect on the theological issues that enter nearly all his major fiction. The first two are more suggestive of the beginning of a qualitative change in Myshkin's character, from Christian soul to Christ figure, that is incubating in Dostoevsky's creative imagination at this time.[3] An extension of Myshkin as Prince Christ is Myshkin's natural, reflexive manner of expressing himself, the incarnationist expectations of his voice to which no other participant in the dialogue of *The Idiot* can lay claim.

Robin Feuer Miller has remarked an initial theme of *The Idiot* as "the impossibility of expressing an idea directly into words."[4] In a similar vein, David Danow explains that a sure sign of the text's prevailing ethos of linguistic impotence is the consistent lack of communication among the novel's principal characters.[5] Dostoevsky's text suggests otherwise. His novels generally explore the question of how, and how effectively, human beings can express ethical claims in a constructed medium like language. *The Idiot* is no exception, but it is too much to say that, because it speculates on the obstacles that impede communication, Dostoevsky's novel is a testament to the impossibility of linguistic signification. Characters like Ganya, Lebedyev, Nastasya Filippovna, and the "young nihilists," to name just a few, understand that the spoken word is a historically charged idiom whose meaning is contingent on the conditions in which it is articulated. Therefore, they are indeed quite successful in manipulating language to great effect throughout the text. Moreover, they are the rule rather than the exception. Among the exceptions to this rule is Myshkin, who, throughout the narrative, never adequately understands the impact of context on the construction of meaning in the material world.

Dostoevsky empowers Myshkin's voice with an inchoate scriptural authority from the moment he enters the Epanchin home,[6] where Lizaveta Prokofyevna demands that Myshkin tell her and her daughters something. Seeing that he comes down from the mountains and is not implicated in the artificially choreographed social relations of nineteenth-century Petersburg society, the respectably bored middle-class Epanchin women immediately romanticize Myshkin's voice for what it might teach them. Myshkin does little to disabuse them of their fantasy. After confessing that "perhaps I really have a notion of instructing,"[7] he discusses the psychology and spectacle of a man condemned to execution. The women are at first disconcerted that he fails to append a judgment to the story, which Alexandra forthwith provides. Myshkin then recounts the tale of Marie, a young woman in a Swiss village who is wrongly persecuted for prurience and subsequently scorned by the rest of the village. Myshkin appeals to the natural goodness of the village children, who inevitably alleviate Marie's misery through their compassion and love at the same time that they verify Myshkin's pedagogic voice.

Recalling the significance Dostoevsky ascribed to "stories" in his *Notebook* entry, Myshkin's narratives may be said to assume the weight of parables that present the Epanchin women with "a model of how to live." In theme and content, these parables possess an irrepressible Christian import. In the way they convey personal experience into a form of art to be consumed by any and everyone within earshot, these parables are "transmuted . . . into symbolic myths."[8] In modality, they present a patina of objectivity as a consequence of Myshkin's refusal to interpret their meaning to the Epanchin women. This feature of Myshkin's voice is perhaps the key to his formidable incarnationist, referential authority. Because he defers moral judgment on people and events, ostensibly to a higher authority, he is viewed by the characters around him as authoritative. As Joseph Frank describes this phenomenon, "The figure of the Prince is surrounded with a pervasive Christian halo that continually illuminates his character, and . . . serves to locate the transcendent nature of his moral and spiritual aspirations."[9]

The events of *The Idiot* are played out in an arena of profoundly idiosyncratic behavior that has its root in the contradiction between economic and spiritual anxieties that informs the majority of the text's characters. To these characters, Myshkin rarely manifests the outward signs of contradiction. His social status is ambiguous; he is without social pretension, and his arrival creates the impression of a spiritual quiet into a storm.[10] If not ideologically pure, Myshkin at first, and frequently thereafter, nevertheless appears ideologically static. Frank contends that what most clearly stamps the Prince is his capacity "for living so totally in each moment of time or in each experience and encounter that he lacks any sense of continuity or consequence."[11] In similar fashion, Dennis Slattery notes: "Tradition, education, anything which promotes an historical perspective, remains foreign to him. . . . Myshkin is of narrow vision. . . . For him the past comprises only private reminiscences insulated from the broader stream of collective history."[12]

Myshkin's tendency to speak mythopoeically in parables distinguished by their lack of conclusion or ethical judgment, along with his basic inability to acclimate himself to the text's unstable social relations, all contribute to the production of his incarnationist voice. As a consequence of this voice, Myshkin and the other characters have profound difficulty communicating with one another. Nonetheless, the text's moral tension thrives on the frequently underscored incompatibility between the Prince's and the others' methods of signification.

Supporting Myshkin's incarnationist voice is a referential mechanism that relies on a stable and anticipated correspondence between word and thing tantamount to a romantic insight to unconditional value.[13] The presence of this mechanism may be confirmed by the characters' reception of the Prince. The Ivolgins and Epanchins of the world recognize Myshkin's initial refusal to judge, a refusal provoked by Myshkin's referential authority: God does not judge those who have been admitted to the kingdom of heaven because there can be no questionable expression of will in His kingdom. The semiotic space that *The Idiot*'s characters avidly scramble to fill is a product of the spatiotemporal dimension of signification. In a world outside time, judgment is no more necessary than ethics; both are obviated with the elimination of choice, which is the ineluctable temporal demand of an historical existence. But Petersburg is not outside time, and Myshkin's rôle as the town's holy fool is assured by his predictable ability to say the wrong thing at the worst possible time.[14]

Ideologically unprepared as he is to enter the unstable contingencies of social relations, which everyone around him can read with varying degrees of fluency, Myshkin never competently learns to align linguistic and social codes in such a way that he can manipulate the effects of his voice with any degree of conscious proficiency. Although he is undeniably physically complicit in the progress of the temporal world and is subsequently forced to make choices and to suffer their consequences, his criterion for right and wrong remains unchanged throughout the text. His is the voice of absolute morality, which requires an atemporal referential capacity to ordain its ethical claims. Myshkin can hardly be blamed for the incarnationist quality of his pedagogic voice. It is not his fault that he does not descend from the mountains into Petersburg society with a full set of the city's ideological coordinates in his moral consciousness; nor can he be expected to assimilate the rules and nuances of constructivist signification in a breath.

It should come as little surprise that Dostoevsky invested one of his characters with a referentially correspondent moral voice. According to George Gutsche, "ethical theory in Russia is well grounded in forms of the Absolute, whether religious or secular, whether Kantian, utilitarian, positivist, Hegelian, Marxist, or Orthodox; and these assumptions about Platonic and Kantian atemporal essences are imbedded implicitly and explicitly in the views of most Russian writers. . . . All, to one degree or another, have based their critical efforts in a soil of certainty, an ultimate reality that lies at the bottom of everything."[15]

Phenomenological studies of Dostoevsky's corpus have traditionally argued that the substance of Dostoevsky's moral sensibility reflects an unmistakable Kantian tendency to distill moral conflict down to the division between selfish and selfless acts. On these interpretations, the individual has a categorical moral imperative to recognize the subjectivity of the other in a selfless act that, by virtue of acknowledging some ideal of community, fulfills the protocol of good behavior. Myshkin's moral voice is therefore thematically consistent with Dostoevsky's Kantian affinities, which underpin the expression of Christian messianism in his fiction.

The moral dimension of *The Idiot* is finally a product of the text's pedagogic aesthetics, which express the tension between Myshkin's incarnationist voice and the radically contingent ethical positions of his various interlocutors. Bakhtin explains the bifurcation of referential processes thus: "Only the mythical Adam, who approached a virginal and as yet unqualified world with the first word, could really have escaped from start to finish this dialogic inter–orientation with the alien word that occurs in the object.

Concrete historical human discourse does not have this privilege; it can deviate from such inter–orientation only on a conditional basis and only to a certain degree."[16] Ironically, Myshkin appears to fit quite comfortably into the category of the mythical Adam who approaches a virginal and as yet unqualified world with the first word. Upon meeting the Prince for the first time, nearly all remark that they have neither seen nor heard the likes of such a man; they are no less foreign to Myshkin's experience. Myshkin's incarnationist voice is placed in tension with conditional modes of reference, and it retains its status by remaining isolated from these modes. Although Myshkin is ineluctably drawn into an "endless and endlessly enriching exchange"[17] with the other characters in the novel, his lack of ideological preparedness to negotiate this exchange makes his pedagogic voice more a structural than a thematic participant in the text's moral dialogue.

Myshkin's apparent inability to participate in the full conversational array of *The Idiot* prompts an interesting question: can Bakhtin's description of the Dostoevskian novel, as a perpetually open polyphony of its characters' unfinished subjectivities, accommodate the referential authority of Myshkin? Put another way, is Myshkin a truly "dialogic" character in the Bakhtinian sense of an unfinished consciousness whose ideas are implicated in the irreducible ideological friction maintained among competing subjects? Addressing this very question, Bakhtin asserts that Myshkin's dialogism is of a "somewhat different character" from the more typical Dostoevskian figure. Bakhtin recalls Dostoevsky's intention that Myshkin carry a "*penetrative word,* that is, a word capable of actively and confidently interfering in the interior dialogue of the other person, helping that person to find his own voice." But Bakhtin is reluctant to endorse Dostoevsky's own commentary because to do so would put an almost monologic constraint on the voice of one of Dostoevsky's major and, for Bakhtin's theory, most intractable protagonists. To diminish the reasons for interpreting Myshkin as a privileged anomaly in a dialogic world, Bakhtin thus qualifies the impact of Myshkin's pedagogic voice: "This penetrative word . . . [is] never, in the case of Myshkin, a decisive voice. It is denied any real ultimate confidence and sovereignty, and is often simply allowed to drop. A firm and integral monologic discourse is unknown to him too. The internal dialogism of his discourse is just as great and anxiety-ridden as that of the other characters."[18]

A rather transparent inconsistency underpins Bakhtin's analysis of Myshkin: Myshkin's interior dialogue is not equivalent to his external monologue. Indeed, while engaged in the kind of morbid, hypersensitive self-reflections that precede his epileptic fits especially, Myshkin reveals a rambling, indecisive interior dialogue rife with anxiety. But the chronic shyness and frequent lack of confidence that accompany his conversation with other characters do not belie the correspondent power of his voice. Bakhtin has elided a crucial distinction: in *The Idiot*, *referential authority is not necessarily pedagogic authority*. The reader should not, as Dostoevsky did not, seek to validate Myshkin's referential authority by his ability to "convert" his audience to Christian *agape*. Quite the contrary. By virtue of the pedagogic dynamic that underwrites *The Idiot*, Myshkin's referential authority is only able to exist as the antithesis of the remaining characters' conditional modes of signification.[19] His capacity to convert other characters is secondary to the signifying mechanism of his voice through which any pedagogic effect is likely to occur.

Developing Bakhtin's reading of Myshkin's dialogism, Caryl Emerson also refers to the concept of *proniknovennoe slovo,* which she translates as the penetrat*ed* word. Emerson's alternate transcription of the term alters the direction of pedagogy between Myshkin and his colloquists. Bakhtin's estimation of Myshkin relies on what he sees as the tendency of Myshkin's voice to penetrate and inform another's consciousness, subsequently vindicating claims for the Prince's dialogic involvement in Dostoevsky's text. But Bakhtin's criticism is dubious in its desire to confer and withhold authority from Myshkin at the same time—a tendency I ascribe to his confusion of the Prince's referential and pedagogic effect. Moreover, Emerson's translation renders unclear by what or whom the Prince's voice is penetrated, and the result of this ambiguity is, ironically, to lessen the persuasiveness of the Bakhtinian position she seeks to espouse. For if Myshkin's ideological position does not enter the stream of *The Idiot*'s dialogue but is instead predominantly entered, the Prince might be shown to represent a sharper monologism than Bakhtin would care to allow.

Emerson's explication of Myshkin's penetrated word extends Bakhtin's:

> The penetrated word does not stand above or outside the discourse of the characters. It does not come down but *across*. . . . The Prince can, and often does, appeal to one of the voices warring inside another person,

and if he reaches an 'authentic voice' he can trigger a major moral rever-
sal. But the penetrated word does not last. It can only enter at a specific
time and place to work a temporary realization. . . . The penetrated word
makes authority real, but only for the moment; it remains personal, historical, and conditional.[20]

Again, this strand of argument conflates the process of signification with
what that process signifies for the other. The latter may, in fact, be considerable. However, if the Prince's voice comes across to his audience, it does so
only after it has come down from the romanticized setting of the Swiss
mountains, whence it brings its inchoate referential apparatus, unprecedented in the society of the Epanchins and their acquaintances. Emerson's
proposal that the Prince's penetrated word is, in the last instance, personal,
historical, and conditional is also at odds with my suggestion that Myshkin's
voice does not, because it cannot, penetrate the dynamic of contingent
social relations that comprises the historical background of Dostoevsky's
text: it is not convincingly historical or conditional in any substantial way.

Emerson's dialogization of Myshkin is necessitated by her efforts to
maintain a clear Bakhtinian split between the way Tolstoy and Dostoevsky
employ discourse in their respective fictions. On her view, "Tolstoyan
discourse strives to rise above specific times and places, it inevitably dehis-
toricizes language—that is, makes it possible to value a word regardless of
when it was spoken and by whom. . . . Either Tolstoy allows a speaker to
assume directly the didactic role of teacher, judge, or preacher, or he presents discourse itself as something more solid and impersonal than it is—
as a direct impression from life, or as something untainted by ideological
preconceptions."[21] These characteristics of discourse could just as easily
apply to Myshkin as to a Tolstoyan hero like Levin.

Although Myshkin does not consciously announce himself as the
repository of referential signification, his example demonstrates time and
again that the incarnationist voice is not easily accommodated to conditional dialogue precisely because it rises above specific times and places.
For example, if anything provokes the penultimate scandal scene of *The
Idiot*, in which the Prince is forced to choose between Aglaia and Nastasya
Filippovna, it is his implacable inclination to inscribe a word with an
absolute value, regardless of when it is spoken and to whom. Myshkin
does choose, and his choice is unequivocally wrong by the standards of
polite Petersburg society because the language of these standards is one the

Prince does not speak. Instead of penetrating the consciousness of others with historically conditioned dialogue, Myshkin translates his voice into parable, just as he transforms his ideologically static life into a work of art, which he then bestows upon his listeners at their request.

But are Myshkin's listeners edified? Does his incarnationist voice accomplish anything in *The Idiot*? As the *Notebooks* intimate, the answers to these questions ostensibly caused Dostoevsky ambivalence and apprehension:

> N.B. The Prince has had only *the slightest effect* on their lives. But everything he might have done and undertaken perishes with him.
>
> *Russia has had its effect on him little by little. His intuitions.* (x)!
>
> But wherever he even made an appearance—everywhere he left a permanent trace.
>
> Hence the infinity of events in the novel (the more wretched persons of all classes), along with the development of the main theme.
>
> (N.B. N.B. N.B.) This is precisely the theme that has to be worked out.[22]

In the space of two sentences, Dostoevsky vacillates between a pedagogically impotent and a subtly but conclusively effective Prince. It is debatable whether Dostoevsky ever significantly reconciled this rather contradictory evaluation of Myshkin's instructive effect in the *Notebooks*. Moreover, some measure of Dostoevsky's ambivalence toward the Prince's pedagogic potential is rather clearly expressed in the novel itself through the unreliable voice of the narrator; it is certainly plausible to imagine that the narrator's lack of assurance about Myshkin's moral voice reflects Dostoevsky's own ambivalence about his protagonist. As a result of the narrator's indeterminate evaluation of Myshkin's character, the narrator's voice also adds to the dialogue on which *The Idiot*'s moral component is constructed.

Dostoevsky's contradictory conception of Myshkin's morally instructive effect additionally informs the divide in critical opinion over whether the novel ultimately bears out the Prince's pedagogic impotence or his influence. Criticism that tends toward the former verdict also tends toward an indirect evaluation of the essentialist elements of Myshkin's voice. For this reason, it deserves a brief synopsis here.

Murray Krieger cites Myshkin's "irrational Christlike transcendence of mere ethical judgment," his "unerring depth of moral perception" as the source of the Prince's impossible moral standard.[23] Though he concedes Myshkin's good intentions, Krieger calls the Prince's moral perfectionism

a "curse of saintliness" that passively pressures others by constantly reminding them of how imperfect they really are. Anthony Cascardi appends a different lexicon to the same propensity of Myshkin's moral pedagogy. For
Cascardi, Myshkin is the "beautiful soul" who is "incapable of bringing [a]
sense of moral obligation to bear fruit in a world composed of actual
beings." Cascardi attributes Myshkin's failure to his inability to participate
flexibly in ethically charged social conditions: "In order adequately and
responsibly to judge another individual, we should understand that person
from within, know everything about them, in order to respond to them as
lived actualities."[24]

The tendency of Myshkin to dehistoricize moral judgment through a
correspondent pedagogic voice creates the "gaps in Christology" to which
Michael Holquist refers. Holquist contends that, as Dostoevskian time sys-
tematically ruptures the chronological connection between moment and
sequence, the metonymic conditions necessary for the emergence of a
man-God like an ideal Myshkin cannot develop in *The Idiot*. Unlike Christ,
whose preordained *telos* was to realize His and humankind's part in a preexisting whole, Myshkin is spiritually isolated in Petersburg. Myshkin's
attempts to duplicate an incarnationist voice like Christ's, without some
kind of suprahistorical validation, end up the same way as what Holquist
describes as the Prince's attempt to live a "unified existence": both are
"constantly exposed by the novel's relentless insistence on the multiplicity
of identities that are merely human, merely personal."[25]

These critics all share a sense of Myshkin's pedagogic failure, which they
ascribe to various components of the Prince's character—his transcendent
moral standard; his atemporal, ahistorical mode of judgment; his naïve
aspiration to unity—that are external manifestations of his incarnationist
voice. Their conclusive assessment of Myshkin's pedagogy is based on the
observation that Myshkin fails to communicate his moral values unprob-
lematically to those around him. Myshkin's values are seen to miscarry, not
as a result of what he does, but as a result of what he does not do.[26] Rather,
the opposite principle governs the instructive effect of Myshkin's voice:
the pedagogic efficacy of the incarnationist voice is a consequence of what
it cannot do, not what it can. Myshkin's correspondent mode of reference
successfully impresses the other characters with the example of its impotence, though the moral significance of this example can never be univocally

demonstrated. Inadequate as Prince Christ, Myshkin is indeed adequate as pedagogue.

Dostoevsky empowers Myshkin's voice with a scriptural authority from the moment he enters the Epanchin home. Even before he offers the Epanchin women his parable of Marie, the Prince reveals a faith in referential language. "Announce Prince Myshkin," he tells the footman, "and the name itself will be a sufficient reason for my visit" (*I*, 18). Myshkin's faith that words can accurately correspond to something essential is constantly challenged in *The Idiot*, most clearly by the process of signification that enables the text's chaotic scandal scenes. Malcolm Jones has described these scenes in which the participants "are overcome by vaguely apprehended ideas which seem momentarily to offer an explanation for what they have not grasped. . . . The techniques of effective story-telling themselves are being undermined. . . . [I]n th[ese] section[s] the narrator abandons (or travesties) such techniques and lets the characters speak whatever rubbish comes into their heads."[27] The scandal scenes are lurid magnifications of a philosophy of language that recognizes and exploits the inescapable temporal restrictions placed on the conveyance of ideas. The scenes powerfully corroborate *The Idiot*'s preponderant ideas that words can be manipulated to mean almost anything and that context figures prominently in the solidification of meaning. They also emphasize the divorce between Myshkin's incarnationist voice and the contingency of value acknowledged by virtually every other character in the text.[28]

Additional examples of Myshkin's inability to comprehend either the temporal constituents of meaning or the much more narrowly applicable value judgments such conditional meaning enables are easily adduced. The Prince assures Nastasya Filippovna that he will never, under any circumstances, reproach her for her prior relationship with Totsky (*I*, 162). Rogozhin observes the untenable magnitude of Myshkin's pity (*I*, 206), and in similar fashion, Aglaia remarks that the Prince's idealism gainsays his professed commitment to real people: "You have no tenderness, nothing but truth, and so you judge unjustly" (*I*, 413). Prince S. admonishes Myshkin for seeking "paradise on earth" (*I*, 330), an atemporal desire that trivializes evidence of real human suffering in favor of a prelapsarian ideal. General Ivolgin is impressed by the "naturalness" of Myshkin's expression

(*I*, 480), which is obviously positioned as a foil to the tendency of the other characters toward artifice and duplicity. After he breaks the vase at the Epanchins' party, the Prince forgets the protocols demanded by context and entreats forgiveness "for *everything*, besides the vase" (*I*, 532). Yevgeny Pavlovitch summarizes the characteristics that contribute to Myshkin's idealism thus: "What's at the bottom of all that's happened is your innate inexperience (mark that word, "innate," prince), and your extra-ordinary simple-heartedness, and then the phenomenal lack of all feeling for proportion in you (which you have several times recognized yourself), and finally the huge mass of intellectual convictions, which you, with your extraordinary honesty, have hitherto taken for real, innate, intuitive convictions!" (*I*, 563). Radomsky's comments strike at the Prince's irrepressible tropism toward abstraction, which appears more as the force of an idea than as the idea's living embodiment.[29]

Myshkin himself recognizes the disparity between his instinctive referential determinacy and the indeterminate, historically inflected discourse of his interlocutors. To Radomsky, he confesses that "my words are incongruous, not befitting the subject, and that's a degradation for those ideas" (*I*, 332). Before the party at the Epanchins, he reflects that "he must restrain himself and be silent, that he might not degrade an idea by his expressing it" (*I*, 502). To the guests at the party, he mentions this anxiety aloud: "I'm always afraid that my absurd manner may discredit the thought or the *leading idea*. I have no elocution" (*I*, 535). As a diagnostician of his place in Petersburg society, Myshkin is both correct and incorrect. He does have elocution, but his elocution is incongruous with the mode of signification common to those around him. Furthermore, although Myshkin appreciates the separation between his and others' modes of expression, he does nothing to modify the referential expectations of his voice to accommodate circumstantial pressures.

The Epanchin's party most fully illustrates the ineluctable operation of Myshkin's incarnationist voice, which tries to affect a correspondence between unconditionally conceived ideals and values and a socially informed, materially contingent context. The narrator reports that "it could never have entered [Myshkin's] head that all this simple frankness and nobility, wit, and refined personal dignity was perhaps only an exquisite artistic veneer. The majority of the guests, in spite of their prepossessing exterior, were rather empty headed people. . . . Myshkin, carried away by the charm of his first impression, had no inclination to suspect this. . . . All this society Myshkin took for true coin, for pure gold without alloy" (*I*, 518–21). Although the narrator's gender and social status are never explicitly revealed, the narrator is presumably an individual with either the means or the opportunity to be privy to the comings and goings of a household like the Epanchins'. One could reasonably expect that such an individual might therefore be tempted to portray the Epanchins' guests, and the social relations they represent, in the kindest possible fashion. But the narrator instead lays bare the artifice that Myshkin does not detect, and in the process makes the Prince seem even further removed from the material reality that surrounds him.

During the party, Myshkin's impassioned denunciation of Roman Catholicism (and, to a lesser degree, of socialism) is symptomatic of his incompatibility with those ideologies that profess spiritual value from a terrestrial altar.[30] According to Myshkin, Roman Catholicism permits temporal, material commitments to vitiate the unconditionally unified truth, exemplified by Christ, to which the Prince's incarnationist voice aspires: "The Pope seized the earth, an earthly throne, and grasped the sword; everything has gone on in the same way since, only they have added to the sword lying, fraud, deceit, fanaticism, superstition, villainy. They have trifled with the most holy, truthful, sincere, fervent feelings of the people; they have bartered it all, all for money, for base earthly power" (*I*, 527). While explicating his "utopian" thoughts, Myshkin considers that "in order to reach perfection one must begin by being ignorant of a great deal. And if we understand things too quickly, perhaps we shan't understand them thoroughly" (*I*, 536). This avowal is yet another confirmation of the Prince's suspicion of the kind of complacent vulgar empiricism that precludes difficult insight into a precultural referent. For Myshkin, the referent of thought and language is not historical but transcendent and absolute, and it is only attainable by one who resists the immediately gratifying allure of material advantage that impedes referential correspondence.

Thus, Myshkin so fervently tries to convince the Epanchins' guests that they are not what they seem to be. Following his "leading idea," he ignores the material reality before him and insists: "I've always heard too much that was bad about you, more than what was good; of your pettiness, the exclusiveness of your interests, your stagnation, your shallow education, and your ridiculous habits. . . . I had heard so often and fully believed myself that society was nothing but manners, and antiquated forms, and that all reality was extinct. But I see now for myself that that cannot be so among us: that may be anywhere else but not in Russia" (*I*, 534–35). Emerging in Myshkin's harangue is a variation of the characteristic Dostoevskian theme of the Russian peasant's pedagogic rôle in the spiritual transformation and salvation of the Russian people. But Myshkin is not speaking to peasants. And the reality of which he speaks is not the immediate impressions that have provoked his speech. He is exercising his incarnationist reflex to speak an ideal image into and onto a material condition that, ideally transformed, corresponds back to the ideal.[31]

    The Idiot's famous penultimate scene, in which Myshkin is forced to choose between Nastasya Filippovna and Aglaia, affords perhaps the most fodder for a statement on the novel's moral tenor. Throughout the narrative, Myshkin has idealized both women. But his image of Aglaia follows an ideal more commensurable with the mundane tradition of courtly love than with his essentially ethereal image of Nastasya Filippovna as the wrongly persecuted angel, the Mary Magdalene whose pure heart has been betrayed by the deceits of the material world and needs to be refitted to the divine plan. When forced to choose between ideals, Myshkin impulsively selects the one to whom he has already sworn his eternal loyalty. His gesture towards Nastasya Filippovna has, in this moment, less to do with what she represents than how she represents it. To choose Aglaia is to choose the earth, but the unbroken commitment of the incarnationist voice is to the atemporal, the transmundane. The incarnationist voice cannot hope to teach Nastasya Filippovna the virtue of an existential value, but it can hope to elevate Aglaia to a faith in the timeless value of an absolute moral imperative to which every human act must, for Myshkin, refer.

    A careful reader of *The Idiot* suspects that Myshkin has to choose Nastasya Filippovna over Aglaia, although the actual ethical reverberations of the choice, through the fluid world of historical contingency, cannot be predicted with nearly the same felicity. When called by Yevgeny Pavlovitch to account for his choice, the divorce between Myshkin's sense of referential truth and Yevgeny Pavlovitch's socially inflected values is the hinge of moral dialogue. The Prince explains to Radomsky that the scene occurred because "they both talked of the wrong thing, utterly wrong" (*I*, 565); that is, both Aglaia and Nastasya Filippovna discoursed in an idiom determined by issues of status and social redemption. Myshkin's sincere conviction, that he loves both women "with two different sorts of love" (*I*, 567), is beyond Radomsky's comprehension. There is no reason to expect Radomsky to think otherwise: he pays lip service to the ideological value of monogamy as taught him by his culture. He rejoins the Prince, "Aglaia Ivanovna loved you like a woman, like a human being, not like an abstract spirit" (*I*, 565); but he does not apprehend that, in Myshkin's hierarchy of value, the abstract spirit ranks higher than the human.

In what may be the most poignant reminder that Myshkin is working within a signifying system that is irreconcilable with the discourse of the other characters, the Prince laments, "Why is it we can never know *everything* about another person, when one ought to, when that other one's to blame!" (*I*, 566). As "that other one," Myshkin verifies his alienation from a human community that lacks the referential insight he appears to demonstrate. Myshkin remains confident that he can make amends with Aglaia if he is granted an opportunity to speak with her: his faith in the correspondent truth value of his voice supersedes all indication that Aglaia *will not* understand his values simply because she *cannot* understand them. As Prince Christ, Myshkin cannot permit contingency to compromise the ideal foundations of his incarnationist voice any more than Christ could have failed the tests in the desert. In wishing that Aglaia might possess his knowledge, not that he might possess hers, the isolation of his incarnationist voice is further substantiated.

If the first feature of Myshkin's incarnationist voice is that it appears to correspond to an atemporal referent of unconditional value, the second feature, which also distinguishes it from the rest of the voices that participate in *The Idiot*'s moral dialogue, is that Myshkin's words must actually be incarnated into a correspondent action in order to validate their truth claims.[32] Feuer Miller targets this second expression of Myshkin's incarnationist voice as one of the earliest sources of moral confusion caused by the Prince. Because Myshkin is both the narrator of the good and the doer of that same good, "characters in the novel mistrust him when he is absent; they cannot define his role."[33] Kovacs concurs, identifying Myshkin's need to enact gestures corresponding to his words as the site of the Prince's dialogic entry into the text. While I disagree with Kovacs's assertion that Myshkin's voice is monologically self-referential—on my reading, the

Prince signifies by referring to some unconditional external authority—
his notion that the other characters are able to exert their own unpre-
dictable volition in the space created between Myshkin's words and the
deeds predicated on those words is persuasive.[34]

There is no semiotic space for referential discrepancy in the Prince's
signifying system: the word, which refers to a thing or objective idea, is
ideally immediately made flesh in an act. As Lebedyev confesses in exaggerated language that does not, however, belie the general principle at
stake, there is nothing *but* space in the socially informed process of signification practiced by Myshkin's interlocutors: "Words and deeds and lies and
truth are all mixed up in me and are perfectly sincere. Deeds and truth
come out in my genuine penitence, I swear it, whether you believe it or
not; and words and lies in the hellish (and always present) craving to get
the better of a man, to make something even out of one's tears of penitence" (*I*, 301). Suggesting that the value of the act is more legitimate than
the value of the word, Lebedyev proffers an empirical conception of social
truth that makes little attempt to reconcile words either to thoughts or to
deeds. Myshkin distrusts this method of signification because it supplies no
evidence of a referential idea. It merely presents itself as the locus of value.
The irony in Myshkin's position is that, after refuting the truth value of the
superficial, the Prince appeals to an unconditionally ideal, not to a deeper
material referent to authorize his voice and gestures.

The effect of this appeal is a widening of the gulf between his and *The
Idiot*'s other characters' signifying systems until they can make no sense
of him. The following conversation, between Myshkin and Lizaveta
Prokofyevna, epitomizes the difficulties that the Prince's audience encounters time and again when they try to comprehend his behavior:

> "Ach, you're a simpleton, a simpleton! Everyone deceives you like a . . .
> like a . . . And aren't you ashamed to trust him? Surely you must see that
> he's cheating you all round?"
>
> "I know very well he does deceive me sometimes," Myshkin brought
> out reluctantly in a low voice, "and he knows that I know it . . ." and he
> broke off.
>
> "Knows it and goes on trusting him! That's the last straw! It's just
> what one would expect of you, though, and there's no need for me to be
> surprised at it. Good Lord! Was there ever such a man!" (*I*, 309)

The answer, of course, is that there was such a man, whose voice was the precedent for Myshkin's. But Lizaveta Prokofyevna's filter for judging the appropriateness of action is a very finite code of sociocultural mores that would see one man swiftly punished for bringing false charges against another. Entrapped in the expectations of surface order and carefully orchestrated social gesture, Lizaveta Prokofyevna perceives the Prince's actions as lacking any sensible referent. This can hardly be her fault, given her material determinants. Insofar as the meaning of his behavior cannot be anchored in the ideological preconceptions of Petersburg society, Myshkin comes to stand as "a signifier without a signified," analogous to the hedgehog given him by Aglaia as a gift.[35] Every character has difficulty trying to figure out what the Prince signifies.

The incarnationist voice is exceptional for the manner, not the substance, of its expression. While Myshkin's voice is structurally pedagogic, teaching others by presenting the example of an unprecedented system of correspondent linguistic reference, it would be premature to categorize the particular ethical content of this instruction. This can only be accomplished by examining the novel's scenes of ideological contestation in which Myshkin engages one or more characters in a moral dialogue. Because of what Frank has called the "monumental plasticity" that epitomizes the respective moral consciousnesses of *The Idiot*'s characters, these effects are never conclusive.[36] But they do evolve to produce a moral tenor that, generated in the pedagogic reciprocity between Myshkin and the others, illustrates a structural model of the production of ethical knowledge.

Myshkin's arrival in Petersburg signals a redescription of the text's preexisting conflicts, all of which are in some way ignited by General Epanchin's and Totsky's plot to marry Nastasya Filippovna off to Ganya. Prior to Myshkin's appearance, everyone implicated in the marriage plan is exclusively concerned with determining the personal, social, and economic consequences of whether the marriage is brought off or falls through. No one expresses the slightest wonder whether the matrimonial scheming is right or wrong, just or unjust. Within minutes of his first conversation with the General, Myshkin introduces an evaluative language to the Epanchin home that has heretofore been absent: "We might perhaps be of use to one another—you to me and I to you—if you were good people, and I had heard that you were good people" (*I*, 23). The General and Ganya immediately suspect that Myshkin is practicing the same kind of sophisticated social machinations in which they themselves are absorbed and are prepared to dismiss him. But when the Prince makes no financial appeal, the General and Ganya are forced to interpret Myshkin's "good" to refer to something other than a material economy. And the General experiences a "change of attitude . . . all in a minute" (*I*, 24). This effect of Myshkin's voice is his first significant pedagogic gesture. It is also, albeit more arguably, the first specifically moral repercussion of his presence in Petersburg, for it inaugurates the honesty and humility that will be repeated in the Prince's interview with Lizaveta Prokofyevna and her three daughters.

From the Prince's remembrance of the condemned man, Alexandra extracts what she perceives to be the moral of the story: "You probably meant to show, prince, that not one instant of life can be considered petty, and that sometimes five minutes is a precious treasure" (*I*, 57). Unsolicited by Myshkin, Alexandra's interposition of the story's moral import is strong evidence of the successfully transmitted pedagogic voice. Compounding Alexandra's impression is the behavior of Lizaveta Prokofyevna, who, after hearing the tale of Marie, unburdens herself to the Prince: "We have nothing but secrets here, prince, you see—nothing but secrets. It has to be so, it's a sort of etiquette; it's stupid. And in a matter which above everything needs frankness, openness and straightforwardness. There are marriages being arranged. I don't like these marriages" (*I*, 77).

It is quite possible that Lizaveta Prokofyevna has been inspired to her outburst by the courage exemplified by the Prince in the story of his spontaneous disregard for social convention and steadfast loyalty to the persecuted village girl.[37] At least three textual clues substantiate this claim. First, Lizaveta is quick to align herself with Myshkin and refer them both into the community of fools (*I*, 77–8) who are misplaced in the age's formal demands. Second, the narrator announces that "Myshkin had succeeded in making a marked impression on the Epanchin family, though he had only been once among them, and then for a short time" (*I*, 174). Third, Lizaveta Prokofyevna's voice gradually emerges as one of the two or three, in addition to Myshkin's, that makes an exceptional contribution to *The Idiot*'s moral climate.

For those characters who are most influenced by him, Myshkin's pedagogic impact apparently inheres in the nature of his idealism, which is not only a structural but also a thematic feature of his voice. In general, the Prince seems to provide an occasion for certain characters to question their values. He infuses a moral component into a world starkly lacking in such immaterial considerations. In his presence, characters become passionate diagnosticians of their culture's social and spiritual crisis. Lizaveta Prokofyevna is symptomatic of this tendency. Enraged by their "ethical" demands against the Prince, she denounces the "young nihilists": "Tfoo! everything is topsy–turvy, everything is upside down. . . . Lunatics! Vain creatures! They don't believe in God, they don't believe in Christ!. . . . you'll end by eating up one another, that's what I prophesy. Isn't that topsy-turvydom, isn't that chaos, isn't it infamy?" (*I*, 275–76). But it is Lebedyev's interpretation of the Apocalypse, to listeners gathered for Myshkin's birthday, that epitomizes the kind of social commentary inspired by the Prince's example:

> Vile as I am, I don't believe in the waggons that bring bread to humanity. For the waggons that bring bread to humanity, without any moral basis for conduct, may coldly exclude a considerable part of humanity from enjoying what is brought. . . . [T]he friend of humanity with shaky moral principles is the devourer of humanity. . . . There must have been an idea stronger than any misery, famine, torture, plague, leprosy, and all that hell, which mankind could not have endured without that idea, which bound men together, guided their hearts, and fructified the "springs of life". . . . Show me any idea binding mankind together today with anything like the power it had in those centuries. And dare to tell me that the "springs of life" have not been muddied and weakened beneath the "star," beneath the network in which men are enmeshed. And don't try to frighten me with your prosperity, your wealth, the infrequency of famine, and the rapidity of the means of communication. There is more wealth, but there is less strength. There is no uniting idea. (*I*, 364, 368)

Myshkin exemplifies the uniting idea that will diminish the multileveled alienation intoned by Lebedyev, but in such a way that it cannot possibly be duplicated. Thus, Lizaveta Prokofyevna can indict the Petersburg youth in one breath, and in the next repudiate Myshkin's immutable trust and generosity toward his detractors (*I*, 276). She can accuse General Ivolgin of shamelessly squandering both his money and his most noble feelings on drink, express a sudden sentiment of true compassion toward him—"We are all sinners. . . . I daresay I am fifty times as great a sinner myself" (*I*, 237)—but nevertheless still send him from the room because his presence is a nuisance to her. Lebedyev can condemn the morally deleterious consequences of valorizing technological progress and acquisitiveness, abet the author of the libelous biographical article on Myshkin, and then become insolent when the guests become unruly at the drunken birthday celebration for the Prince that he himself instigated (*I*, 404). Their grim depictions of cultural artifice and spiritual fragmentation notwithstanding, Lizaveta Prokofyevna and Lebedyev are still socially determined beings for whom the Prince's atemporal moral standards are unattainable. They manifest the deep contradiction among economic, social, and moral pressure that Myshkin transcends through idealism.

If Myshkin's idealism inspires an expression of spiritual fortitude, however precarious and tentative, in Lizaveta Prokofyevna and Lebedyev, it inspires something quite different in many of the other characters.[38] For example, although Nastasya Filippovna's erratic behavior is established by the narrator well in advance of Myshkin's encounter with her, the onset of her madness might be traced to her conversation with the Prince at her birthday party. Treating her as he did the young Swiss girl Marie, Myshkin refuses to reproduce the contempt in which the other characters hold Nastasya Filippovna; he simply does not recognize the social codes that she has allegedly transgressed to earn her shame. Instead, he refutes the grounds for her persecution and voices his unqualified and unconditional loyalty to her with a marriage proposal. Regardless of Myshkin's motives at this moment, the implications of his profession are fairly clear: the Prince idealizes Nastasya Filippovna, much as he does everyone, and no one quite knows how to process the previously unprecedented candor of his voice, least of all Nastasya Filippovna:

> "Won't you feel ashamed when people tell you afterwards that your wife used to live with Totsky as his kept mistress?"
>
> "No, I shan't be ashamed . . . It wasn't your doing that you were with Totsky."
>
> "And you will never reproach me with it?"
>
> "Never."
>
> "Be careful; don't answer for your whole life!" (*I*, 162)

When she ultimately rejects the marriage proposal, she identifies Myshkin's idealization of her, which she understands about as well as he understands her anxiety, as the reason:

> "I shall be afraid of ruining you, and of your reproaching me with it afterwards."
>
> . . .
>
> "Is it possible?" moaned Myshkin, wringing his hands.
>
> "Did you think I meant it. . . .You called me perfection this evening; a fine sort of perfection who, simply to boast of trampling on a million and a princedom, is going into the gutter! What sort of wife should I make you after that?" (*I*, 163–64)

These exchanges establish a dynamic between the Prince and Nastasya Filippovna that will be repeated until the end of the novel. Although it may not serve any positive end, Myshkin has "an influence over her" (*I*, 114) that does contribute to the moral import of *The Idiot* and may also be termed pedagogic. But Nastasya Filippovna's self-perception, which has been sedimented by the ignoble desires of Totsky, General Epanchin, Ganya, and Rogozhin, cannot be directly altered by Myshkin's most compassionate intentions. Myshkin's expression of moral certainty has no equivalent referent in Nastasya Filippovna's moral consciousness. Unlike the other characters in the novel, she is sincerely convinced that Myshkin represents a divinely attractive, yet impossible ideal and not a benign sort of idiot: it takes a Mary Magdalene to recognize a Christ. Her apparent cruelty toward him is not motivated by scorn, spite, or hatred, but by her self–persecutorial— and correct—belief that she will never be able to correspond to the ideal on which he bases his perception of her. In his relationship with her, the Prince's inability to maneuver within the signifying system of Petersburg convention thus provokes the most dire consequences. Myshkin ultimately represents a greater moral burden than she can bear.[39]

It is significant that only Myshkin judges her ensuing behavior to be mad. The other characters, conditioned as they are both to the manifold contingencies of historical existence and to the social expectations placed on an individual in a specific circumstance, seem far less surprised by Nastasya Filippovna's erratic, self-destructive actions. She is the (however hyperbolical) classic picture of the woman scorned, with no recourse for

dignified empowerment in the arbitrarily constructed system of social justice that condemns her. The chaos that attends her may appropriately be
termed scandalous, but the language of scandal is, by definition, fairly predictable for anyone raised on and into the various ideologies of Petersburg
society, a group that excludes Myshkin. His genuine astonishment that he
might be called to fight a duel with the officer he insults in Nastasya
Filippovna's defense further indicates his incapacity to read and judge the
social text before him. A duel does not actually mean anything for Myshkin
until he leaves the isolated world of the sanitarium, where his mental convalescence is nearly tantamount to an ideological cleansing, and immerses
himself in dynamic social conditions.

Minor characters who engage in dialogue with Myshkin also corroborate the pedagogic force of his voice. Prepared to prevail upon the Prince's
generosity, Keller asks for less money after speaking with him. Keller's
response to Myshkin's pedagogic example is fairly typical of the response
Myshkin routinely provokes from the text's secondary figures: "Even the
preacher, Bourdaloue, would not have spared a man; but you've spared
one, and judged me humanely! To punish myself and show that I am
touched, I won't take a hundred and fifty roubles; give me only twenty-
five, and it will be enough! That's all I want, for a fortnight, at any rate. I
won't come for money within a fortnight. I did mean to treat Agashka; but
she's not worth it. Oh, God bless you, dear prince!" (*I*, 301). Similarly
informed by Myshkin's unconditional kindness, Antip Burdovsky sends
him a letter conceding that he has wrongly besmirched the Prince: "I am
quite persuaded, my dear sir, that you are perhaps better than other men.
. . . [Y]ou have helped my mother, and for that I am bound to be grateful to you, even though it be weakness. In any case, I look upon you differently and think it only right to tell you so. And thereafter I suppose
there can be no more relations of any sort between us" (*I*, 310).

Kovacs asseverates that "Myshkin's basic impulse, the internal idea of
his lyrical theme, is to awaken the thought, the social consciousness and
self-consciousness of the 'unfortunate of all classes,' to instill in them the
idea of their innocence."[40] If "innocence" be taken to mean their prelapsarian, correspondent relationship with a transcendent ethical principle,
then Kovacs's understanding of Myshkin's pedagogic intent appears sound.
Nevertheless, the reaction inspired by Myshkin, even from minor characters,
continues to be difficult to assess. Keller's florid assurance is almost too

beautifully phrased to be sincere. The warning that he will likely be back with his hand out after two weeks seems a safety net to remind him not to get too carried away by his own gracious rhetoric. Indeed, the fact that he introduces a vocabulary imitative of Myshkin's values is a sign that the Prince's discourse, the pattern of his voice, has in some way entered the moral consciousness of yet another character. But it is not clear whether Keller is genuinely touched by the Prince or even whether a dubiously uttered respect for the Prince is better than none.

On the other hand, Burdovsky's sincerity is almost guaranteed by the reluctance with which he acknowledges Myshkin's values. Attending his sincerity is the conviction, conditioned by the earlier inflammatory rhetoric of his companions, that the letter will provide Myshkin with the excuse to become self–righteous and repeat what Edward Wasiolek has called "the cycle of hurt and be hurt." As Wasiolek observes, "The Prince pays for the hurt that is visited on him by accepting it and suffering it, and by suffering it he breaks the vicious circle of hurting and being hurt, and by breaking the circle, he effects changes in others."[41] Put in terms of my analysis of Myshkin's incarnationist voice, the Prince breaks the cycle of hurt and be hurt because he is never entirely implicated in it. He influences it, as it influences him. But the temporal determinants of the cycle do not assimilate Myshkin. Burdovsky wrongly assumes that the Prince will use the letter as ammunition against him because, like every other character in the novel, he has never encountered someone who would not so use the letter.

Because it cannot be contextualized, the moral import of the incarnationist voice does not produce a sustained positive effect, even in those characters who are to some degree receptive to it. Once the initial furor over Myshkin's presence settles and the characters are faced with the task of processing the existential significance of an immaterial moral standard, they typically deflect the legitimacy of the moral burden unintentionally bestowed by Myshkin by calling him an idiot. They fault him for their dubious behavior, not themselves. Their judgment of the Prince is enabled by the same thing that precludes their successful imitation of him. They lack a consistently acknowledged and lived faith in something that transcends the temporal, the mundane. Even Lizaveta Prokofyevna and Lebedyev, who eloquently lament the loss of Christ in Russia, do not attempt to use Myshkin's precedent to set an unconditional moral example for their family, friends, or acquaintances. Given this response to Myshkin by the aforementioned characters, what kind of perspective on the Prince's pedagogic voice is provided by those, like Ippolit and Rogozhin, who are initially hostile toward him?

Dostoevsky's narrator suggests that Ippolit has consistent access to Myshkin's voice, despite the young man's illness, which often renders him immobile. When he is not present at scenes where the Prince speaks, he learns from others what was said (*I*, 286). Ippolit is a formidable component of the text's moral dialogue. He is also notably similar to Myshkin in a variety of ways. To Lizaveta Prokofyevna, he states his life's goal thus: "I wanted to live for the happiness of all men, to discover and proclaim the truth" (*I*, 287). There is not a single other character, besides Myshkin, whose professed aspirations reach so far spiritually beyond material indulgence of the most common kind. Ippolit's confession is structured around the parable of a general who, for no practical reason, visits prisoners and shows them acts of kindness. Ippolit explains the potentially instructive consequences of the general's charity in language imbued with the kind of idealism one might associate with Myshkin:

> In scattering the seed, scattering your "charity," your kind deeds, you are giving away, in one form or another, part of your personality, and taking into yourself part of another; you are in mutual communion with another, a little more attention and you will be rewarded with the knowledge of the most unexpected discoveries. You will come at last to look upon your work as a science; it will lay hold of all your life, and may fill up your whole life. On the other hand, all your thoughts, all the seeds scattered by you, perhaps forgotten by you, will grow up and take form. He who has received them from you will hand them on to another. And how can you tell what part you may have in the future determination of the destinies of humanity? (*I*, 392)

This is a nearly perfect demotic expression of a Christian Utopianism. Were Ippolit able to commit himself to charitable deeds commensurable with his spoken ideal, his similarity to Myshkin would be further magnified. He does appear to comprehend the value of action; the whole spectacle of his confession, with its intentionally apocalyptic resonance, is designed as a form of protest (*I*, 402) on behalf of an outraged humanity.

But the capacity to fuse a word to an absolute referent before translating both into a correspondent ideal gesture is beyond Ippolit. He does not possess an incarnationist voice. He resembles Nastasya Filippovna in that he consistently hurts others, especially Myshkin, because he cannot reconcile his desire for the ideal with the brutal reality of his material condition. Myshkin thus comes to represent a locus of enormous moral ambivalence for Ippolit. He cannot resist the Prince—"I lay down at ten o'clock to-day meaning not to get up again till *the time* came. But you see I changed my mind, and got up once more to come to you . . . so you see I had to" (*I*, 542)—ostensibly for what Myshkin might teach him. Neither can he allow himself to concede Myshkin's moral integrity, delighting in the anxiety he provokes from the Prince over the Aglaia–Nastasya Filippovna affair: "Aha! You seem to be losing your indifference and beginning to be surprised. I'm glad that you're ready to be like a human being at last. I'll comfort you for that" (*I*, 544).

Ippolit's perception of Myshkin may, in fact, be summarized in the young man's own words: "Though I have been a cad to you, because . . . why should I be a loser?" (*I*, 546). One may ascribe the prominent ellipsis in this sentence to the two competing moral standards at work in Ippolit's consciousness. According to his spiritual ideal of kindness, there can be no reason for Ippolit's behavior toward the Prince. If there can be no reason for the behavior, then Ippolit has betrayed his ideal. If he has betrayed the ideal, then he is the loser that he cannot permit himself to be. The fact is that he has betrayed this ideal. Rather than blame himself, he blames Myshkin, whose moral example has evidently had a pedagogic effect, though certainly not the effect the Prince intends.

Although physically absent from much of *The Idiot*'s moral dialogue, Rogozhin is nevertheless Myshkin's most intimate interlocutor. The dynamic of their conversation helps to delineate an urgent picture of the stakes of Myshkin's presence in Petersburg. Their competition for Nastasya Filippovna is merely a distilled figure of the intense moral conflict that characterizes their relationship. Sidney Monas argues that Rogozhin is unconcerned with the artifice of gentility, society, social life; he wants only to possess, to accumulate—and Nastasya Filippovna is something to be added to the pile.[42] On Monas's view, Rogozhin's desire both roots him in, and removes him from, the economic expectations governing a certain class of Petersburg society. His desires are not regulated by the status their satisfaction will confer (though the status will most assuredly follow just the same). Rogozhin's sentiment toward Myshkin is an extension of this contradictory logic: he is at once attracted to, and enraged by, the Prince's divorce from material pressures. We have seen the Prince elicit some version of the same reaction from other characters. In such cases, it was Myshkin's moral idealism that compelled another's anxiety. Moral anxiety also derives from the relationship between Myshkin and Rogozhin, but it is the repercussion of a more deeply repressed conflict.

The contradiction at the heart of the relationship between Rogozhin and Myshkin is based on Rogozhin's oppressive desire to possess the Prince's body.[43] Both Myshkin's absence and presence have an effect on Rogozhin. When they are apart from each other, Myshkin enters Rogozhin's consciousness predominantly as a thing to be had, not as an idea whose moral significance might represent an alternative to his making a fetish of capital. Rogozhin expresses his ambivalence toward Myshkin thus: "When you are not before me I feel anger against you at once, Lyov Nikolayevitch. Every minute of these three months that I haven't seen you I have been angry with you, on my word, I have. I felt I could have poisoned you! I tell you now. You haven't been sitting a quarter of an hour with me, and all my anger is passing away and you are dear to me as you used to be. Stay with me a little" (I, 201–2). When the Prince and Rogozhin are separated, the reader is always made to feel that Rogozhin is close by, arresting Myshkin's body with his eyes. Total separation from the Prince inspires an unmitigatedly murderous impulse in Rogozhin. When they are together, Rogozhin becomes susceptible to Myshkin's pedagogic voice because the preliminary requirement of the Prince's physical propinquity is being met.

Their first private dialogue represented by the narrator is suffused with moral and religious import. In response to Rogozhin's question whether Myshkin believes in God, the Prince recalls parables of his experience with the magnificent religiosity of the Russian peasant, concluding, "There is work to be done, Parfyon! There is work to be done in our Russian world, believe me!" (I, 214). Uttered as a parting salvo, Myshkin prepares to leave Rogozhin's house, but he is first asked whether the two may exchange crosses. After Myshkin delightedly agrees, he is blessed by Rogozhin's mother at the latter's request. In both these gestures, Rogozhin demonstrates his recognition and assimilation of the Prince's values. The scene ends:

"Don't be afraid! Though I've taken your cross, I won't murder you for your watch!" [Rogozhin] muttered indistinctly, with a sudden strange laugh.

But all at once his whole face changed; he turned horribly pale, his lips trembled, his eyes glowed. He raised his arms, embraced Myshkin warmly, and said breathlessly:

"Well, take her then, since it's fated! She is yours! I give in to you! . . . Remember Rogozhin!" (*I*, 215)

It is possible to read Rogozhin's surrender of Nastasya Filippovna as his tremendous effort to exemplify the Prince's selflessness, knowing full well that he will fail once the immediate physical reminder of Myshkin's generosity is gone and the process of material accumulation again dominates his consciousness. Rogozhin does not categorically give in to Myshkin after the scene on his threshold is over and Myshkin again disappears from sight: he remains attentive to Nastasya Filippovna's activity and always hovers nearby. But the bizarre triangle of desire that develops among them is empowered by the Prince. Myshkin's immediate moral example lessens Rogozhin's desire for Nastasya Filippovna at the same time that it drives her more urgently into Rogozhin's arms. Since he cannot modify the absolute expression of his persona, the Prince has no way to forestall the impending catastrophe he incites.

Rogozhin serves another prominent function in *The Idiot*'s moral dynamic: he is the recipient of Myshkin's own self-disclosure and is given the opportunity to remark the influence of another character on the Prince. Addressing Rogozhin about Nastasya Filippovna's behavior, Myshkin declares, "Do you know that a woman is capable of torturing a man with her cruelty and mockery without the faintest twinge of conscience, because she thinks every time she looks at you: 'I'm tormenting him to death now, but I'll make up for it with my love, later'" (*I*, 354). Rogozhin instantly comprehends the repercussions of Myshkin's experience with Aglaia in the Prince's statement: "I say, prince, have you come in for the same treatment? . . . I never heard you say such things before" (*I*, 354). Rogozhin proceeds to afford Myshkin a more comprehensive insight into Nastasya Filippovna's and Aglaia's desires. For once, Myshkin does not serve as sounding-board for another's anxiety. He is the student whose consciousness is forever altered by a particularly timely lesson.

Inspired by the Prince's abstract observation about the way women treat men, Rogozhin leads Myshkin to understand something about the complexion of desire as it is expressed, with all its blemishes, between people of this earth. Eagerly announcing the start of his "new life" (*I*, 355) after their conversation, Myshkin confirms Rogozhin's pedagogic effects.

There are only two other instances in *The Idiot* where Myshkin appears to assimilate the voice of another character in such a way as to place himself at the receiving end of the pedagogic relationship. Both instances involve Aglaia. She conveys to Myshkin a detailed account of how to load and fire a pistol, which he then repeats virtually word-for-word to Keller in order to demonstrate that he is not as theoretically naïve as others imagine him about Petersburg social convention. On a second occasion, Myshkin reveals that he has very much taken to heart one of Aglaia's many criticisms of him: "You said something very clever just now. You were speaking of my uncertainty about Ippolit. 'There's nothing but truth in it, and so it's unjust.' I shall remember that and think it over" (*I*, 415). The absolute moral referent for the incarnationist voice makes it unlikely that Myshkin is lying when he tells Aglaia that he will ponder her comment. The comment itself strikes at the very core of what the incarnationist voice represents to the other characters who participate in *The Idiot*'s moral dialogue; it distinguishes the anomalous example of a mode of reference that transcends the temporal determinants of social signification.

Myshkin's initial receptivity to Aglaia's observation suggests that he may finally be becoming familiar with Petersburg social codes and with the constructivist signifying mechanism used to manipulate them. Facing historical pressures, Myshkin demonstrates ideological flexibility by appealing to Aglaia's very human concern for his well-being. However, whatever ideological progress Aglaia is able to bring about in Myshkin's incarnationist voice and moral consciousness seems peremptorily undermined in the scene during which the Prince chooses Nastasya Filippovna over her younger rival. No single character in *The Idiot* has more on the line in her relationship with Myshkin than Aglaia. Myshkin has idealized both women, but his persistent attention to Nastasya Filippovna is predicated on the immutable value he confers on the assumption of another's suffering. By offering herself as an alternative to Nastasya Filippovna, Aglaia self-consciously offers the temporally contingent as an alternative to a romanticized ideal.

In structure, Myshkin's selection conveys his commitment to his unimpeachable image of Nastasya Filippovna as a thing unconditionally worth serving. Aglaia's only mistake is presenting herself as someone who has suffered less at the hands of Petersburg society than Nastasya Filippovna. For this, she is alienated from his most urgent sympathies at a crucial moment and verifies the failure of her pedagogic voice to inform his. One of the scene's most profound ironies is that, having chosen Nastasya Filippovna, Myshkin's voice goes silent; neither his words nor his gestures serve to palliate either woman's anxiety. His absolute ethical voice only drives them both to despair further.

Myshkin realizes that he has gravely mishandled his relationship with Aglaia only upon learning that she refuses to see him. His proposed means of reconciling himself to her is simply to reiterate what instigated the rift in the first place: "I don't quite know how, but I am to blame. . . . There's something in all this I can't explain to you, Yevgeny Pavlovitch. I can't find the words, but . . . Aglaia Ivanovna will understand! Oh, I've always believed that she would understand" (*I*, 567). Speaking with a voice intimately implicated in Petersburg social relations, Yevgeny Pavlovitch disabuses the Prince of his optimism: "No, prince, she won't understand" (*I*, 567). The essential divorce between Myshkin's incarnationist voice and the process by which knowledge is signified in a human community continues intact. The words the Prince finds so difficult to utter are inaccessible without a sure grasp of the context that requires them. Myshkin reflexively assumes blame for the catastrophe, but he can provide no evidence that he understands why he is to blame. That evidence would only be forthcoming were the Prince to comprehend the value of Aglaia's historically conditioned love. And his belief in her compassion is another egregious example of his implacable tendency to impress something material with his ideal estimation of it.

The narrator's response to Myshkin's decision to remain with Nastasya Filippovna signals a turn in the tone of the narrative report: "If we should be asked for an explanation . . . how the spiritual condition of our hero was to be defined at that instant . . . we should, we admit, find it very difficult to answer. . . . In presenting all these facts and declining to attempt to explain them, we have no desire to justify our hero in the eyes of the reader. . . . [N]ot only the Epanchins, but everyone directly or indirectly connected with them had thought proper to break off all relations with Myshkin" (*I*, 561). As Feuer Miller observes, this narrative moment is an acute point of crisis in the act of reading; hitherto, the conventional problems attending the credibility of a narrator's commentary on events have ostensibly always been present, but they have not been foregrounded as they are now. With the narrator's peremptory disavowal of Myshkin's company, the reader is abruptly forced to become even more actively engaged in judging the relative legitimacy of the text's competing ethical ideologies. Feuer Miller does not miss the point that the narrator's sudden distance from Myshkin makes the narrator's voice a formidable pedagogic instrument in the text.[44] No other voice, not even Myshkin's, has the power to alter the complexion of *The Idiot*'s moral import as swiftly as one able to toss the entire narrative's meaning temporarily up for grabs.

The narrator does, however, offer a possible conduit to interpretive stability by suggesting that Yevgeny Pavlovitch possesses a privileged voice in the task of sifting through the text's competing ethical positions. Coming as it does fast on the heels of the narrator's refusal to accept responsibility for the chronicle, the narrator's validation of Yevgeny Pavlovitch's "forcible and psychologically deep words . . . spoken plainly and unceremoniously . . . in friendly conversation with Myshkin" (*I*, 561) is obviously problematic, since it is difficult to decide whether it should be trusted or be counted among the commentary for which the narrator has abjured accountability. Of course, it would be nice to be able to speak with confidence about the legitimacy and accuracy of a narratorial report, but in the absence of such confidence, the best an ethical reading can do is try to acquire overlapping textual evidence to substantiate an interpretive claim whose veracity might otherwise be diminished if based solely on the evidence of a single narratorial comment. Such a process is a fine example of responsible ethical criticism in that it treats the narratorial voice as a series of temporally contingent voices from whose tension may be distilled a narratorial perspective that might be judged stable without being dogmatically authoritative.

Gleaning examples over the course of the text, one finds that, from a variety of perspectives, the narrator has indeed provided a comprehensive picture of Yevgeny Pavlovitch by the time of his final conversation with Myshkin. Krieger supplies an inventory of diverse personality traits—cold-blooded; realistic; skeptical; but of fine and intelligent face;

furthermore, possessing heart—that adequately validates a personality and a voice that are never allegorized as a figure of something outside the flow of historical time.[45] Yevgeny Pavlovitch's criticism of the manner in which Myshkin has handled the affair frankly targets dubious properties of the Prince's voice: "From the very first . . . it began with falsity. What begins in a lie must end in a lie; that's a law of nature" (*I*, 563). In his speculation "whether there was reality, whether there was genuineness in [Myshkin's] emotions, whether there was natural feeling or only intellectual enthusiasm" (*I*, 564), Yevgeny Pavlovitch detects the inclination toward abstract idealization that underpins the incarnationist manner of reference. As he expresses his astonishment at Myshkin's desire to love Aglaia and Nastasya Filippovna with "two different sorts of love" (*I*, 567), he repeats the antithetical relationship between Petersburg social codes and the Prince's ahistorical values. He therefore serves to recapitulate the stakes of the ethical reading developed in this chapter.

Dostoevsky offers at least two additional pieces of evidence to support the contention that Yevgeny Pavlovitch articulates a moral alternative to Myshkin's essentialism. He earns the trust of Kolya Ivolgin, the young boy whose lived commitment to charitable acts is epitomized in his sincere caring toward General Ivolgin, his frequently opprobrious father. And he begins to develop an intimate relationship with Vera Lebedyev on account of their mutual concern for the Prince's well-being once the latter has been returned to the sanitarium.[46] Like Kolya, Vera is kind and compassionate; she is also humble. She thus enacts the moral values that Myshkin exemplifies[47] but without the incarnationist constraints that impede Myshkin's full participation in *The Idiot*'s moral dialogue.

I have said that a novel's moral dimension is most evidently empowered by the intrusion of a textual element that interrupts a certain perceived stasis in the events being narrated. The train that transports Myshkin from the mountains inaugurates the text's first pedagogic dynamic, as the Prince introduces a referential mode of signification whose repercussions for Petersburg society must then be tested and recorded. The often chaotic speed of subsequent scenes and conversations maintains the moral tensions generated by Myshkin's arrival. At the center of *The Idiot*'s action is Nastasya Filippovna, a hyperkinetic figure who arguably experiences the Prince's pedagogic example most desperately and then extends her internal conflict out to whatever characters happen to be implicated in her

social circle. When, at the end of the novel, Nastasya Filippovna is mur-
dered, the scene's final tableau eliminates the source of the text's principal
moral dynamic. Nastasya Filippovna lies perfectly still on her deathbed,
and Myshkin can say nothing to remedy the situation. Having observed a
similar silence on the occasion of Myshkin's mismanagement of the scene
between Nastasya Filippovna and Aglaia, the reader can hardly be surprised by the Prince's reaction to Nastasya Filippovna's death: never comfortably integrated into the social dialogue performed by those around
him, the correspondent mechanism of Myshkin's incarnationist voice is
finally shattered, and his gestures are therefore powerless to ameliorate
Rogozhin's inchoate madness. When the police arrive, Myshkin "could
understand no questions he was asked and did not recognize the people
surrounding him" (*I*, 594). Frank's commentary on Myshkin's fate is
smart, succinct, and pertinent. Sitting vigil with the raving Rogozhin over
the corpse, the Prince "passe[s] altogether beyond the bounds of all social
codes,"[48] codes he has abutted but has never penetrated.

The structural conflict of *The Idiot* between unconditionally referential and historically contingent processes of signification seems fairly deci-
sively reconciled by the final impotence of Myshkin's voice as an immediate
material event. But the removal of Myshkin's pedagogic voice is not succeeded by a concomitant erasure of its instructive effects. To claim that the
Prince is a moral failure because his voice no longer signifies and his gestures no longer impress[49] is to deny the possibility that a failed attempt at
signification can still be pedagogically instructive; moreover, incomplete
knowledge is still knowledge. The narrator does indicate that certain persons of the story—Lebedyev, Keller, Ganya, Ptitsyn, and many others,
"go on living as before . . . hav[ing] changed but little" (*I*, 595). However,
others—Lizaveta Prokofyevna, Kolya, Yevgeny Pavlovitch, Vera Lebedyev
—express sincere concern for Myshkin's well-being. They demonstrate a
commitment to solidarity that is contrary to the fundamentally narcissistic atmosphere otherwise characteristic of Petersburg. In their compassion
for Myshkin, these characters thus bring a small portion of the social order
closer to the parabolic example of community illustrated by the Prince in
Marie's Swiss village.[50]

Myshkin's epigrammatic parable was originally commissioned by Lizaveta Prokofyevna, and she figures prominently in the novel's concluding
sequence. Throughout the narrative, Lizaveta Prokofyevna stands steadfastly

behind Myshkin under pressures that cause others nothing but indigna-
tion. Faced with the evidence of Aglaia's love for him, she surprises herself
by endorsing the Prince's candidacy for matrimony: "'In what way is the
Prince not what is wanted?' And that protest of her own heart was what
gave Lizaveta Prokofyevna more trouble than anything" (*I*, 493). After the
disastrous betrothal gathering at the Epanchin estate, she declares her loyalty to Myshkin despite the low esteem in which she knows he is held by
her most distinguished acquaintances and benefactors: "Be sure, once for
all, that whatever happens, whatever may come you'll always be our
friend, mine anyway. I can answer for myself" (*I*, 541). In her willingness
to espouse an attitude overtly at odds with social expectations, Lizaveta
Prokofyevna indeed resembles Myshkin. But she does not come to stand
in as his amanuensis, brandishing an unrealistic moral ideal to which she
would make the material world correspond.

Lizaveta Prokofyevna's measurable turn toward solidarity with
Myshkin notwithstanding, the last words of the novel, which she utters
to Yevgeny Pavlovitch, remind the reader that in the temporal world any
ethical ideology is contingent upon material circumstances: "We've had
enough of following our whims; it's time to be reasonable. And all this, all
this life abroad, and this Europe of yours is all a fantasy, and all of us abroad
are only a fantasy. . . . [R]emember my words, you'll see it for yourself!"
(*I*, 597). She now rejects what she and her daughters had earlier romanticized as the source of a new and intriguing form of moral significance.
The metonymic import of her denunciation of European culture is the
abjuration of its alleged product, Myshkin's incarnationist voice. Lizaveta
Prokofyevna's moral consciousness has been influenced by Myshkin's
absolute standard of value, but it is beyond her power to duplicate that
standard. This is not to say that she, or any of the other characters who
have learned from Myshkin's example, should be condemned for ultimately failing to maintain a conclusive alternative to the Prince's ethical
position. In the ethical tension between Myshkin and his interlocutors,
what emerges in the text's moral dimension is the theoretical precept that
there can be no "ultimately" in history. There can only be a dialogue of
ethical positions that stabs at arresting conditional truths.

In a recent interview, Nicholas Rzhevsky asked Vadim Kozhinov to discuss the Bakhtinian notion that Dostoevsky's novels contain no last word,
no ideological resolution. Kozhinov replied by citing an essay entitled,

"Towards the Completion of the Dostoevsky Book," in which two "totally different concepts of the author" appear, "the author who appears in Dostoevsky's novels" and "the real author, Dostoevsky." Kozhinov proceeds to argue that the implied author of the texts grants the characters total freedom to explore their personal truths, whilst the author Dostoevsky distances himself from his characters' dialogue and engages the objective world, where he believes truth can be discovered. On Kozhinov's view, Dostoevsky "leaves the last word for himself," and "there is no relativism in Dostoevsky's world at all."[51] Kozhinov's words are compelling because they are as much a profession of faith as they are a statement of epistemological certainty. Dostoevsky's faith that the truth could somehow be told was hard-won and genuine, but it always remained faith, not accomplished fact. The novels are a record of that faith, but they no more accomplish the fact than the author did in his personal life.

Following Kozhinov's expression, there is as little conclusive moral truth in Dostoevsky's novels as there is relativism in the author's world. These two perspectives are not incompatible; in the novels, they combine to produce ethical positions that are determined by specific social conditions. By rejecting Myshkin without rejecting morality, *The Idiot* makes this clear. An ethical reading of *The Idiot* ultimately searches in vain for any "'as yet unspoken future word'"[52] that might bring order to the text. Such a search could only be conducted by one willing to confer pedagogic authority on an atemporal moral voice for whom the future is accessible because it has no means to differentiate what will be from what is. Myshkin is this voice. He has his chance to impress an ideal moral order on Petersburg social relations. He cannot. And it is hard to imagine that another Myshkin would engender a different pedagogic effect than the first in an historically contingent world. Wobbly center intact, Dostoevsky's novel remains an ambivalent narrative that does not accommodate thematic closure. As such, the process of sorting through the characters' attempts to address and resolve the text's various moral tensions is a model of how to conduct nonmonologic, nonreductive ethical readings of literature.

To force a moral on, or to extract a codified lesson from, *The Idiot* (or any other text, for that matter) is to perform the kind of reading to which ethical criticism's opponents have legitimately objected. Such ethical readings open themselves to a host of difficulties because ethics, in general, is a fundamentally contingent business, and a proselytizing critique often appears to pretend to a degree of authority quite uniformly disallowed by the contemporary critical milieu for at least two reasons. Some reject reductive, authoritative literary critique outright as hostile to what they see as the relative status of any ideological position. These critics are wary of critical or theoretical attempts to return to any mode of knowledge production that may be used to legitimize oppressive expressions of cultural capital and institutional control. Others take issue not so much with authoritative interpretive claims as with any authoritative claims that are incommensurable with their own.

Both groups are commonly indicted with politicizing literary study, with using literary texts to advance an agenda that reflects ethical concerns about the best way to live and how best to achieve it. Contemporary criticism whose object is the "politics of identity" is perhaps the most common strand of such practice; attempts to articulate the significance of a particular subject carry an implicit message that the subject being represented deserves such attention, that it is unjust, hence wrong, to do otherwise. Such critique makes it seem as though what really matters most when reading a text, even if the text happens to be a human subject, is what the text signifies. I have no principled objection to the best of this type of critique, but all of it tends to create the impression that ethics and politics are inseparable because the political position inevitably requires an ethical foundation. And this is simply not the case. It might very well be that politicized criticism must trade in thematic agenda in order to be effective, but ethical literary criticism need not promote any values at all.

Interestingly, even the most prolific writers on, and espousers of, ethical readings characteristically demonstrate an ineluctable tendency to thematize the object of their interpretation. This does not help the case for a nonreductive, nonmonologic ethical critique, one that cannot subsequently be dismissed out of hand as just another form of the political. As I have tried to show, the best way to retain a place for ethical literary readings as an alternative to thematic textual commentary is to focus on how a text conveys its ideological positions, not on the substantive significance of the positions themselves. This entails investigating the way ethical voices function in literary texts as pedagogic participants in moral dialogue with other voices.

Directed toward the formal rhetorical strategies and linguistic structures whereby ethical discourse proceeds, ethical criticism helps to elucidate the expression and validation of truth claims. That ethical criticism can contribute to a field of such enduring concern is a testament to its continued value as a method of literary analysis. Perhaps it may also serve to hold the final judgment on ethical criticism in abeyance a while longer.

NOTES

1. Plato's argument is much more complex than popularly imagined; hence, there is no single reference for his critical operation in *The Republic*. Readers interested in the way Plato arrives at his conclusions about the role of the poet and poetry in the ideally realized state should consult approximately the last third of Book Two, and the first half of Book Three, of *The Republic*, ed. James Adam (Cambridge: Cambridge University Press, 1963).

2. See Christopher Clausen, *The Moral Imagination: Essays on Literature and Ethics* (Iowa City: University of Iowa Press, 1986): "As is well known, few poets or critics denied the instructive functions of literature before the middle of the nineteenth century. Didacticism was not merely *a* respectable view of poetic purposes; it was . . . virtually the *only* respectable view" (2).

3. As Martha Nussbaum presents this scenario, "The sense that we are social beings puzzling out, in times of great moral difficulty, what might be, for us, the best way to live—this sense of practical importance, which animates contemporary ethical theory and has always animated much of great literature, is absent from the writings of many of our leading literary theorists" (*Love's Knowledge: Essays on Philosophy and Literature* [Oxford: Oxford University Press, 1990], 170).

On literary criticism's gradual divestment of its "encumbering moral and social attachments" from the 1930s onward, see Gerald Graff, *Professing Literature: An Institutional History* (Chicago: University of Chicago Press, 1987), 147–48. See also Clausen, "Moral Inversion and Critical Argument," *Georgia Review* 42 (spring 1988): 10–11; Clausen, "Morality, Poetry, and Criticism," *Kenyon Review* 5 (fall 1983): 74–75; and Wayne Booth, *The Company We Keep: An Ethics of Fiction* (Berkeley: University of California Press, 1988), 25–44.

4. See David Parker, *Ethics, Theory, and the Novel* (Cambridge: Cambridge University Press, 1994), 32–33 for a synoptic account of ethical criticism's resurgence in the 1980s. For an equally succinct summary of the ambivalence inspired by this resurgence, see Lawrence Buell, "In Pursuit of Ethics," *PMLA* 114 (January 1999): 11–12.

Geoffrey Galt Harpham elaborates the status of ethical literary criticism in the late twentieth century in his contribution, "Ethics," to *Critical Terms for Literary Study*, 2d edition, ed. Frank Lentricchia and Thomas McLaughlin (Chicago: University of Chicago Press, 1995). It is worth noting that this entry was one of the new additions to the 1995 edition, which served to update the first edition published five years earlier.

5. In so doing, I make myself a respondent to Colin McGinn's observation that "some attempt should be made to come to terms with the embeddedness of the ethical in the fictional. For this we need new methods and styles with which to discuss stories and morals" (*Ethics, Evil, and Fiction* [Oxford: Clarendon Press, 1997], 175).

6. See Robert Scholes, "The Novel as Ethical Paradigm?" *Novel* 21 (winter 1988): 189.

7. See Adam Zachary Newton, *Narrative Ethics* (Cambridge: Harvard University Press, 1995), 32–33.

8. Clausen, "Moral Inversion," 11.

9. Nussbaum says the same thing somewhat differently: "We will need to maintain as much self-consciousness as possible about our method and our implicit ends, asking what evaluative content they themselves express" (*Love's Knowledge*, 186).

10. Don Bialostosky, *Wordsworth, Dialogics, and the Practice of Criticism* (Cambridge: Cambridge University Press, 1992), 124.

11. Newton, *Narrative Ethics,* 37.

12. Bialostosky, *Wordsworth,* 78.

13. See Thomas M. Kavanagh, "Uneasy Theories: The Ethics of Narration in Contemporary French Criticism," *Criticism* 28 (fall 1986): 456. See also Daniel R. Schwarz, who, citing Bialostosky's contribution to the dialogic imperative governing what I am calling responsible ethical criticism, argues that "we need to learn how to enter into a dialogue with diverse approaches, to see their point of view, to understand that interpretive communities become narrow enclaves unless they conceive themselves as part of larger intellectual communities" ("The Ethics of Reading: The Case for Pluralistic and Transactional Reading," *Novel* 21 [winter/spring 1988]: 202). His injunction "When reading criticism we need to be aware of the theoretical assumptions that produce a reading and examine whether we belong to the community of readers who share those assumptions" (203) is somewhat roughly analogous to my related claim that ethical critics must be up front about their own interpretive methods if they are not to be dismissed as dogmatic and proselytizing. In his inventory of characteristics for the ethical critic, who must be "honest about . . . theoretical and methodological assumption . . . dialogic in tone . . . pluralistic in his response to texts and to other critical views . . . aware of the mysteries of language, the possibility of indeterminacy, disorder, and misunderstanding" (217), Schwarz is very close to my own way of thinking about the preconditions of responsible ethical readings.

Along similar lines, Kavanagh observes that "the 'truth' relevant to literature and criticism is a function of their shared subjectivity, their shared openness to dialogue, and their shared concern with value and ethics as a corollary to the potential universality of their dialogue" ("Uneasy Theories," 456).

14. See Derek Attridge, "Singularities, Responsibility: Derrida, Deconstruction, and Literary Criticism," in *Critical Encounters: Reference and Responsibility in Deconstructive Writing* (New Brunswick, N.J.: Rutgers University Press, 1995): "Some texts, then, largely texts of modernity, do *not* lend themselves to the transcendent reading that has dominated the history of literature, thwarting the urge to move through the writing to a self-sufficient, preexisting theme, intention, historical or psychological cause, referent, model, or moral, and thwarting too the formalizing drive which would divorce the text from questions of reference, ethics, and history" (113).

15. Mikhail Bakhtin, *The Dialogic Imagination: Four Essays*, ed. Michael Holquist, trans. Caryl Emerson and Michael Holquist (Austin: University of Texas Press, 1981), 259, 300.

16. Reprinted in *Love's Knowledge*, 171–72. Ironically, Nussbaum's ethical readings, which are characteristically silhouetted against the Aristotelian standard of the Good Life, have themselves been viewed as enacting many of the critical moves for which ethical readings are often dismissed. Hilary Putnam observes that "Aristotle is centrally concerned with the connection between happiness and character and with the vicissitudes that can shape character. For this reason it is natural that his position would be congenial to a philosopher who is also a talented student of literature. But there are dangers in becoming wedded to just one picture of our moral life—and not least in the reading of literary works" ("Taking Rules Seriously—A Response to Martha Nussbaum," *New Literary History* 15 [autumn 1983]: 197). Robert Eaglestone sees a profound methodological flaw in Nussbaum's tendency to pretend that the "moral truths she finds in texts are directly available, mediated only by the keen sight of the critic and are not the result of any act of interpretation. This is the significance of her term 'commentary'— it seems to suggest a neutral, passive 'explaining' of a text, rather than an active interpretation" (*Ethical Criticism: Reading after Levinas* [Edinburgh: Edinburgh University Press, 1997], 55).

17. John Gardner, *On Moral Fiction* (New York: Basic Books, 1977), 129, 100, 23.

18. Thus, in articulating a standard for moral judgment of literary texts, McGinn holds that "it really is hideous to desire the suffering of the innocent, vile to exploit the weak, foul to betray a friend—each of these acts evokes revulsion and disgust in us" (*Ethics, Evil, and Fiction*, 103). Arguing that "a moral failing in a literary work is at the same time an aesthetic failing," Frank Palmer is led to conclude that "whatever is to be counted as a moral failing will normally militate in some way against the spirit of love that shines through the creative act" (*Literature and Moral Understanding* [Oxford: Clarendon Press, 1992], 174–75). Such idealistic humanism is reiterated by Victor Haines: "A world cannot be imagined immediately or mediately without the creative matrix of truth, beauty, *and* virtue. The

174 NOTES TO PAGE 7

constitution of a text is a true, aesthetic, and moral endeavor—the proper aim of *good* interpretation" ("No Ethics, No Text," *Journal of Aesthetics and Art Criticism* 47 [winter 1989]: 41). Even Richard Rorty apparently cannot resist thematizing his standard for the ethical evaluation of a text, stating that "reading some books decreases our self-centeredness by reminding us that others are in pain—pain of a sort which we may be likely to cause, or which we might be able to relieve. Reading other books increases our self-centeredness by reminding us of the pos-sibility of self-making, the possibility that we might make our own lives into works of art" ("Duties to the Self and to Others: Comments on a Paper by Alexander Nehamas," *Salmagundi* 111 [summer 1996]: 60).

19. Peter Brooks, "Aesthetics and Ideology: What Happened to Poetics?" *Critical Inquiry* 20 (spring 1994): 520–21, 513.

20. James S. Hans suggests the opposite: "If there is no larger audience for ethi-cal criticism anymore—and no means of disseminating such work—then it becomes the responsibility of the critics and scholars who are left behind to address the crucial ethical questions that reside in any important piece of literature" (*The Value(s) of Literature* [Albany: State University of New York Press, 1990], 15).

21. Tobin Siebers, *Morals and Stories* (New York: Columbia University Press, 1992), 25. Clausen echoes this sentiment: "The motives behind what has come to be known as political or ideological criticism are inescapably moral ones, and any attack on the possibility of moral judgment as such weakens the only ground from which political criticism can be persuasively mounted. Without defensible moral judgments, no exploited group has any moral claims against any other group, and there is consequently no reason for literary critics or anyone else whose interests are not directly affected to get involved. This relativistic view of political struggle, although sometimes met with in extreme statements of Marxist doctrine, is absolutely fatal to adversary politics" ("Moral Inversion," 13).

Jameson's own position on ethical criticism is perhaps best represented in *The Political Unconscious: Narrative as a Socially Symbolic Act* (Ithaca: Cornell University Press, 1981), where he attempts to provide a way to expose the pretense of "the process of cultural 'universalization' (which implies the repression of the opposi-tional voice, and the illusion that there is only one genuine 'culture')," a process he identifies as "the specific form taken by what can be called the process of legiti-mation in the realm of ideology and conceptual systems" (87). One feature of this process is the commonplace practice of decoding texts through what he calls "*ethi-cal* criticism" (59). On Jameson's account, ethical criticism is always restrictive, whether it is searching for the "meaning" of life, for knowledge about "human nature," or representing certain idiosyncratic projections of human "experience" as materially real "wisdom" (59). In this respect, ethical criticism merely reflects the way "all ethics lives by exclusion and predicates certain types of Otherness or evil" (60). Jameson is suspicious of ethical criticism because it does not present itself as one code among others. When ethical criticism is so practiced, such a suspicion seems justifiable. However, Jameson's forthright intention in *The Political Unconscious* to discover how "history as a ground and as an absent cause can be conceived in such a way as to resist . . . transformation back into one optional code among others" (101) puts us somewhat at odds. For Jameson, ethics are an ideological representation of the objectively real infrastructural foundation of classical historical materialism and as such must never be mistaken for real knowledge.

Jameson's repudiation of the ethical in favor of the political and scientific comes to stand for *the* Marxist attitude toward ethics in Harpham's otherwise excellent study of ethics and literature, *Getting it Right: Language, Literature, and Ethics* (Chicago: University of Chicago Press, 1992). Harpham argues that, following Jameson, the comprehensive Marxist position on ethical inquiry is an "extreme form of historicist skepticism" (11) characterized by "resentment and belligerence" (9). These attitudes are incommensurable with the principled resistance that Harpham says is necessary to produce ethical readings that negotiate the Scylla and Charybdis of "stilted maxims" and "apologias, bad faith, and false consciousness" (45). "Everyone," Harpham maintains, agrees that the "mark of ethicity itself . . . is the structural interference of two value systems" (104). I would include myself in this everyone, since I find Harpham's conception of ethicity to be, in essence, correct.

22. Simon Stow, "Unbecoming Virulence: The Politics of the Ethical Criticism Debate," *Philosophy and Literature* 24 (April 2000): 185, 191, 195.

23. Michael Sprinker, "We Lost It at the Movies," *MLN* 112:3 (April 1997): 395, 397.

24. Allan Bloom, *The Closing of the American Mind* (New York: Simon and Schuster, 1987), 25–26, 39.

25. Richard A. Posner, "Against Ethical Criticism," *Philosophy and Literature* 21 (1997): 18.

26. Patricia Meyer Spacks tries to collapse this dilemma: "Ethical interpretations prove no more univocal than any other variety, but interpreters' voices, for all their multiplicity, remain inevitably and invariably ethical" ("The Novel as Ethical Paradigm," *Novel* 21 [winter 1988]: 187).

27. Michael Bérubé, *Public Access: Literary Theory and American Cultural Politics* (London: Verso, 1994), 108.

28. See John Searle, "Literary Theory and Its Discontents," *New Literary History* 25 (summer 1994): 637–68. On the much ballyhooed interpretive nihilism that allegedly follows from Derrida's assertions of the impossibility of authoritative linguistic determinacy, John D. Caputo writes, "Derrida is not arguing that 'anything goes' nor is he turning truth over to caprice, but he is arguing strongly for a democratic open-endedness that makes those who have appointed themselves the Guardians of Truth nervous" (*Deconstruction in a Nutshell: A Conversation with Jacques*

Derrida, ed. John D. Caputo [New York: Fordham University Press, 1997], 58). Peter Baker reinterprets Derrida's now notorious "There is nothing outside the text" as a way of saying that "every human response (even the writing of books) is always an ethical response, caught up in conflicting networks of power, violence, and domination" (*Deconstruction and the Ethical Turn* [Gainesville: University Press of Florida, 1995], 129). So it would seem that deconstruction might be commensurable with political and ethical thinking after all.

29. This because, irrespective of the intention of the language user, an "ethical mandate" inheres in language use (Newton, *Narrative Ethics,* 25). Another way of confirming the ethicity of language is provided by Eaglestone, again in his reading of Levinas: "It is from this understanding of language as the relation to the other expressed, not represented, that the ethical importance of language emerges. Language is where and how we are put into question by the other, and drawn to our responsibilities" (*Ethical Criticism,* 122). Further, as Booth is quick to note, the word *ought* "is used by an astonishing number of writers who claim that there are no firm moral or ethical principles" ("The Ethics of Teaching Literature," *College English* 61 [September 1998]: 43).

30. A clear and succinct introductory discussion of this engagement may be found in Derek Attridge, "Innovation, Literature, Ethics: Relating to the Other," *PMLA* 114 (January 1999): 20–31. Eaglestone's *Ethical Criticism* is perhaps the most comprehensive book-length text discussing Derrida and Levinas.

31. See Simon Critchley, *The Ethics of Deconstruction: Derrida and Levinas* (Oxford: Blackwell, 1992), 195.

32. Murray Krieger, "In the Wake of Morality: The Thematic Underside of Recent Theory," *New Literary History* 15 (autumn 1983): 125, 129–30.

33. Christopher Norris, "The Ethics of Reading and the Limits of Irony: Kierkegaard Among the Postmoderns," *Southern Humanities Review* 23 (winter 1989): 8, 19, 28.

34. John Elliott is a bit more severe in his estimation that "deconstruction's effectiveness takes hold when its own historical and ethical assumptions match those that are either latently or blatantly available in the literary work itself" ("The Ethics of Repression: Deconstruction's Historical Transumption of History," *New Literary History* 23 [1992]: 733). While it is not exactly characteristic of his assessment, Norris himself displays ambivalence toward the ethical value of deconstruction, commenting that what deconstruction "tends to overlook . . . is that whole dimension of human involvement that gives moral concepts their characteristic 'thickness,' or their relevance to the complex situations of everyday life" (*Deconstruction and the Interests of Theory* [Norman: University of Oklahoma Press, 1989], 182). This seems fair to me; it is tantamount to saying that deconstruction is ethical, but not overtly or practically so.

35. Krieger's discovery of a repressed thematic element in the story of contemporary critical theory is the kind of ethical interpretation traditionally

practiced on literary texts: the critic looks for the theme of a novel, poem, or play and then looks for the moral of the theme ("Wake," 119–36). Roger Seamon, who also detects an undeniable thematic aspect of any textual narrative, takes a somewhat unorthodox approach to the function of textual themes: themes "convey to audiences what story is to be made out of sentences. The story flows, so to speak, from the theme, rather than the theme following from the story. . . . The thematic statements of critics do not extract the propositional implications of stories, but inform readers of what story the critic thinks is being told" ("The Story of the Moral: The Function of Thematizing in Literary Criticism," *Journal of Aesthetics and Art Criticism* 47 [summer 1989]: 230). Seamon demonstrates this assertion by proposing two readings of "The Prodigal Son." The common reading of this parable yields the moral that "there is joy in the presence of the angels of God over one sinner that repenteth" (231). However, if the same story were to be titled "The Prodigal Father" and conveyed the moral "Waste not your heart on the unworthy, lest you lose the love of the righteous" (231), one would find, after rereading the parable, that it was indeed a different story (231). The same sentence tokens would elicit entirely different responses.

36. J. Hillis Miller, *The Ethics of Reading* (New York: Columbia University Press, 1986), 1.

37. Christopher Norris, *Paul de Man, Deconstruction and the Critique of Aesthetic Ideology* (London: Routledge, 1988), 106.

38. Hillis Miller, *Ethics*, 59. Critchley corroborates Hillis Miller's argument, asserting that "an unconditional categorical imperative or moment of affirmation is the source of the injunction that produces deconstruction and is produced through deconstructive reading" (*Ethics of Deconstruction*, 41). Caputo also remarks the ethical responsibility inhering in the act of critical engagement (*Deconstruction in a Nutshell*, 53); and Norris, the ethical responsibility for the effects of the act (*Derrida* [Cambridge: Harvard University Press, 1987], 205).

39. J. Hillis Miller, "Is There an Ethics of Reading?" in *Reading Narrative: Form, Ethics, Ideology*, ed. James Phelan (Columbus: Ohio State University Press, 1989), 99. The very ethics of Hillis Miller's assertion of the ineluctable ethical imperative inhering in the relationship between reader, text, and world has been greeted with skepticism by Norris, who views Hillis Miller's inability to differentiate between an ontological ethical necessity and a linguistic necessity as an abrogation of responsibility (Eaglestone, *Ethical Criticism*, 81). Put simply, on Eaglestone's reading of Norris's critique, Hillis Miller "cannot tell whether he is responding to an ethical demand or a linguistic demand" (93) when he insists on the inevitable ethicity of reading.

40. See Peter Baker, *Deconstruction*, 68.

41. See Eaglestone, *Ethical Criticism*, 177.

42. See Robert Bernasconi, "Deconstruction and the Possibility of Ethics," in *Deconstruction and Philosophy: The Texts of Jacques Derrida*, ed. John Sallis (Chicago:

University of Chicago Press, 1987), 135. Attridge identifies a violence at the heart of such a deconstructionist ethical relation in which one individual labors to respect another's position at that same time that he or she attempts to judge it against his or her own ("Singularities," 119). Recognizing the implications of this struggle, Peter Baker maintains that "*ethical deconstruction consists in a self-articulating resistance to intersubjective violence*" (*Deconstruction*, 97).

43. Booth, *Company*, 287. Clausen expresses the consequences of missing the subtleties surrounding the object of ethical criticism, which is less a moral truth than a critical process: "Moral categories and intentions may be analyzed in a variety of ways, in literature as in politics and everyday life. We need not, of course, take all intentions at face value —or, more shallow still, take the intention for the literary achievement. Faults like these have sometimes made moral criticism seem narrow or merely naive. They have not, however, made it dispensable. At the most, they have driven critics to disguise moral observations in the terminology of esthetics, politics, or psychoanalysis" (*Moral Imagination*, 175).

44. Siebers, *Morals and Stories*, 207.

45. Gerald Graff, *Beyond the Culture Wars: How Teaching the Conflicts Can Revitalize American Education* (New York: W. W. Norton, 1992), 255.

46. On this tendency, see Booth, "Ethics," 47–48.

47. Ibid., 43–44.

48. Ibid., 48–52.

49. The myth of an ideological view from nowhere would still be an ethical position, since "any critical act is an expression of values, an offering of a context of significance whose application another reader may dispute" (Clausen, *Moral Imagination*, 22). Clausen's adamancy about sincerely reorienting criticism toward an ethical mode is largely based on the premise that "we should be clearer about what we are doing when we judge a book to be well or badly written" (*Moral Imagination*, xi), since an exclusively aesthetic standard of literary evaluation is impossible.

50. See Jerome McGann, "Canonade," *New Literary History* 25 (summer 1994): 488.

51. Richard Rorty, *Contingency, Irony, and Solidarity* (Cambridge: Cambridge University Press, 1989), 82.

52. David Sidorsky, "Modernism and the Emancipation of Literature from Morality: Teleology and Vocation in Joyce, Ford, and Proust," *New Literary History* 15 (autumn 1983): 144.

53. Alasdair MacIntyre, *After Virtue*, 2d edition (Notre Dame: University of Notre Dame Press, 1981), 216, 211.

54. Nussbaum, *Love's Knowledge*, 5. See also Kavanagh: narration's "variegated texture of the aleatory and the indeterminate uses language as a mirror to the chaotic, chance-driven incoherence of life and the real. While we may always

attempt to 'interpret' this real, to detect patterns of causality and meaning through which we might control and understand it, the particular power of narrative lies in its ability to subvert, undermine, and render impossible any imposition of fixed patterns of consequence and determinism upon the real" ("Uneasy Theories," 457).

55. Paul Ricoeur, *Time and Narrative,* trans. Kathleen McLaughlin and David Pellauer (Chicago: University of Chicago Press, 1984), 1:52.

56. See Richard T. Eldridge, *On Moral Personhood: Philosophy, Literature, Criticism, and Self-Understanding* (Chicago: University of Chicago Press, 1989), 12, 20.

57. See Martha Nussbaum, "Reply to Richard Wollheim, Patrick Gardiner, and Hilary Putnam," *New Literary History* 15 (autumn 1983): 204. As Alexander Nehamas notes, Nussbaum is attracted to the morally pedagogic potential of literature for its ability to represent the fine detail of the situations that come to serve as options for ethical reflection ("What Should We Expect from Reading?" *Salmagundi* 111 [summer 1996]: 35); however, Nussbaum also suggests that such detail loses its potential moral value when it is paraphrased or summarized (36). Thus, Nehamas is skeptical about just how morally instructive literature may in the end be, since he doubts readers' ability to avoid "abstracting general lessons from the situations depicted by literature" (37).

58. Rorty, *Contingency,* 9, 73, 80.

59. Justin Gosling, "Literature and Moral Understanding: A Philosophical Essay on Ethics, Aesthetics, Education, and Culture," *Review of English Studies* 182 (May 1995): 308.

60. Rorty, *Contingency,* 80–81.

61. Barbara Herrnstein-Smith, *Contingencies of Value: Alternative Perspectives for Critical Theory* (Cambridge: Harvard University Press, 1988), 172.

62. McGinn, *Ethics, Evil, and Fiction,* 175.

63. MacIntyre, *After Virtue,* 28–29.

64. There are, of course, too many layers of ideological material represented in narrative texts to calculate, in any kind of general way, the number of potential combinations of such tension. It is perhaps more productive to consider sources of such tension, as does James Phelan, who, referring to "instabilities" in narrative, differentiates between "those occurring within the stories, instabilities between characters, created by situations, and complicated and resolved through actions," and "those created by the discourse, instabilities—of value, belief, opinion, knowledge, expectation—between authors and/or narrators, on the one hand, and the authorial audience on the other" ("Narrative Discourse, Literary Character, and Ideology," *Reading Narrative: Form, Ethics, Ideology*, ed. James Phelan [Columbus: Ohio State University Press, 1989], 133–34). Once they become a source from which an ethical position issues, any of the participants in these instabilities may be studied for its contribution to a text's moral dialogue.

65. Nussbaum, *Love's Knowledge*, 390.

66. Palmer, *Literature and Moral Understanding*, 110.

67. In *Love's Knowledge*, Nussbaum introduced a series of questions interrogating the role of voice in the narrative articulation of ethical philosophy in literature, but her interest was synoptic, provided in the context of a comprehensive overview of the different ways that readers may make sense of the epistemological value of literary representation, and the questions were left largely unanswered.

68. Jeffrey T. Nealon, "The Ethics of Dialogue: Bakhtin and Levinas," *College English* 59 (February 1997): 131.

69. Citing Gérard Genette, Richard Aczel offers one of the broadest definitions of textual voice: "Rather than constituting linguistically axiomatic, text-immanent properties, textual voices will be construed as the product of a dialogue between the reader and 'the traces [the narrating instance] has left—the traces it is considered to have left—in the narrative discourse it is considered to have . . . produced'" ("Hearing Voices in Narrative Texts," *New Literary History* 29 [1998]: 494).

70. Ibid., 483, 494.

71. The potential traces of authorial presence in narrative voice prompts William E. Cain's assertion that ethical critics ought to be aware of the "profound ways in which creative writers have themselves theorized about art as a means through which a person might come to lead a better life" ("The Ethics of Criticism: Does Literature Do Any Good?" *College English* 53 [April 1991]: 470).

72. See Schwarz on the need to locate the significance of the voice of critical texts in the act of interpretation ("Ethics of Reading," 203).

73. Mikhail Bakhtin, "The Problem of Speech Genres," in *Speech Genres and Other Late Essays*, ed. Caryl Emerson and Michael Holquist, trans. Vern W. McGee (Austin: University of Texas Press, 1986), 92, 99.

74. Bakhtin, *Problems of Dostoevsky's Poetics*. ed. and trans. Caryl Emerson (Minneapolis: University of Minnesota Press, 1984). Therefore, though Bakhtin's general thoughts about the phenomenon of voice as an expression of a character's worldview and entire individuality (293) seem right on target, the Bakhtinian notion of pedagogic dialogue, where "someone who knows and possesses the truth instructs someone who is ignorant of it and in error" (81), seems somewhat wide of the mark. Of course, there are cases of pedagogy in literature that are choreographed as simple proselytizing, but these are worst-case pedagogic scenarios that should not serve to nullify the value of a pedagogy that proceeds through a dialogue expressive of more than one possibility in a literary text. Bakhtin's observation seems better fitted to what might be termed "pedagogic monologue."

75. Sandy Petrey, *Realism and Revolution: Balzac, Stendhal, Zola, and the Performances of History* (Ithaca: Cornell University Press, 1988), 85, 132, 134.

76. Ibid., 7, 131, 133.

77. Bakhtin, *Dialogic*, 263. Bakhtin uses the term "dialogization" to refer to a theoretical and structural principle of narrative whereby the last word on a text's meaning never comes. On Bakhtin's view, the novel is conventionally "open"; that is, it contains no aesthetic provision for a monologic interpretive voice, coming either from within or without the text itself, to eliminate the opposition among competing narrative voices in favor of a single, authoritative textual import. In a discussion of responsible ethical criticism, Bakhtin's notion of "dialogization" is less useful than one might imagine for at least two reasons.

First, although the tension among competing voices is both a structural feature of the novel and a significant target of ethical textual practice, ethical readings —like any other—must nevertheless have a terminus that somehow pulls together the various lines of argument that the critic follows while constructing his or her interpretation of a text. Our minds are simply unable to resist making some kind of sense of the data with which they come into contact; furthermore, readers close off a variety of what they might consider trivial interpretive possibilities in order to open up a much smaller number of possibilities that are more significant to them (see Wayne Booth, "Are Narrative Choices Subject to Ethical Criticism?" in *Reading Narrative: Form, Ethics, Ideology*, ed. James Phelan [Columbus: Ohio State University Press, 1989], 65). Ethical critics are no exception to this human proclivity in the act of reading; however, they do face the demand of acknowledging that evaluative categories like "trivial" and "significant" are not universal and that no responsible ethical criticism should dogmatically pretend that they are. Through his discussion of dialogization, Bakhtin is clearly trying to emphasize an aesthetic textual feature that makes dogmatic, reductive readings of literary narrative a dubious textual practice. But ethical readings do draw *conclusions* that need not, however, be authoritatively *conclusive* (see Peter J. Rabinowitz, "End Sinister: Neat Closure as Disruptive Force," in *Reading Narrative*, ed. James Phelan, 122). Rather, responsible ethical readings understand that the precise nature of their conclusions are provisional, predicated on historically determined biases whose ideological coordinates are not transcended uncritically.

Second, aligned with his assertions regarding the definitional dialogic openness of the novel is Bakhtin's idea that "it is quite possible to imagine and postulate a unified truth that requires a plurality of consciousnesses, one that cannot in principle be fitted into the bounds of a single consciousness, one that is, so to speak, by its very nature *full of event potential* and is born at a point of contact among various consciousnesses" (*Problems*, 81). This contention does not so much contradict Bakhtin's understanding of the novel's dialogic openness as it offers a much more forthright admission of the possibility of a unified interpretive moment that is concomitantly sensitive to the manifold ideological determinants lending themselves to a unified interpretation's making. The levels of meaning denoted by the terms grouped beneath the rubric of "dialogism" are, in fact, a fine example of the way that the same signifiers can be shown to yield different connotations by the same critic. However, since Bakhtin's highly nuanced usage of the term "dialogic" can potentially be reduced to stand for an aesthetic structure or interpretive category that recognizes no stable product of textual practice, it is an inefficient designation for ethical criticism.

CHAPTER 2

1. Thomas Mann, *Letters to Paul Amann, 1915–1952*, ed. Herbert Wegener, trans. Richard and Clara Winston (Middletown: Wesleyan University Press, 1960), 42.

2. For a comprehensive account of these opponents, see Herbert Lehnert and Eva Wessell, *Nihilismus der Menschenfreundlichkeit* (Frankfurt am Main: Vittorio Klostermann, 1991), 11–19.

3. Thomas Mann, *Reflections of a Non-Political Man*, trans. Walter D. Morris (New York: Frederick Ungar Publishing Co., 1983), 311–12.

4. All of the following works draw an ideological connection between the *Reflections* and *The Magic Mountain*, though the connection never serves to elaborate Hans Castorp's moral education: Ernest Bisdorff, *Thomas Mann und die Politik* (Luxembourg: Editions du Centre, 1966), 28–30; Ronald Hayman, *Thomas Mann: A Biography* (New York: Scribner, 1995), 324, 335–36, 347–48; Richard Koc, "Magical Enactments: Reflections on 'Highly Questionable' Matters in *Der Zauberberg*," *Germanic Review* 68 (summer 1993): 114; Helmut Koopmann, "Die Lehren des *Zauberbergs*," in *Das "Zauberberg" Symposium 1994 in Davos*, ed. Thomas Sprecher (Frankfurt am Main: Vittorio Klostermann, 1995), 68–77; Hans Mayer, "On the Political Development of an Unpolitical Man," in *Critical Essays on Thomas Mann*, ed. Inta M. Ezergailis (Boston: G. K. Hall and Co., 1988), 199–202; Hans Wißkirchen, "Der Einfluß Heinrich Manns auf den *Zauberberg*," in *Auf dem Weg zum "Zauberberg": Die, Davoser Literaturtage, 1996*, ed. Thomas Sprecher (Frankfurt am Main: Vittorio Klostermann, 1997), 143–64; and Jürgen Scharfschwerdt, *Thomas Mann und der deutsche Bildungsroman* (Stuttgart: W. Kohlhammer Verlag, 1967), 109–13.

5. Koopman (Die Lehren des *Zauberbergs*, 74–77) and Hayman (*Thomas Mann*, 298, 324) suggest the way that the argument developed in the *Reflections* contributes to the characterization of Settembrini, a connection to which Mann himself alluded in a letter of September 5, 1920, to Julius Bab: "Der Civilisationsliterat tritt in Gestalt eines italienischen Freimaurers persönlich darin auf" (*Briefe, 1889–1936* [Frankfurt am Main: S. Fischer Verlag, 1962], 183). Bisdorff notes that Mann's internal dialogue in the wartime writing is a primary source for the dialogue between Settembrini and Naphta (*Thomas Mann und die Politik*, 30), an observation more fully elaborated by T. J. Reed in *Thomas Mann: The Uses of Tradition* (Oxford: Clarendon Press, 1974), 239–46, 256–57. However, these critiques stop short of engaging the question of the ethical dynamics of Mann's novel.

6. Hermann J. Weigand, *Thomas Mann's Novel "Der Zauberberg": A Study* (New York: AMS Press, 1971), 3.

7. Compare Henry Hatfield, who sees Hans Castorp moving from "shapelessness to form" (*From the Magic Mountain: Mann's Later Masterpieces* [Ithaca: Cornell University Press, 1979], 62).

8. For Mann's related self-perception as pedagogue, see Osman Durrani, "The Tearful Teacher: The Role of Serenus Zeitblom in Thomas Mann's *Doktor Faustus*," *Modern Language Review* 80 (July 1985): 655.

9. All of the following works discuss in some detail the way the relationship between Thomas and Heinrich informs the *Reflections:* Alfred Kantorowicz, *Heinrich und Thomas Mann: Die persönlichen, literarischen und weltanschaulichen Beziehungen der Brüder* (Berlin: Aufbau-Verlag, 1956), 17–51; Ernst Keller, *Der unpolitische Deutsche: Eine Studie zu den "Betrachtungen eines Unpolitischen" von Thomas Mann* (Bern: Francke Verlag, 1965), 17–43; Hermann Kurzke, "Die Quellen der *Betrachtungen eines Unpolitischen*," *Internationales Thomas-Mann-Kolloquium 1986 in Lübeck*, ed. Eckhard Heftrich and Hans Wysling (Bern: Francke Verlag, 1987), 298–302; Hayman (*Thomas Mann*, 287–91, 295–303), Mayer ("Political Development," 200–202), and Reed (*Mann*, 190–210).

10. See Judith Marcus, *Georg Lukács and Thomas Mann: A Study in the Sociology of Literature* (Amherst: University of Massachusetts Press, 1987), 29–30.

11. Erich Heller, *The Ironic German: A Study of Thomas Mann* (Boston and Toronto: Little, Brown and Co., 1958), 132.

12. Ibid., 138, 140

13. See Hayman: "The [*Zivilisationsliterat*] is the archetypal literary man who uses words in the ostensibly reasonable way Western civilization has encouraged; Thomas aligns himself—and German culture—with anti-rationalism. This gives him the right to ignore facts he'd have to confront if he were trying to be objective" (*Thomas Mann*, 290).

14. Only in this sense can Georg Lukács's observation that Mann rejects a "moral world order" be understood (*Essays on Thomas Mann*, trans. Stanley Mitchell [New York: Howard Fertig, 1978], 14).

15. As Reed puts this, "External realities had grown increasingly remote from intensely experienced private concerns, and were drawn into the works which stated those concerns as mere material, drained of independent existence and value, not imaginatively penetrated but acquired and manipulated" (*Mann*, 225).

16. See Reed, who argues for the inadequacy of a purely aesthetic approach to the literary *Bildungsroman* ("The Uses of Tradition," in *Modern Critical Interpretations: Thomas Mann's The Magic Mountain*, ed. Harold Bloom [New York: Chelsea House, 1986], 53).

17. Those interested in a more general account of the characters' pedagogic positions should see C. E. Williams, "Not an Inn, but an Hospital," in *Modern*

Critical Interpretations, 40–41. For additional description, see Irvin Stock, "*The Magic Mountain*," *Modern Fiction Studies* 32 (winter 1986): 496–510; see also W. H. Bruford, "'Bildung' in *The Magic Mountain*," in *Modern Critical Interpretations,* for extended analyses of Settembrini (70–73) and Naphta (75–78).

18. Marcus, *Georg Lukács and Thomas Mann,* 99.

19. Thomas Mann, *The Magic Mountain*, trans. H. T. Lowe-Porter (New York: Vintage International, 1992), 32.

20. Compare Bruford, whose inability to find a compelling representation of social relations in the novel sounds more like a manufactured occasion to renounce a Lukácsian reading of Mann than an accurate reading of Hans Castorp's material conditions: "In general, we have the merest glimpses of industrial and commercial life, always from above, and we hear nothing at all about the landowning and farming classes, and the agricultural workers under them, nor about the millions of factory hands. Whole aspects of the nation's life, like party politics or the social movement are similarly hardly touched upon. So the well-known dictum of Georg Lukács, that Thomas Mann gives us a picture of the 'total social reality of the time' by bringing together in one place a 'representative cross-section of its society,' must be taken with more than a grain of salt" ("'Bildung,'" 69).

21. Weigand, *Thomas Mann's Novel,* 91. For Mann's use of other literary texts, especially Whitman's poetry, in constructing *The Magic Mountain's* infrastructure, see Joseph Warner Angell, "Preface," in *The Yale Zauberberg-Manuscript: Rejected Sheets Once Part of Thomas Mann's Novel*, ed. James F. White (Bern: Francke Verlag, 1980), viii.

22. The narrator has occasion to address an observation or pronouncement in a way that aligns the narrator, the reader, and Hans Castorp; for example, of the young man's growing infatuation with Clavdia Chauchat, the narrator speculates, "When a man is in Hans Castorp's state . . . he longs, above all, to have her of whom he dreams aware that he dreams, let reason and common sense say what they like to the contrary. Thus are we made" (*MM*, 142). Readers of *The Magic Mountain* might also find significant the text's only pronominal reference to the second-person singular, which occurs as part of a description of how to find the Berghof's management: "You reached it after passing the hall, the garderobe, the kitchens" (*MM*, 131). As it stands, such a construction certainly corroborates the thesis that Mann intends to make the reader complicit in Hans Castorp's experience in the cure. But the "you" form is a free translation of Mann's German, which reads as follows: "*Wenn man, jenseits der Halle, an der Garderobe und den Küchen . . . verfolgte . . . ,*" where *man* is more strictly rendered in English as 'one' (Thomas Mann, *Der Zauberberg* [Frankfurt am Main: Fischer Taschenbuch Verlag, 1967], 139.

23. Lukács calls Settembrini a "harbinger of progress *sans phrase*," and argues that "he makes no self-criticism, has neither doubts nor reservations, which is why—although he has no personal stake in it—he is such an uncritical standard-bearer of the capitalist system" (*Essays,* 38).

24. Weigand finds something mischievous in the way Hans Castorp appropriates Settembrini's "finely chiselled phrases" for his own experimental ends (*Thomas Mann's Novel,* 118).

25. For a protracted examination of Settembrini's reluctance, or inability, to leave the Berghof, see Alexander Nehamas, "Nietzsche in *The Magic Mountain,*" in *Modern Critical Interpretations*, 106–9.

26. I have provided my own English translation of the text's original French.

27. Those critics who do address the issue of who "wins" the rhetorical debates between Settembrini and Naphta do not share a consensus. For example, Hayman views Naphta as Settembrini's intellectual superior (*Thomas Mann,* 348). Bruford maintains the opposite ("'Bildung,'" 78). Lukács first states that their debates "end in a draw" (*Essays,* 36), but then adds that Naphta can always defeat Settembrini in argument because his anticapitalist stance is also intensely self-critical, while Settembrini simply toes the bourgeois line (38n. 11).

28. Marcus (*Georg Lukács and Thomas Mann,* 145) traces this position, that everything is moral that serves the coming of socialism, to Lukács.

29. Compare Stock ("Magic Mountain," 508–10), who discerns the resonance of Settembrini's humanistic rhetoric in Hans Castorp's affirmation of life.

30. Hayman cites the moment when Mann began to conceive the goal of the novel as the synthesis between mind and body (*Thomas Mann,* 313–14).

31. Nehamas marks the growing narrative distance between the reader and Hans Castorp as the novel progresses ("Nietzsche," 116).

32. Lukács, *Essays,* 36.

33. See Heller, *Ironic German,* 132.

34. Compare the assurance of Koc, who, for example, sees Hans Castorp's decision to leave the private sphere of the cure and to become complicit in public national events as a product of the engineer's intense experience with psychoanalysis, of which the seance is the greatest symptom. On Koc's reading, Hans Castorp deflects his attention from individual psychology to social politics because he is afraid that continued introspection will force him to negotiate traumatic repressed psychical material ("Magical Enactments," 115).

35. See Bruford, "'Bildung,'" 78; Hayman, *Thomas Mann,* 348; and Lukács, *Essays,* 36, 38n. 11.

CHAPTER 3

1. Albert Camus, *Lyrical and Critical Essays*, ed. Philip Thody, trans. Ellen Conroy Kennedy (New York: Vintage, 1970), 104.

2. Albert Camus, *Resistance, Rebellion, and Death*, trans. Justin O'Brien (New York: Vintage, 1960), 28.

3. See James W. Woelfel, *Camus: A Theological Perspective* (Nashville: Abingdon Press, 1975), 49. Susan Tarrow cites the following excerpt from one of Camus's

186 Notes to Pages 64-80

essays: "Is it possible, legitimate, to be in history while using as points of reference values that go beyond history?" (*Exile from the Kingdom: A Political Rereading of Albert Camus* [University: University of Alabama Press, 1985], 195).

4. Albert Camus, *The Myth of Sisyphus and Other Essays*, trans. Justin O'Brien (New York: Vintage, 1955), 73.

5. David Sprintzen, *Camus: A Critical Examination* (Philadelphia: Temple University Press, 1988), 273.

6. See Donald Lazere, *The Unique Creation of Albert Camus* (New Haven: Yale University Press, 1973), 102; and Lev Braun, *Witness of Decline: Albert Camus—Moralist of the Absurd* (Rutherford, N. J.: Fairleigh Dickinson University Press, 1974), 142–49, for elaboration on Camus's distrust of socialist realism and of the historicism that underlay it.

7. See Albert Camus, *Notebooks, 1942–1951*, trans. Justin O'Brien (New York: Alfred A. Knopf, 1965): "Why am I an artist and not a philosopher? Because I think according to words and not according to ideas" (113).

8. Albert Camus, *The Rebel: An Essay on Man in Revolt*, trans. Anthony Bower (New York: Alfred A. Knopf, 1956), 259.

9. Stephen G. Kellman, *The Plague: Fiction and Resistance* (New York: Twayne, 1993), 101.

10. Camus, *Rebel*, 258, 262–63.

11. Camus, *Notebooks, 1942–1951*, 120.

12. Stephen Spender, "Albert Camus, Citizen of the World," *New York Times Book Review,* 1 August 1948, 1.

13. Orville Prescott, "Outstanding Novels," *Yale Review* 38 (autumn 1948): 189.

14. Jean-Paul Sartre, *Situations*, trans. Benita Eisler (New York: George Braziller, 1965), 75.

15. Ibid., 97–98.

16. Tarrow, *Exile,* 133.

17. There are, of course, exceptions. Lazere observes, "The philosophical dialogues between Rieux, Tarrou, Paneloux, and Rambert, although substantial thematically, tend to make stilted, bombastic fiction. . . . After the first reading, without the suspense and emotional involvement in the characters' fates, Rieux, Tarrou, Cottard, and Paneloux do not retain enough individual complexity or appeal to become much more than the abstract voices of philosophical positions" (*Unique Creation,* 176). Of the Oranais, Bloom writes, "Either the relatively innocent suffer an affliction from outside, or the at least somewhat culpable are compelled to suffer the outward sign of their inward lack of grace. Truth doubtless lies in between, in our lives, but to represent so mixed a truth in your novel you must be an accomplished novelist, and not an essayist, or writer of quasi-philosophical tales" (*Albert Camus*, ed. Harold Bloom [New York: Chelsea House, 1989], 4). Tarrow

ascribes the lack of dialogue to the novel's "stifling atmosphere," in which "time stands still, each day resembles the next, and even the words at one's disposal lose their impact" (*Exile*, 124).

18. Laurence M. Porter, "From Chronicle to Novel: Artistic Elaboration in Camus's *La Peste*," *Modern Fiction Studies* 28 (winter 1982–83): 591.

19. Serge Doubrovsky, "The Ethics of Albert Camus," in *Critical Essays on Albert Camus*, ed. Bettina L. Knapp (Boston: G. K. Hall and Co., 1988), 161.

20. Colin Davis, "Interpreting *La Peste*," *Romantic Review* 85 (January 1994): 133, 139.

21. Raymond Stephanson presents the most extreme version of referential instability: "If the threat of plague in part follows from its invisibility and lack of imaginative coordinates, then an equally unsettling implication is that once an image or symbol has been supplied, the imaginative structure finally fails to 'contain' plague. Pestilence ultimately refuses to yield to the very act of imaginative appropriation it has precipitated and threatens to obliterate the self" ("The Plague Narratives of Defoe and Camus: Illness as Metaphor," *Modern Language Quarterly* 48 [September 1987]: 239).

22. Emmett Parker, *Albert Camus: The Artist in the Arena* (Madison: University of Wisconsin Press, 1965), 112–13.

23. Shoshana Felman, "Narrative as Testimony: Camus's *The Plague*," in *Reading Narrative: Form, Ethics, Ideology*, ed. James Phelan (Columbus: Ohio State University Press, 1989), 257, 258.

24. In a subsequent discussion, Felman magnifies the possibility that an accurate representation of material history is not limited to evidence collected empirically: "In *The Plague*, the event is witnessed insofar as it is fully and directly *experienced*. In *The Fall*, the event is witnessed insofar as it is *not experienced*, insofar as it is literally *missed*. The suicide in effect is *not seen* and the falling in itself is not perceived. . . . *The Fall* bears witness, paradoxically enough, to the *missing* of the fall" ("The Betrayal of the Witness: Camus's *The Fall*," in *Testimony: Crises of Witnessing in Literature, Psychoanalysis, and History*, ed. Shoshana Felman and Dori Laub, M.D. [New York: Routledge, 1991], 168–69).

25. In addition to the text itself, two entries from the 1942–1951 *Notebooks* lead to this premise. In the first, Camus notes regarding those separated by the disease "those moments when they let themselves sink into the plague and long for the relaxation it provides. Cottard says: it must be good in prison. And the inhabitants: the plague perhaps frees from everything" (55). The second appears thus: "Plague. All fight—and each in his way. The only cowardice is falling on one's knees. . . . Many new moralists appeared and their conclusion was always the same: one must fall on one's knees. But Rieux replied: one must fight in such and such a way. . . . In any fighting group one needs men who kill and men who cure. I have chosen to cure. But I know that I am fighting" (82).

26. During the Second World War, while he was composing *The Plague*, Camus made the following statement about language's ability to correspond to an external, objective referent: "Indulging in metaphysics means accepting paradoxes, and the metaphysics of language follows this rule. Either, in fact, our words translate only our impressions, and, partaking of their contingency, are deprived of any precise meaning; or else our words represent some ideal and essential truth, and consequently have no contact with tangible reality, which they can in no way affect. Thus we can name things only with uncertainty, and our words become certain only when they cease to refer to actual things" (*LCE*, 230–31).

27. See Davis: "Certainly, the narrator adopts a rhetoric of authority which implies clear understanding" ("Interpreting *La Peste*," 130). For the narrator's own comments on his sources and use of them, see Albert Camus, *The Plague*, trans. Stuart Gilbert (New York: Vintage International, 1991), 6–7.

28. Porter, "From Chronicle to Novel," 590. Felman is most emphatic on this point: "[The] bridging between narrative and history is possible since the narrator is both an *informed* and an *honest* witness [*témoin fidèle*]. Once endowed with language through the medium of the witness, *history speaks for itself*. All the witness has to do is to *efface himself*, and let the *literality of events* voice its own *self-evidence*" ("Narrative," 256).

29. Sprintzen provides a more exhaustive account of Oran's bourgeois ideology and its material consequences (*Camus*, 89–102). However, his account stops short of addressing the effects of bourgeois culture on ethical practice. Tarrow glosses Oran's ethical status: "The Oranais are smugly settled in their petty bourgeois existence, careless of moral problems and unmoved by the beauty of the world of nature" (*Exile*, 134).

30. Camus's own perception of the bourgeoisie is difficult to define since no stable referent for the term emerges in either his fictional or his nonfictional writings. Emmett Parker (*Albert Camus*) proposes that, during the war, Camus used the term *bourgeoisie* to represent "that highest, upper-class strata of French society—*la grande bourgeoisie*—whose financial holdings would almost automatically create a 'conflict of interests' whenever they participated personally in political affairs. It is unlikely that he meant the term to encompass the entire middle class, which in its broadest definition would include small shopkeepers, professionals, white-collar workers, and even small stockholders" (79); as Camus understood it, this group was notable for its "lack of imagination" (80), a characteristic certainly applicable to the majority of Oranais, not just to Oran's upper-class citizens. Moreover, according to Lazere (*Unique Creation*, 181), Camus himself was of "lower-working-class origin." His father was a "simple salaried foreman" (Olivier Todd, *Albert Camus: A Life*, trans. Benjamin Ivry [New York: Alfred A. Knopf, 1997], 3), and these circumstances are likely to have colored the son's estimation of middle-class values.

31. This is one of the facts that allow Philip Thody to claim that Rieux's voca-tion itself "makes it impossible to elude . . . moral and philosophical problems" (*Albert Camus* [New York: St. Martin's Press, 1989], 108).

32. While explicating the inadequacies of language in Camus's text, Brian Fitch observes, "Language can have no real grasp on the concrete reality of human suf-fering" (*The Narcissistic TEXT: A Reading of Camus's Fiction* [Toronto: University of Toronto Press, 1982], 16).

33. According to Richard Shryock, Rieux is *the* discursive standard in *The Plague*, and the characters with a discursive position different from Rieux's are inevitably destroyed ("Discourse and Polyphony in *La Peste*," *Symposium* 44 [spring 1990]: 60–63).

34. See Porter, "From Chronicle to Novel," 595.

35. See Patrick McCarthy, *Camus* (New York: Random House, 1982), 227.

36. Sprintzen, *Camus*, 91.

37. Ibid., 167.

38. Germaine Brée classifies time in *The Plague* as the "antagonism between the mechanical tick of a clock presiding over the monotonous and grotesque hecatombs of human beings and the generous and free flow of a time rich in human emotion" (*Camus* [New York: Harcourt, Brace and World, 1964], 109).

39. Tarrow, *Exile*, 124.

40. In this context, the old patient who occupies himself counting beans all day is outside of time (ibid., 139).

41. The other appears in connection with a report on Oran's dwindling food supply. As a result of profiteering, "poor families were in great straits, while the rich went short of practically nothing" (*P*, 236–37).

42. Tarrow notes that "an undiluted concentration on the battle against the plague could be just as dangerous as the plague itself" (*Exile*, 135).

43. See Edward J. Hughes, *Albert Camus: La Peste* (Glasgow: University of Glasgow French and German Publications, 1988): "In the case of Paneloux . . . [Camus] points out the deficiencies inherent in tidy theological systems, arguing that such an outlook robs one of contact with life, for all its muddle and contra-diction" (42).

44. Camus, *Notebooks, 1942–1951*, 50.

45. Felman maintains that, by the time he was writing *The Fall*, Camus had come to realize that "the Plague is such that, by its very nature, it cannot be testi-fied to by any *alliance*" ("Betrayal," 182). If this observation on the impossibility of collective witnessing in the face of plague is accurate, then perhaps Camus already had some intimation of it during the composition of *The Plague*, a possibility that might account for the sharp disparity between the reaction of the general popula-tion of Oranais and the main characters' individual ethical responses to the abate-ment of the epidemic.

CHAPTER 4

1. Joseph Conrad, *Notes on Life and Letters* (London: J. M. Dent and Sons, 1970), 13; cited in the text as *NLL*.

2. Joseph Conrad, *The Nigger of the "Narcissus,"* ed. Robert Kimbrough (New York: W. W. Norton, 1979), xiii.

3. Joseph Conrad, *Life and Letters*, ed. G. Jean-Aubry (London: William Heinemann, 1927), 205.

4. Joseph Conrad, *A Personal Record* (New York: Harper and Brothers Publishers, 1912), 150–51.

5. See R. A. Gekoski, *Conrad: The Moral World of the Novelist* (New York: Harper and Row, 1978), 27.

6. John Batchelor, *Lord Jim* (London: Unwin Hyman, 1988), 43.

7. Benita Parry, "*Lord Jim*," in *Marlow*, ed. Harold Bloom [New York: Chelsea House Publishers, 1992], 144.

8. Vincent Pecora, "*Heart of Darkness* and the Phenomenology of Voice," *ELH* 52 (winter 1985): 997–1000. Ironically, Ian Watt reads these signals of the texts' overt metaphysical skepticism as the greatest evidence of Conrad's authorial presence: "Under cover of Marlow's probing of the meaning of the past, Conrad smuggled in the ancient privilege of the narrator by the backdoor, and surreptitiously reclaimed some of the omniscient author's ancient rights to the direct expression of the wisdom of hindsight" (*Conrad in the Nineteenth Century* [Berkeley: University of California Press, 1979], 212).

9. Eric Tretheway, "Language, Experience, and Selfhood in Conrad's *Heart of Darkness*," *Southern Humanities Review* 22 (spring 1988): 106.

10. Parry begins her reading of Marlow's perception of imperialism with an observation very similar to mine (*"Lord Jim,"* 128), but she is far more persuaded than I that Marlow inevitably and conclusively endorses the fiction of imperialism.

11. Compare Ralph W. Rader, "*Lord Jim* and the Formal Development of the English Novel," in *Reading Narrative: Form, Ethics, Ideology*, ed. James Phelan (Columbus: Ohio State University Press, 1989), whose reading of *Lord Jim* presumes the existence of an ontologically real natural source of evil in the character of Gentleman Brown.

12. Watt, *Conrad*, 208–9.

13. See Charles Eric Reeves, "A Voice of Unrest: Conrad's Rhetoric of the Unspeakable," *Texas Studies in Literature and Language* 27 (spring 1985): 289. Raymond Gates Malbone is careful to remind us that, although Conrad's impressionism permits a fairly broad interpretive engagement with his texts, the technique does not authorize any and all exegetical claims ("'How to Be': Marlow's Quest in *Lord Jim*," *Twentieth Century Literature* 10 [April 1964–January 1965]: 178).

14. Joseph Conrad, *Lord Jim*, 2d edition, ed. Thomas Moser (New York: W. W. Norton, 1968), 137.

15. Watt, *Conrad*, 212. Writing specifically on *Lord Jim*, a number of critics discuss Conrad's attempt to create an affinity between Marlow and the reader: see Batchelor, *Lord Jim*, 88; Gekoski, *Conrad*, 92, 94; and Albert J. Guerard, *Conrad: The Novelist* (Cambridge: Harvard University Press, 1958), 142, 153.

16. An access whose authority is open to some debate; see D. C. R. A. Goonetilleke, *Joseph Conrad: Beyond Culture and Background* (New York: St. Martin's Press, 1990): "The most fundamental irony of the tale is that Marlow is narrating experiences whose full import . . . he (and his immediate circle of listeners) is unaware of" (75).

17. Joseph Conrad, *Heart of Darkness*, 3d edition, ed. Robert Kimbrough (New York: W. W. Norton, 1988), 8.

18. Jacques Berthoud sees Marlow's ambivalence as a product of his awareness that cultural value is arbitrary and so cannot be absolutized (*Joseph Conrad: The Major Phase* [Cambridge: Cambridge University Press, 1978], 47). For a different perspective on Marlow's moral baggage at the beginning of *Heart of Darkness*, see Robert S. Baker, who reads Marlow as "caught up in the hopeless endeavor of maintaining a rigid code in a world that permitted anything but the shallow assurances of an unbending morality" ("Joseph Conrad," *Contemporary Literature* 22 [winter 1981], 117).

19. Since I am more concerned with qualifying the natives' voice as the structural antithesis of capitalism and imperialism than I am with quantifying its ideological "meaning"—an operation, I have in effect been arguing that the text impedes, even if the reader undertakes it in good faith—I find no pressing need to address Chinua Achebe's charges that Joseph Conrad is a "thoroughgoing racist" (257) in part because he makes no effort to represent the natives' voice(s) in any but a stereotypically pejorative Eurocentric fashion (255–56) that best suits the needs of his narrative ("An Image of Africa: Racism in Conrad's *Heart of Darkness*," in *Heart of Darkness*, ed. Robert Kimbrough [New York: W. W. Norton, 1988]). I will, however, suggest that Achebe's bald condemnation of Conrad and *Heart of Darkness* only holds up if the reader takes Marlow as the direct ideological amanuensis of Conrad, a feat I believe the text again prevents if a reader were for some reason inclined to make the identification in the first place. In addition, the natives' structural status—no matter how provincially or, more accurately, ambiguously Conrad depicts its import—as the ethical alternative to the socioeconomic savagery of imperialism might permit the judgment that Conrad's racism is not quite as thoroughgoing as Achebe would have one believe. For an exhaustive and elegant response to Achebe's charges, see Bruce Fleming, "Brothers under the Skin: Achebe on *Heart of Darkness*," *College Literature* 19/20 (October 1992–February 1993): 90–99.

20. David Galef, "On the Margins: The Peripheral Characters in Conrad's *Heart of Darkness*," *Journal of Modern Literature* 17 (summer 1990): 131.

21. Galef provides a brief inventory of those places in the text where Marlow's classification of his and Kurtz's relationship—prior to his meeting the Chief of the Inner Station—betrays an imagined commitment with no real material basis (131–32). For synoptic remarks on Marlow and Kurtz's romanticism, see also Harold Bloom, "Introduction," in *Marlow*, ed. Harold Bloom (New York: Chelsea House Publishers, 1992).

22. Jeremy Hawthorn pronounces judgment on the moral ambiguity generated in referential space: "Not only is the detachability of language from belief and accurate reference a *symbol* for moral insubstantiality and duplicity, it is also a *means* whereby this duplicity is effected" (*Joseph Conrad: Narrative Technique and Ideological Commitment* [London: Edward Arnold, 1990], 198).

23. Frances B. Singh, "The Colonialistic Bias of *Heart of Darkness*," *Conradiana* 10 (1978): 50.

24. Michael Levenson, "The Value of Facts in the *Heart of Darkness*," *Nineteenth-Century Fiction* 40 (December 1985): 275.

25. Watt, *Conrad,* 235.

26. Goonetilleke, *Joseph Conrad,* 82. Berthoud's belief that Kurtz sincerely maintains the ideology of European imperialism to the last leads him to contend that "Marlow's strength . . . his capacity to serve a moral idea," is subverted rather than stabilized when the two men meet in the wilderness (*Joseph Conrad,* 58).

27. Pecora, *"Heart of Darkness,"* 1007.

28. Juliet McLauchlan identifies the "confirmation of the validity of [Kurtz's] ideals, intentions, even his words" as the "great moral center of *Heart of Darkness*," though she ascribes a considerably different value to them ("The 'Value' and 'Significance' of *Heart of Darkness*," *Conradiana* 15 [1983]: 10).

29. Levenson, "Value of Facts," 279.

30. On the ethical meaning of *Lord Jim,* Hillis Miller writes that "the text does not permit the reader to decide among alternative [interpretive] possibilities, even though those possibilities themselves are identified with precise determinate certainty" (*Fiction and Repetition: Seven English Novels* [Cambridge: Harvard University Press, 1982], 35, 40). His observation, if watered down a bit, is no less applicable to *Heart of Darkness.*

31. George Cheatham, "The Absence of God in *Heart of Darkness*," *Studies in the Novel* 28 (fall 1986): 309.

32. Hawthorn, *Joseph Conrad,* 199; Levenson, "Value of Facts," 277.

33. See Batchelor, *Lord Jim,* 149; and Daphna Erdinast Vulcan, *Joseph Conrad and the Modern Temper* (Oxford: Clarendon Press, 1991), 108.

34. Watt, *Conrad,* 316.

35. Responding to criticism, after Henry James, that Conrad's decision to use Marlow as a narrative device was a lapse in artistic judgment, Dorothy Van Ghent

makes the point that Marlow *must* exist in *Lord Jim* because Jim's case explores relative, not absolute moral issues, so the text requires a relativist consciousness to filter and present the facts ("On *Lord Jim*," in *Twentieth Century Interpretations of Lord Jim: A Collection of Critical Essays*, ed. Robert E. Kuehn [Englewood Cliffs, N.J.: Prentice-Hall, 1969], 76). As a comment on the narrative form of Conrad's text, Van Ghent's observation is agreeable. I would add that the reader's estimation of Marlow's relativist consciousness is not necessarily Marlow's own. Throughout *Heart of Darkness* and *Lord Jim*, Marlow struggles for the same absolute moral insight that he projects onto Kurtz and Jim.

36. Michael Sprinker argues that, because of the imperialist dynamic that Jim reproduces in Patusan, *Lord Jim* is not a novel about "universally human ethical problems" but about "moral sanctions imposed upon a particular class or class fraction at a specific period in its history," which Marlow "*quite unself-consciously* extols in his celebration of Jim's heroism in bringing peace and order to the country" ("Fiction and Ideology: *Lord Jim* and the Problem of Literary History," in *Reading Narrative; Form, Ethics, Ideology*, ed. James Phelan [Columbus: Ohio State University Press, 1989], 242; emphasis added).

37. Batchelor observes that the attempt to speak the language of romanticism convincingly "seems to strain Marlow's linguistic and personal resources" (*Lord Jim*, 112).

38. Erdinast Vulcan, *Joseph Conrad*, 36.

CHAPTER 5

1. Posner, "Against Ethical Criticism," 8.

2. Fyodor Dostoevsky, *The Notebooks for The Idiot*, ed. Edward Wasiolek, trans. Katharine Strelsky (Chicago: University of Chicago Press, 1967), 198.

3. Except on their methods of pedagogy, I do not propose to make an exhaustive comparison of the similarities between Myshkin and Christ. Such studies have already been deftly performed; see Victor Terras, The Idiot: *An Interpretation* (Boston: Twayne, 1990), 72–84; and Elizabeth Dalton, *Unconscious Structure in* The Idiot: *A Study in Literature and Psychoanalysis* (Princeton: Princeton University Press, 1979), 68–86. I do not believe that they exaggerate the possibility of viewing Myshkin as a Christ figure.

4. Robin Feuer Miller, *Dostoevsky and The Idiot: Author, Narrator, and Reader* (Cambridge: Harvard University Press, 1981), 205.

5. David K. Danow, *The Dialogic Sign: Essays on the Major Novels of Dostoevsky* (New York: Peter Lang, 1991), 55.

6. See Dalton, *Unconscious Structure*, 69.

7. Fyodor Dostoevsky, *The Idiot*, trans. Constance Garnett (New York: Bantam Classic, 1981), 56.

8. Feuer Miller, *Dostoevsky*, 171, 187.

9. Joseph Frank, "A Reading of *The Idiot*," *Southern Review* 5 (April 1969), 309.

10. See Edward Wasiolek, *Dostoevsky: The Major Fiction* (Cambridge: M.I.T. Press, 1964), 103.

11. Joseph Frank, *Dostoevsky: The Stir of Liberation, 1860–1865* (Princeton: Princeton University Press, 1986), 129.

12. Dennis Patrick Slattery, *The Idiot: Dostoevsky's Fantastic Prince* (New York: Peter Lang, 1983), 133–34.

13. Arpad Kovacs elaborates Myshkin's romanticism in terms that recall the conventional depiction of the romantic poet as moral legislator: "Myshkin idealizes and poeticizes in his 'novella' [of Marie] the 'triumph of virtue,' of 'singular good,' which are based on a personal origin, on the principle of the premoral purity of man, his inherent innocence and the 'natural law of compassion.' . . . This principle organizes the hero's monologic discourse, and constructs from these events a *sentimental idyll* with a 'moral' which Myshkin then advances as an ideal model for a happy life on this earth" ("The Poetics of *The Idiot*: On the Problem of Dostoevsky's Thinking about Genre," in *Critical Essays on Dostoevsky*, ed. Robin Feuer Miller [Boston: G. K. Hall and Co., 1986], 120). The overlap between Myshkin's character and traditional romantic rhetoric is at times remarkable. For example, one of Walton's early descriptions of Victor Frankenstein could, at times, be ascribed to the Prince; both possess "an intuitive discernment; a quick but never-failing power of judgment; a penetration into the causes of things, unequalled for clearness and precision" (Mary Shelley, *Frankenstein*, ed. Johanna M. Smith [Boston: Bedford Books of St. Martin's Press, 1992], 36–37).

14. Harriet Murav ascribes pedagogic potential to the character of the holy fool, who "uses his secret knowledge to provoke and manipulate others" (*Holy Foolishness: Dostoevsky's Novels and the Poetics of Cultural Critique* [Stanford: Stanford University Press, 1992], 93).

15. George Gutsche, *Moral Apostasy in Russian Literature* (DeKalb: Northern Illinois University Press, 1986), 6.

16. Bakhtin, *Dialogic Imagination*, 279.

17. Gary Saul Morson and Caryl Emerson, "Introduction: Rethinking Bakhtin," in *Rethinking Bakhtin: Extensions and Challenges*," ed. Gary Saul Morson and Caryl Emerson (Evanston: Northwestern University Press, 1989), 58.

18. Bakhtin, *Problems*, 241–42.

19. Kovacs argues the opposite, that Myshkin is monologic until he tries to actualize his words in deeds, after which his pathos of sincerity is undermined and he is dialogized in the external world ("Poetics," 117).

20. Caryl Emerson, "The Tolstoy Connection in Bakhtin," in *Rethinking Bakhtin: Extensions and Challenges*," ed. Gary Saul Morson and Caryl Emerson (Evanston: Northwestern University Press, 1989), 157.

21. Ibid., 158.

22. Dostoevsky, *Notebooks*, 193.

23. Murray Krieger, "Dostoevsky's 'Idiot': The Curse of Saintliness," in *Dostoevsky: A Collection of Critical Essays*, ed. René Wellek (Englewood Cliffs, N.J.: Prentice-Hall, 1962), 48–49.

24. Anthony J. Cascardi, *The Bounds of Reason: Cervantes, Dostoevsky, Flaubert* (New York: Columbia University Press, 1986), 131–32.

25. Michael Holquist, *Dostoevsky and the Novel* (Princeton: Princeton University Press, 1977), 110–11, 112.

26. Cascardi, *Bounds of Reason,* 130.

27. Malcolm V. Jones, *Dostoevsky after Bakhtin* (Cambridge: Cambridge University Press, 1990), 135.

28. It is on the subject of this distinction between Myshkin's reflexive unconditional language and the other characters' acceptance of the contingency of value that Feuer Miller's extensive work on *The Idiot*'s readers might be read most profitably. Feuer Miller contends that there are three readers of Dostoevsky's text: the real reader (a nonideal, everyday self), the implied reader (generally critical of, and responsive to, the narrator's recounting), and the narrator's reader (generally uncritical of the narrator's recounting) (*Dostoevsky*, 4–5). According to Feuer Miller, each of these readers corresponds to one of three authors of Dostoevsky's text. The real reader corresponds to Dostoevsky, the nonideal, historical being who composed the novel. The implied reader corresponds to the implied author, whose ideal perspective subsumes the narrower contextual vision of the narrator, who is a member of Petersburg society and is implicated in the text's events. Feuer Miller claims that the real reader is given the task of sifting through the various appeals made by *The Idiot*'s multileveled narrative structure on the implied and the narrator's reader.

I find Feuer Miller's categories a compelling, though not always entirely clear scaffolding for a reader-response-oriented criticism. One way of clarifying her categories might be to read them as structural analogues of the opposed processes of signification that I claim govern Dostoevsky's novel. Because it is implicated in the temporal social conditions represented in the text, the narrator's voice is thoroughly conditioned by contingency and demurs from authoritative pronouncement (*Dostoevsky*, 104–5); it also becomes profoundly hostile to Myshkin's incarnationist voice as the novel progresses. Authority more comfortably resides in the voice of the implied author, whose voice, like Myshkin's, is gradually undermined by the temporal demands placed on dialogue and eventually surrenders to the manifold stabs at fixed signification that follow Myshkin's recrudescent idiocy.

29. Slattery, *The Idiot,* 197.

30. Frank, "Reading," 326.

31. Frank proposes that Myshkin's epileptic fits represent the closest that the Prince comes to recognizing his unearthly ideal in the normal conditions of earthly existence ("Reading," 315). This would nicely account for why Myshkin,

who throughout the party is gradually comprehending the gap between his ideal and the materially real, succumbs to a violent fit that brings the festivities to a peremptory end.

32. For a source for Myshkin's need to translate his moral words into moral actions, see Nicholas Rzhevsky's concise summary of Dostoevsky's fourth *feuilleton* for the *St. Petersburg News:* "Man is not a real presence in the world unless he asserts his existence by moral action in the concrete life of society" (*Russian Literature and Ideology: Herzen, Dostoevsky, Leontiev, Tolstoy, Fadeyev* [Urbana: University of Illinois Press, 1983], 94).

33. Feuer Miller, *Dostoevsky*, 171.

34. Kovacs, "Poetics," 117–18.

35. Jones, *Dostoevsky after Bakhtin,* 140.

36. Frank, "Reading," 310. After acknowledging the "modulations and nuances of egoism" that are reflected by *The Idiot's* characters, Frank supplies something of a moral hierarchy into which he fits different characters according to the degree to which they manifest certain egoistic tendencies. According to this hierarchy, characters like Ganya and Totsky are lowest on the moral scale in that they pursue "some personal utilitarian advantage, or the satisfaction of some physical appetite." Characters like Nastasya Filippovna, Rogozhin, and Ippolit occupy the second tier of the scale because, though their egoism takes a "self-destructive form," they have a "genuine capacity for some sort of moral-spiritual experience." Aglaia, Lizaveta Prokofyevna, Radomsky, and the Prince represent the third tier, who combine "admirable qualities of mind and heart," but who also erect an "inner barrier to the attainment of a total selflessness" ("Reading," 310–11). The clarity of this hierarchy is at once its strength and its weakness. Frank maintains that Dostoevsky's characters can and often do move fluidly between these categories. But in the practice of ethical textual readings, one must not succumb to the temptation to impose a preconceived thematic structure on a text. One must allow the text's structural dynamics to expose an ethical tendency and import.

37. Slattery makes the case that "Lizaveta's 'clear view' is an act of recognition not simply of the prince, but also of his effect on the thought and behavior of Petersburg society" (*The Idiot,* 114).

38. Thus Slattery's observation that "[Myshkin's] love of a pure ideal arouses the ideals of those who constellate around him. They define themselves through him even as they judge him to be mad" (109) must be carefully qualified. Indeed, the Prince ostensibly compels others to measure their values against his, but he arouses vastly dissimilar reactions from them.

39. Krieger, "Curse," 48.

40. Kovacs, "Poetics," 120.

41. Wasiolek, *Dostoevsky,* 104.

42. Sidney Monas, "Across the Threshold: *The Idiot* as a Petersburg Tale," in *New Essays on Dostoevsky*, ed. Malcolm V. Jones and Garth M. Terry [Cambridge: Cambridge University Press, 1983], 85.

43. The sexual component of Rogozhin's desire—for Nastasya Filippovna, as well—is problematized by the constant textual reminders that associate the Rogozhin family with the Russian *skoptsy*, who practiced self-mutilation in the name of God (see ibid., 84).

44. Robin Feuer Miller, "The Role of the Reader in *The Idiot*," in *Critical Essays on Dostoevsky*, ed. Robin Feuer Miller (Boston: G. K. Hall and Co., 1986), 111, 113.

45. Krieger, "Curse," 50. Krieger and Jeremy Smith, who also discusses the ethical position of Radomsky (*Religious Feeling and Religious Commitment in Faulkner, Dostoyevsky, Werfel, and Bernanos* [New York: Garland Publishing, 1988], 189–91), finally observe inadequacies in the moral voice of Yevgeny Pavlovitch.

46. Krieger, "Curse," 50.

47. See Richard Peace, *Dostoevsky: An Examination of the Four Major Novels* (Cambridge: Cambridge University Press, 1971), 98.

48. Frank, "Reading," 328.

49. See Smith, *Religious Feeling*, 189.

50. Slattery, *The Idiot*, 215.

51. Nicholas Rzhevsky, "Kozhinov on Bakhtin," *New Literary History* 25 (spring 1994): 436.

52. Smith, *The Idiot*, 199.

BIBLIOGRAPHY

Achebe, Chinua. "An Image of Africa: Racism in Conrad's *Heart of Darkness*." In *Heart of Darkness,* edited by Robert Kimbrough, 251–62. New York: W. W. Norton, 1988.

Aczel, Richard. "Hearing Voices in Narrative Texts." *New Literary History* 29, no. 3 (1998): 467–500.

Amoia, Alba. *Albert Camus*. New York: Continuum, 1989.

Angell, Joseph Warner. "Preface." *The Yale Zauberberg-Manuscript: Rejected Sheets Once Part of Thomas Mann's Novel*. Edited by James F. White. Bern: Francke Verlag, 1980.

Attridge, Derek. "Innovation, Literature, Ethics: Relating to the Other." *PMLA* 114, no. 1 (January 1999): 20–31.

———. "Singularities, Responsibility: Derrida, Deconstruction, and Literary Criticism." *Critical Encounters: Reference and Responsibility in Deconstructive Writing,* 106–26. New Brunswick, N.J.: Rutgers University Press, 1995.

Baker, Peter. *Deconstruction and the Ethical Turn*. Gainesville: University Press of Florida, 1995.

Baker, Robert S. "Joseph Conrad." *Contemporary Literature* 22, no. 1 (winter 1981): 116–26.

Bakhtin, Mikhail. *The Dialogic Imagination: Four Essays*. Translated by Caryl Emerson and Michael Holquist. Edited by Michael Holquist. Austin: University of Texas Press, 1981.

———. *Problems of Dostoevsky's Poetics*. Translated and edited by Caryl Emerson. Minneapolis: University of Minnesota Press, 1984.

———. "The Problem of Speech Genres." In *Speech Genres and Other Late Essays,* translated by Vern W. McGee, edited by Caryl Emerson and Michael Holquist, 60–102. Austin: University of Texas Press, 1986.

Barthes, Roland. "*La Peste*: Annales d'une epidemie ou roman de la solitude?" *Bulletin du Club du meilleur livre* (February 1955): 4–8.

Batchelor, John. *Lord Jim*. London: Unwin Hyman, 1988.

Bernasconi, Robert. "Deconstruction and the Possibility of Ethics." In *Deconstruction and Philosophy: The Texts of Jacques Derrida,* edited by John Sallis, 122–39. Chicago: University of Chicago Press, 1987.

Berthoud, Jacques. *Joseph Conrad: The Major Phase*. Cambridge: Cambridge University Press, 1978.

Bérubé, Michael. *Public Access: Literary Theory and American Cultural Politics*. London: Verso, 1994.

Bialostosky, Don. *Wordsworth, Dialogics, and the Practice of Criticism*. Cambridge: Cambridge University Press, 1992.

Bisdorff, Ernest. *Thomas Mann und die Politik*. Luxembourg: Editions du Centre, 1966.

Bloom, Allan. *The Closing of the American Mind*. New York: Simon and Schuster, 1987.

Bloom, Harold. "Introduction." In *Albert Camus*, edited by Harold Bloom, 1–6. New York: Chelsea House, 1989.

————. "Introduction." In *Marlow*, edited by Harold Bloom, 1–3. New York: Chelsea House, 1992.

Booth, Wayne. "Are Narrative Choices Subject to Ethical Criticism?" In *Reading Narrative: Form, Ethics, Ideology*, edited by James Phelan, 57–78. Columbus: Ohio State University Press, 1989.

————. *The Company We Keep: An Ethics of Fiction*. Berkeley: University of California Press, 1988.

————. "The Ethics of Teaching Literature." *College English* 61, no. 1 (September 1998): 41–55.

Bovè, Paul. *In the Wake of Theory*. Hanover, N.H.: Wesleyan University Press, 1992.

Braun, Lev. *Witness of Decline: Albert Camus—Moralist of the Absurd*. Rutherford, N.J.: Fairleigh Dickinson University Press, 1974.

Braverman, Albert S., and Larry Nachman. "Nature and the Moral Order in *The Magic Mountain*." *Germanic Review* 53, no. 1 (winter 1978): 1–12.

Brée, Germaine. *Camus*. New York: Harcourt, Brace and World, 1964.

Brooks, Peter. "Aesthetics and Ideology: What Happened to Poetics?" *Critical Inquiry* 20, no. 3 (spring 1994): 509–23.

Bruford, W. H. "'Bildung' in *The Magic Mountain*." In *Modern Critical Interpretations: Thomas Mann's The Magic Mountain*, edited by Harold Bloom, 67–83. New York: Chelsea House, 1986.

Buell, Lawrence. "In Pursuit of Ethics." *PMLA* 114, no. 1 (January 1999): 7–19.

Cain, William E. "The Ethics of Criticism: Does Literature Do Any Good?" *College English* 53, no. 4 (April 1991): 467–76.

Camus, Albert. *Lyrical and Critical Essays*. Edited by Philip Thody. Translated by Ellen Conroy Kennedy. New York: Vintage, 1970.

————. *The Myth of Sisyphus and Other Essays*. Translated by Justin O'Brien. New York: Vintage, 1955.

————. *Notebooks, 1935–1942*. Translated by Philip Thody. New York: Alfred A. Knopf, 1963.

————. *Notebooks, 1942–1951*. Translated by Justin O'Brien. New York: Alfred A. Knopf, 1965.

————. *The Plague*. Translated by Stuart Gilbert. New York: Vintage International, 1991.

————. *La Peste*. Paris: Gallimard, 1947.

————. *The Rebel: An Essay on Man in Revolt*. Translated by Anthony Bower. New York: Alfred A. Knopf, 1956.

————. *Resistance, Rebellion, and Death.* Translated by Justin O'Brien. New York: Vintage, 1960.

Caputo, John D. *Deconstruction in a Nutshell: A Conversation with Jacques Derrida,* edited by John D. Caputo. New York: Fordham University Press, 1997.

Cascardi, Anthony J. *The Bounds of Reason: Cervantes, Dostoevsky, Flaubert.* New York: Columbia University Press, 1986.

Cheatham, George. "The Absence of God in *Heart of Darkness.*" *Studies in the Novel* 28, no. 3 (fall 1986): 304–13.

Clausen, Christopher. *The Moral Imagination: Essays on Literature and Ethics.* Iowa City: University of Iowa Press, 1986.

————. "Moral Inversion and Critical Argument." *Georgia Review* 42, no. 1 (spring 1988): 9–22.

————. "Morality, Poetry, and Criticism." *Kenyon Review* 5, no. 4 (fall 1983): 74–89.

Conrad, Joseph. *A Personal Record.* New York: Harper and Brothers, 1912.

————. *Heart of Darkness.* 3d ed. Edited by Robert Kimbrough. New York: W. W. Norton, 1988.

————. *Life and Letters.* Edited by G. Jean-Aubry. London: William Heinemann, 1927.

————. *Lord Jim.* 2d ed. Edited by Thomas Moser. New York: W. W. Norton, 1996.

————. *Notes on Life and Letters.* London: J. M. Dent and Sons, 1970.

————. *The Nigger of the "Narcissus."* Edited by Robert Kimbrough. New York: W. W. Norton, 1979.

Cordes, Alfred. *The Descent of the Doves: Camus' Journey to the Spirit.* Washington, D.C.: University Press of America, 1980.

Critchley, Simon. *The Ethics of Deconstruction: Derrida and Levinas.* Oxford: Blackwell, 1992.

Dalton, Elizabeth. *Unconscious Structure in The Idiot: A Study in Literature and Psychoanalysis.* Princeton: Princeton University Press, 1979.

Danow, David K. *The Dialogic Sign: Essays on the Major Novels of Dostoevsky.* New York: Peter Lang, 1991.

Davis, Colin. "Interpreting *La Peste.*" *Romanic Review* 85 (January 1994): 125–42.

Dostoevsky, Fyodor. *The Idiot.* Translated by Constance Garnett. New York: Bantam Classic, 1981.

————. *The Notebooks for The Idiot.* Edited by Edward Wasiolek. Translated by Katharine Strelsky. Chicago: University of Chicago Press, 1967.

Doubrovsky, Serge. "The Ethics of Albert Camus." In *Critical Essays on Albert Camus,* edited by Bettina L. Knapp. Boston: G. K. Hall, 1988.

Durrani, Osman. "The Tearful Teacher: The Role of Serenus Zeitblom in Thomas Mann's *Doktor Faustus.*" *Modern Language Review* 80 (July 1985): 652–58.

Eaglestone, Robert. *Ethical Criticism: Reading after Levinas*. Edinburgh: Edinburgh University Press, 1997.

Eldridge, Richard T. *On Moral Personhood: Philosophy, Literature, Criticism, and Self-Understanding*. Chicago: University of Chicago Press, 1989.

Elliott, John. "The Ethics of Repression: Deconstruction's Historical Transumption of History." *New Literary History* 23 (1992): 727–45.

Emerson, Caryl. "The Tolstoy Connection in Bakhtin." In *Rethinking Bakhtin: Extensions and Challenges,* edited by Gary Saul Morson and Caryl Emerson, 149–72. Evanston: Northwestern University Press, 1989.

Felman, Shoshana. "The Betrayal of the Witness: Camus' *The Fall*." In *Testimony: Crises of Witnessing in Literature, Psychoanalysis, and History,* edited by Shoshana Felman and Dori Laub, M.D., 165–203. New York: Routledge, 1991.

———. "Narrative as Testimony: Camus' *The Plague*." In *Reading Narrative: Form, Ethics, Ideology,* edited by James Phelan, 250–71. Columbus: Ohio University Press, 1989.

Fitch, Brian T. *The Narcissistic TEXT: A Reading of Camus' Fiction*. Toronto: University of Toronto Press, 1982.

Fleming, Bruce. "Brothers under the Skin: Achebe on *Heart of Darkness*." *College Literature* 19, no. 3/20, no. 1 (October 1992–February 1993): 90–99.

Frank, Joseph. *Dostoevsky: The Stir of Liberation, 1860–1865*. Princeton: Princeton University Press, 1986.

———. "A Reading of *The Idiot*." *Southern Review* 5 (April 1969): 302–31.

Galef, David. "On the Margins: The Peripheral Characters in Conrad's *Heart of Darkness*." *Journal of Modern Literature* 17, no. 1 (summer 1990): 117–38.

Gardner, John. *On Moral Fiction*. New York: Basic Books, 1977.

Gekoski, R. A. *Conrad: The Moral World of the Novelist*. New York: Harper and Row, 1978.

Giroux, Henry A. "Academics as Public Intellectuals: Rethinking Classroom Politics." In *PC Wars: Politics and Theory in the Academy,* edited by Jeffrey Williams, 294–307. New York: Routledge, 1995.

Goonetilleke, D. C. R. A. *Joseph Conrad: Beyond Culture and Background*. New York: St. Martin's Press, 1990.

Gosling, Justin. "Literature and Moral Understanding: A Philosophical Essay on Ethics, Aesthetics, Education, and Culture." *Review of English Studies* 182 (May 1995): 308–10.

Graff, Gerald. *Beyond the Culture Wars: How Teaching the Conflicts Can Revitalize American Education*. New York: W. W. Norton, 1992.

———. *Professing Literature: An Institutional History*. Chicago: University of Chicago Press, 1987.

Guerard, Albert J. *Conrad: The Novelist*. Cambridge: Harvard University Press, 1958.

Gutsche, George. *Moral Apostasy in Russian Literature*. DeKalb: Northern Illinois University Press, 1986.

Haines, Victor Yelverton. "No Ethics, No Text." *Journal of Aesthetics and Art Criticism* 47, no. 1 (winter 1989): 35–42.

Hampson, Robert. *Joseph Conrad: Betrayal and Identity*. New York: St. Martin's Press, 1992.

Hans, James S. *The Value(s) of Literature*. Albany: State University of New York Press, 1990.

Harpham, Geoffrey Galt. "Ethics." *Critical Terms for Literary Study*, 2d ed., edited by Frank Lentricchia and Thomas McLaughlin. Chicago: University of Chicago Press, 1995.

————. *Getting It Right: Language, Literature, and Ethics*. Chicago: University of Chicago Press, 1992.

Hatfield, Henry. *From the Magic Mountain: Mann's Later Masterpieces*. Ithaca: Cornell University Press, 1979.

Hawthorn, Jeremy. *Joseph Conrad: Narrative Technique and Ideological Commitment*. London: Edward Arnold, 1990.

Hayman, Ronald. *Thomas Mann: A Biography*. New York: Scribner, 1995.

Heller, Erich. *The Ironic German: A Study of Thomas Mann*. Boston and Toronto: Little, Brown and Co., 1958.

Herrnstein-Smith, Barbara. *Contingencies of Value: Alternative Perspectives for Critical Theory*. Cambridge: Harvard University Press, 1988.

Holquist, Michael. *Dostoevsky and the Novel*. Princeton: Princeton University Press, 1977.

Hughes, Edward J. *Albert Camus: La Peste*. Glasgow: University of Glasgow French and German Publications, 1988.

Jameson, Fredric. *The Political Unconscious: Narrative as a Socially Symbolic Act*. Ithaca: Cornell University Press, 1981.

Jones, Malcolm V. *Dostoyevsky after Bakhtin*. Cambridge: Cambridge University Press, 1990.

Kantorowicz, Alfred. *Heinrich und Thomas Mann: Die persönlichen, literarischen und weltanschaulichen Beziehungen der Brüder*. Berlin: Aufbau–Verlag, 1956.

Kavanagh, Thomas M. "Uneasy Theories: The Ethics of Narration in Contemporary French Criticism." *Criticism* 28 (fall 1986): 445–58.

Keller, Ernst. *Der unpolitische Deutsche: Eine Studie zu den "Betrachtungen eines Unpolitischen" von Thomas Mann*. Bern: Francke Verlag, 1965.

Kellman, Stephen G. *The Plague: Fiction and Resistance*. New York: Twayne, 1993.

Koc, Richard. "Magical Enactments: Reflections on 'Highly Questionable' Matters in *Der Zauberberg.*" *Germanic Review* 68, no. 3 (summer 1993): 108–15.

Koopmann, Helmut. "Die Lehren des *Zauberbergs.*" In *Das "Zauberberg" Symposium 1994 in Davos,* edited by Thomas Sprecher, 59–80. Frankfurt am Main: Vittorio Klostermann, 1995.

Kovacs, Arpad. "The Poetics of *The Idiot*: On the Problem of Dostoevsky's Thinking about Genre." In *Critical Essays on Dostoevsky,* edited by Robin Feuer Miller, 116–26. Boston: G. K. Hall, 1986.

Krieger, Murray. "Dostoevsky's 'Idiot': The Curse of Saintliness." In *Dostoevsky: A Collection of Critical Essays,* edited by René Wellek, 32–52. Englewood Cliffs, N.J.: Prentice-Hall, 1962.

————. "In the Wake of Morality: The Thematic Underside of Recent Theory." *New Literary History* 15 (autumn 1983): 119–36.

Kurzke, Hermann. "Die Quellen der *Betrachtungen eines Unpolitischen.*" In *Internationales Thomas–Mann–Kolloquium 1986 in Lübeck,* edited by Eckhard Heftrich and Hans Wysling, 291–310. Bern: Francke Verlag, 1987.

Lazere, Donald. *The Unique Creation of Albert Camus.* New Haven: Yale University Press, 1973.

Lehnert, Herbert, and Eva Wessell. *Nihilismus der Menschenfreundlichkeit.* Frankfurt am Main: Vittorio Klostermann, 1991.

Levenson, Michael. "The Value of Facts in the *Heart of Darkness.*" *Nineteenth-Century Fiction* 40, no. 2 (December 1985): 261–80.

Lukács, Georg. *Essays on Thomas Mann.* Translated by Stanley Mitchell. New York: Howard Fertig, 1978.

MacIntyre, Alasdair. *After Virtue.* 2d ed. Notre Dame: University of Notre Dame Press, 1981.

Malbone, Raymond Gates. "'How to Be': Marlow's Quest in *Lord Jim.*" *Twentieth Century Literature* 10 (April 1964–January 1965): 172–80.

Mann, Thomas. *Briefe, 1889–1936.* Frankfurt am Main: S. Fischer Verlag, 1962.

————. *Letters to Paul Amann, 1915–1952.* Edited by Herbert Wegener. Translated by Richard and Clara Winston. Middletown, Conn.: Wesleyan University Press, 1960.

————. *The Magic Mountain.* Translated by H. T. Lowe–Porter. New York: Vintage International, 1992.

————. *Reflections of a Non-Political Man.* Translated by Walter D. Morris. New York: Frederick Ungar Publishing Co., 1983.

————. *Der Zauberberg.* Frankfurt am Main: Fischer Taschenbuch Verlag, 1967.

Marcus, Judith. *Georg Lukács and Thomas Mann: A Study in the Sociology of Literature.* Amherst: University of Massachusetts Press, 1987.

Mayer, Hans. "On the Political Development of an Unpolitical Man." In *Critical Essays on Thomas Mann,* edited by Inta M. Ezergailis, 191–206. Boston: G. K. Hall, 1988.

McCarthy, Patrick. *Camus*. New York: Random House, 1982.

McGann, Jerome. "Canonade." *New Literary History* 25, no. 3 (summer 1994): 487–504.

McGinn, Colin. *Ethics, Evil, and Fiction*. Oxford: Clarendon Press, 1997.

McLauchlan, Juliet. "The 'Value' and 'Significance' of *Heart of Darkness*." *Conradiana* 15, no. 1 (1983): 3–21.

Miller, J. Hillis. *The Ethics of Reading*. New York: Columbia University Press, 1986.

————. *Fiction and Repetition: Seven English Novels*. Cambridge: Harvard University Press, 1982.

————. "Is There an Ethics of Reading?" In *Reading Narrative: Form, Ethics, Ideology*, edited by James Phelan, 79–101. Columbus: Ohio State University Press, 1989.

Miller, Robin Feuer. *Dostoevsky and The Idiot: Author, Narrator, and Reader*. Cambridge: Harvard University Press, 1981.

————. "The Role of the Reader in *The Idiot*." In *Critical Essays on Dostoevsky*, edited by Robin Feuer Miller, 103–116. Boston: G. K. Hall, 1986.

Monas, Sidney. "Across the Threshold: *The Idiot* as a Petersburg Tale." In *New Essays on Dostoyevsky*, edited by Malcolm V. Jones and Garth M. Terry, 67–93. Cambridge: Cambridge University Press, 1983.

Morson, Gary Saul, and Caryl Emerson. "Introduction: Rethinking Bakhtin." In *Rethinking Bakhtin: Extensions and Challenges*, edited by Gary Saul Morson and Caryl Emerson, 1–60. Evanston: Northwestern University Press, 1989.

Murav, Harriet. *Holy Foolishness: Dostoevsky's Novels and the Poetics of Cultural Critique*. Stanford: Stanford University Press, 1992.

Nagel, Thomas. *The View from Nowhere*. Oxford: Oxford University Press, 1986.

Nealon, Jeffrey T. "The Ethics of Dialogue: Bakhtin and Levinas." *College English* 59, no. 2 (February 1997): 129–48.

Nehamas, Alexander. "Nietzsche in *The Magic Mountain*." In *Modern Critical Interpretations: Thomas Mann's The Magic Mountain*, edited by Harold Bloom, 105–16. New York: Chelsea House, 1986.

————. "What Should We Expect from Reading?" *Salmagundi* 111 (summer 1996): 27–58.

Newton, Adam Zachary. *Narrative Ethics*. Cambridge: Harvard University Press, 1995.

Norris, Christopher. *Deconstruction and the Interests of Theory*. Norman: University of Oklahoma Press, 1989.

————. *Paul de Man, Deconstruction, and the Critique of Aesthetic Ideology*. London: Routledge, 1988.

————. *Derrida*. Cambridge: Harvard University Press, 1987.

————. "The Ethics of Reading and the Limits of Irony: Kierkegaard among the Postmoderns." *Southern Humanities Review* 23 (winter 1989): 1–35.

Nussbaum, Martha Craven. *Love's Knowledge: Essays on Philosophy and Literature.* Oxford: Oxford University Press, 1990.

————. "Reply to Richard Wollheim, Patrick Gardiner, and Hilary Putnam." *New Literary History* 15 (autumn 1983): 201–8.

Palmer, Frank. *Literature and Moral Understanding.* Oxford: Clarendon Press, 1992.

Parker, David. *Ethics, Theory, and the Novel.* Cambridge: Cambridge University Press, 1994.

Parker, Emmett. *Albert Camus: The Artist in the Arena.* Madison: University of Wisconsin Press, 1965.

Parry, Benita. "Lord Jim." In *Marlow,* edited by Harold Bloom. New York: Chelsea House Publishers, 1992.

Peace, Richard. *Dostoevsky: An Examination of the Four Major Novels.* Cambridge: Cambridge University Press, 1971.

Pecora, Vincent. "*Heart of Darkness* and the Phenomenology of Voice." *English Literary History* 52, no. 4 (winter 1985): 993–1015.

Petrey, Sandy. *Realism and Revolution: Balzac, Stendhal, Zola, and the Performances of History.* Ithaca: Cornell University Press, 1988.

Phelan, James. "Narrative Discourse, Literary Character, and Ideology." In *Reading Narrative: Form, Ethics, Ideology,* edited by James Phelan, 132–46. Columbus: Ohio State University Press, 1989.

Plato. *The Republic.* Edited by James Adam. Cambridge: Cambridge University Press, 1963.

Porter, Laurence M. "From Chronicle to Novel: Artistic Elaboration in Camus' *La Peste.*" *Modern Fiction Studies* 28 (winter 1982–83): 589–95.

Posner, Richard A. "Against Ethical Criticism." *Philosophy and Literature* 21, no. 1 (1997): 1–27.

Prescott, Orville. "Outstanding Novels." *Yale Review* 38 (Autumn 1948): 189.

Putnam, Hilary. "Taking Rules Seriously—A Response to Martha Nussbaum." *New Literary History* 15 (autumn 1983): 193–200.

Rabinowitz, Peter J. "End Sinister: Neat Closure as Disruptive Force." In *Reading Narrative: Form, Ethics, Ideology,* edited by James Phelan, 120–31. Columbus: Ohio State University Press, 1989.

Rader, Ralph W. "*Lord Jim* and the Formal Development of the English Novel." In *Reading Narrative: Form, Ethics, Ideology,* edited by James Phelan, 220–35. Columbus: Ohio State University Press, 1989.

Reed, T. J. *Thomas Mann: The Uses of Tradition.* Oxford: Clarendon Press, 1974.

————. "The Uses of Tradition." In *Modern Critical Interpretations: Thomas Mann's The Magic Mountain,* edited by Harold Bloom, 53–66. New York: Chelsea House, 1986.

Reeves, Charles Eric. "A Voice of Unrest: Conrad's Rhetoric of the Unspeakable." *Texas Studies in Literature and Language* 27 (spring 1985): 284–310.

Ricoeur, Paul. *Time and Narrative,* vol. 1. Translated by Kathleen McLaughlin and David Pellauer. Chicago: University of Chicago Press, 1984.

Rorty, Richard. *Contingency, Irony, and Solidarity.* Cambridge: Cambridge University Press, 1989.

———. "Duties to the Self and to Others: Comments on a Paper by Alexander Nehamas." *Salmagundi* 111 (summer 1996): 59–67.

Rzhevsky, Nicholas. "Kozhinov on Bakhtin." *New Literary History* 25, no. 2 (spring 1994): 429–44.

———. *Russian Literature and Ideology: Herzen, Dostoevsky, Leontiev, Tolstoy, Fadeyev.* Urbana: University of Illinois Press, 1983.

Sartre, Jean-Paul. *Situations.* Translated by Benita Eisler. New York: George Braziller, 1965.

Scharfschwerdt, Jürgen. *Thomas Mann und der deutsche Bildungsroman.* Stuttgart: W. Kohlhammer Verlag, 1967.

Scholes, Robert. "The Novel as Ethical Paradigm?" *Novel* 21, no. 1 (winter/spring 1988): 188–96.

Schwarz, Daniel R. "The Ethics of Reading: The Case for Pluralistic and Transactional Reading." *Novel* 21, no. 1 (winter/spring 1988): 197–218.

Seamon, Roger. "The Story of the Moral: The Function of Thematizing in Literary Criticism." *Journal of Aesthetics and Art Criticism* 47 (summer 1989): 229–36.

Searle, John. "Literary Theory and Its Discontents." *New Literary History* 25, no. 3 (summer 1994): 637–65.

Shelley, Mary. *Frankenstein.* Edited by Johanna M. Smith. Boston: Bedford Books of St. Martin's Press, 1992.

Shryock, Richard. "Discourse and Polyphony in *La Peste.*" *Symposium* 44 (spring 1990): 58–66.

Sidorsky, David. "Modernism and the Emancipation of Literature from Morality: Teleology and Vocation in Joyce, Ford, and Proust." *New Literary History* 15 (autumn 1983): 137–53.

Siebers, Tobin. *Morals and Stories.* New York: Columbia University Press, 1992.

Singh, Frances B. "The Colonialistic Bias of Heart of Darkness." *Conradiana* 10, no. 1 (1978): 41–54.

Slattery, Dennis Patrick. *The Idiot: Dostoevsky's Fantastic Prince.* New York: Peter Lang, 1983.

Smith, Jeremy. *Religious Feeling and Religious Commitment in Faulkner, Dostoyevsky, Werfel and Bernanos.* New York: Garland Publishing, 1988.

Spacks, Patricia Ann Meyer. "The Novel as Ethical Paradigm." *Novel* 21 (winter 1988): 181–88.

Spender, Stephen. "Albert Camus, Citizen of the World." *New York Times Book Review,* 1 August 1948.

Sprinker, Michael. "Fiction and Ideology: *Lord Jim* and the Problem of Literary History." In *Reading Narrative: Form, Ethics, Ideology,* edited by James Phelan, 236–49. Columbus: Ohio State University Press, 1989.

———. "We Lost It at the Movies." *MLN* 112, no. 3 (April 1997): 385–99.

Sprintzen, David. *Camus: A Critical Examination.* Philadelphia: Temple University Press, 1988.

Stampfl, Barry. "Marlow's Rhetoric of (Self-) Deception in *Heart of Darkness.*" *Modern Fiction Studies* 37, no. 2 (summer 1991): 183–96.

Stephanson, Raymond. "The Plague Narratives of Defoe and Camus: Illness as Metaphor." *Modern Language Quarterly* 48 (September 1987): 224–41.

Stock, Irvin. "The Magic Mountain." *Modern Fiction Studies* 32, no. 4 (winter 1986): 487–519.

Stow, Simon. "Unbecoming Virulence: The Politics of the Ethical Criticism Debate." *Philosophy and Literature* 24, no. 1 (April 2000): 185–96.

Tarrow, Susan. *Exile from the Kingdom: A Political Rereading of Albert Camus.* University: University of Alabama Press, 1985.

Terras, Victor. *The Idiot: An Interpretation.* Boston: Twayne, 1990.

Thody, Philip. *Albert Camus.* New York: St. Martin's Press, 1989.

Todd, Olivier. *Albert Camus: A Life.* Translated by Benjamin Ivry. New York: Alfred A. Knopf, 1997.

Tretheway, Eric. "Language, Experience, and Selfhood in Conrad's *Heart of Darkness.*" *Southern Humanities Review* 22, no. 2 (spring 1988): 101–11.

Van Ghent, Dorothy. "On *Lord Jim.*" In *Twentieth Century Interpretations of* Lord Jim: *A Collection of Critical Essays,* edited by Robert E. Kuehn, 68–81. Englewood Cliffs, N.J.: Prentice-Hall, 1969.

Vulcan, Daphna Erdinast. *Joseph Conrad and the Modern Temper.* Oxford: Clarendon Press, 1991.

Wasiolek, Edward. *Dostoevsky: The Major Fiction.* Cambridge: M.I.T. Press, 1964.

Watt, Ian. *Conrad in the Nineteenth Century.* Berkeley: University of California Press, 1979.

Weigand, Hermann J. *Thomas Mann's Novel "Der Zauberberg": A Study.* New York: AMS Press, 1971.

Williams, C. E. "Not an Inn, but an Hospital." In *Modern Critical Interpretations: Thomas Mann's "The Magic Mountain,"* edited by Harold Bloom, 37–51. New York: Chelsea House, 1986.

Wißkirchen, Hans. "Der Einfluß Heinrich Manns auf den *Zauberberg.*" In *Auf dem Weg zum "Zauberberg": Die Davoser Literaturtage, 1996,* edited by Thomas Sprecher, 143–64. Frankfurt am Main: Vittorio Klostermann, 1997.

Woelfel, James W. *Camus: A Theological Perspective*. Nashville: Abingdon Press, 1975.

Wysling, Hans. "Probleme der *Zauberberg*–Interpretation." In *Ausgewählte Aufsätze 1963–1995,* edited by Thomas Sprecher and Cornelia Bernini, 231–47. Frankfurt am Main: Vittorio Klostermann, 1996.

INDEX

absurd, theory of the, 71
Achebe, Chinua, 191–92n. 19
Aczel, Richard, 180n. 69
aesthetics: aestheticism in *Magic Mountain,* 50–51, 54–56, 58, 68; Conrad on relationship between morality and, 99–106; dialogue between ideological components of text and, 3–4; Mann on aestheticism, 40–44
After Virtue (MacIntyre), 20–21
Allegories of Reading (de Man), 80
allegory, 80–81
Althusser, Louis, 81, 82
Amann, Paul, 35
Aristotle, 173n. 16
Arnold, Matthew, 1
art: Camus on, 71–74, 186n. 7; Conrad on, 99, 100–102; Lukács on, 39, 40; Mann on, 40–44; modernist movement in, 19; and *Zivilisationsliterat* (European literary man), 38–40
Attridge, Derek, 173n. 14, 176n. 30, 178n. 42
Austen, Jane, 15

Bab, Julius, 182n. 5
Baker, Peter, 176n. 28, 178n. 42
Baker, Robert S., 191n. 18
Bakhtin, Mikhail, 5, 28, 32, 139–41, 142, 167, 180n. 74, 181–82n. 77
Barthes, Roland, 27, 70, 78–80, 81, 82, 94, 95, 97
Batchelor, John, 193n. 37
Beckett, Samuel, 15
Beethoven, Ludwig van, 41
Berthoud, Jacques, 191n. 18, 192n. 26

Bérubé, Michael, 10–11
Bialostosky, Don, 4, 34, 172n. 13
Bildungsroman, 183n. 16
Bisdorff, Ernest, 182nn. 4–5
Bloom, Allan, 9
Bloom, Harold, 186–87n. 17, 192n. 21
Booth, Wayne, 1, 14–18, 71, 176n. 29
bourgeoisie: Camus on, 188–89n. 30; in *Heart of Darkness,* 118–19; in *The Idiot,* 137; in *The Magic Mountain,* 46–51, 54–55, 60, 185n. 23, 185n. 27; in *The Plague,* 83–84, 87, 95, 97, 188n. 29
Bové, Paul, 1
Braun, Lev, 186n. 6
Brée, Germaine, 189n. 38
Brooks, Peter, 7, 19
Bruford, W. H., 184n. 20, 185n. 27
Buell, Lawrence, 171n. 4

Cain, William E., 180n. 71
Camus, Albert: on art versus philosophy, 186n. 7; on bourgeoisie, 188–89n. 30; class background of, 189n. 30; on dialogue, 72; on Dostoevsky, 71–72; on ethical fiction, 70, 71–76, 98; on formalism, 72; on history, 70, 186n. 3; humanism of, 70–71; on language, 188n. 26; Mann compared with, 73; on monologic text, 71–72; on philosophical writing versus thesis-mongering, 73–74; on realism, 72–73; relativism of, 70–71; resistance sympathies of, 27, 84; review of Sartre's *Nausea* by, 71; on socialist realism, 72–73, 75, 186n. 6; as teacher, 76; and theory of the

Camus, Albert (*continued*)
    absurd, 71; on truth, 70, 83. *See also Plague, The* (Camus); and other works by Camus
canon formation, 18–20
capitalism, 102–4, 115–17, 122, 123, 124
Caputo, John D., 175n. 28, 177n. 38
Cascardi, Anthony, 144
characters: author's own theoretical voice in, 27; dialogue of, 31–34; MacIntyre on, 24; and pedagogic voice and moral dialogue, 24–26, 28–31; and signification modes, 29. *See also* specific novels
Christ figure, 136, 143–45, 149, 155, 193n. 3
classroom teaching, 15–18
Clausen, Christopher, 3, 171n. 2, 174n. 21, 178n. 43, 178n. 49
Closing of the American Mind, The (Bloom), 9
Conrad, Joseph: on art, 99; on fiction versus history, 101–2; and racism, 191–92n. 19; on relationship between morality and aesthetics, 99–106. *See also Heart of Darkness* (Conrad); *Lord Jim* (Conrad); and other works by Conrad
conscientiousness, 38
constitutive signification, 29–31, 135
Critchley, Simon, 177n. 38
criticism. *See* ethical criticism

Danow, David, 136
Davis, Colin, 80, 188n. 27
de Man, Paul, 12–13, 80
deconstructionist criticism, 6, 11–14, 175–76n. 28, 176n. 34, 177n. 38, 178n. 42
Derrida, Jacques, 11–12, 175–76n. 28, 176n. 30

Dewey, John, 16
dialogic imperative, 4, 172n. 13
dialogic overtones, 28, 181–82n. 77
dialogism, 140–42, 149–50, 181–82n. 77, 195n. 19
"dialogization," 181n. 77
dialogue: Camus on, 71–72; in narratives, 31–34, 180n. 74, 181–82n. 77. *See also* specific novels
Dickens, Charles, 10
Dostoevsky, Fyodor: attitude of, toward religious faith, 27, 139; Camus on, 71–72; and character development of Prince Myshkin, 135–36, 143; compared with Tolstoy, 142; Kantian affinities of, 139; on moral action, 196n. 32. *See also Idiot, The* (Dostoevsky)
Doubrovsky, Serge, 80

Eaglestone, Robert, 19, 173n. 16, 176nn. 29–30, 177n. 39
Eagleton, Terry, 7
either/or fallacy, 14–20
Elliott, John, 176n. 34
Emerson, Caryl, 141–42
Enlightenment, 26, 39, 53, 67
Ethical Criticism (Eaglestone), 176n. 30
ethical literary criticism: audience for, 174n. 20; and canon formation, 18–20; categories of potentially bad ethical criticism, 5–11, 34, 168–69, 178n. 43; characteristics for ethical critic, 172n. 13; and classroom teaching, 15–18; and deconstructive ethics, 6, 11–14, 175–76n. 28, 176n. 34, 177n. 38, 178n. 42; definition of, 1, 3; dialogue between aesthetic structures and ideological components of text, 3–4; and either/or fallacy, 14–20; and humanism, 5–7; and

narrative, 20–24; objections to, 2, 3, 5, 19, 134–35, 168–69, 174–75n. 21; pedagogic voice and moral dialogue, 4–5, 24–34; and Plato, 1; and politics, 7–9, 169, 174–75n. 21; and relativism, 9–11; responsible ethical criticism, 2–3, 8, 34, 80, 89, 134–35, 169–70. *See also* specific novels and novelists

Fall, The (Camus), 187n. 24, 189n. 45
Felman, Shoshana, 81–82, 187n. 24, 188n. 28, 189n. 45
Fitch, Brian, 189n. 32
Flaubert, Gustave, 42
Fleming, Bruce, 192n. 19
fool, 138, 194n. 14
formalism, 72
Forster, E. M., 10
Foucault, Michel, 7, 12
Fountainhead, The (Rand), 37
Frank, Joseph, 137, 138, 151, 166, 196n. 31, 196n. 36
Frankenstein (Shelley), 194n. 13
Freud, Sigmund, 12, 13

Galef, David, 192n. 21
Gardner, John, 6–7
generic criticism, 6
Genette, Gérard, 180n. 69
Getting It Right (Harpham), 175n. 21
Goethe, Johann Wolfgang von, 42
Good Life standard, 173n. 16
Goonetilleke, D. C. R. A., 191n. 16
Graff, Gerald, 15, 171n. 3
Gutsche, George, 139

Haines, Victor, 173–74n. 18
Hans, James S., 174n. 20
Hard Times (Dickens), 10
Harpham, Geoffrey Galt, 171n. 4, 175n. 21

Hatfield, Henry, 183n. 7
Hawthorn, Jeremy, 192n. 22
Hayman, Ronald, 182nn. 4–5, 185n. 27, 185n. 30
Heart of Darkness (Conrad): alternative interpretive possibilities of, 118, 192n. 30; authorial presence in, 105, 190n. 8; beginning of, with third-person description, 106; "brutes" in, 112–13; capitalism and imperialism in, 102–4, 107–9, 112–13, 115–17, 131, 192n. 26; characters named with abstract nouns in, 106–7; competing pedagogic voices in dialogue of, 32, 112; concluding words of, 120; different interpretations of Kurtz, 28; Kurtz's death in, 115–16; Kurtz's escape plans in, 114–15; Kurtz's horror in, 24–25, 28, 115–17, 127, 130, 132; Kurtz's voice in, 104, 111–20, 122–25, 130, 192n. 28; and limits of language to express "truth," 103; and Marlow on power of vision, 109–10; Marlow's ambivalence in, 105–6, 107, 109, 191n. 18; Marlow's lie to Kurtz's Intended in, 118–22, 124, 127; Marlow's moral consciousness in, 28, 30, 33, 99–100, 102–22, 123, 131, 132–33, 193n. 35; Marlow's narratorial voice in, 107–8; Marlow's relationship with Kurtz in, 192n. 21, 192n. 26; and Marlow's view of labor, 108–9; and Marlow's view of truth, 109–11; moral dialogue in, 33; narrator of, 106–7; natives' culture and jungle in, 110–16, 119, 120, 191n. 19; relationship between *Lord Jim* and, 105–6, 120–24, 127, 131, 132–33

Hegel, G. W. F., 139
Heller, Erich, 41–42
hermeneutics, 6
Herrnstein-Smith, Barbara, 23
historical criticism, 6
history: Conrad on fiction versus, 101–2; and narrative, 188n. 28
Holquist, Michael, 144
Homer, 20
Horace, 1
humanism: of Camus, 70–71; and ethical literary criticism, 5–7; in *The Magic Mountain,* 26, 39, 50–56, 59, 60, 67

idealism, 145–46, 148–49, 152–55, 196n. 38
Idiot, The (Dostoevsky): Aglaia in, 142–43, 145, 148–49, 151, 159, 161, 162, 163, 165, 166, 167, 196n. 36; authorial presence in, 27, 196n. 28; Bakhtin on, 139–41; Burdovsky in, 156, 157; concluding words of, 167; critics on, 27, 139–44; and Dostoevsky's development of Myshkin's character, 135–36, 143; Epanchin home in, 137, 145, 146–48, 151–52; Filippovna in, 196n. 36; Ganya in, 136, 151–52, 155, 166, 196n. 36; gulf between Myshkin's and other characters' signifying systems, 150–51; Ippolit in, 158–159, 196n. 36; Keller in, 156–57, 166; Kolya Ivolgin in, 165, 166; Lebedyev in, 136, 150, 153, 154, 157, 166; Lizaveta Prokofyevna in, 137, 150–58, 166–67, 196nn. 36–37; madness of Nastasya Filippovna in, 154–56; madness of Rogozhin in, 166;

marriage plan of Ganya to Nastasya Filippovna, 151–52; minor characters' reaction to Myshkin in, 156–58; moral dialogue in, 33, 34, 151, 167–68; moral hierarchy of characters in, 196n. 36; murder of Nastasya Filippovna in, 166; and Myshkin as Christ figure, 136, 143–45, 149, 155, 193n. 3; Myshkin's life goal in, 158; and Myshkin as recipient in pedagogic relationship, 161–62; and Myshkin as representative of reductive ethical criticism, 34; Myshkin's choice between Aglaia and Nastasya Filippovna in, 142–43, 148–49, 159, 162–65; Myshkin's Christian virtues in, 33, 136, 137, 138–39, 141, 143–45, 157, 158, 196n. 36; Myshkin's epileptic fits in, 141, 195n. 31; Myshkin's idealism in, 145–46, 148–49, 152–55, 197n. 38; Myshkin's incarnationist voice and referential signification in, 135–51, 157, 163, 165; Myshkin's monologism versus dialogism, 140–42, 149–50, 196n. 19; Myshkin's parables in, 137, 138, 145, 152, 160, 166; Myshkin's pedagogic impotence versus Myshkin's influence in, 143–45, 166; Myshkin's pedagogic voice in, 151–61; Myshkin's romanticism in, 194n. 13; Myshkin's voice and moral consciousness in, 30–31, 34, 135, 136–68; narrator of, 143, 146–47, 154, 158, 163–65, 195–96n. 28; Nastasya Filippovna in, 33, 136, 142–43, 145, 148–49, 151, 154–56, 159, 161, 162–66, 196n. 36, 197n. 43; Radomsky in,

146, 148–49, 196n. 36, 197n. 45;
real reader, implied reader, and
narrator's reader of, 195–96n. 28;
Rogozhin in, 145, 155, 158,
159–62, 166, 196n. 36, 197n. 43;
Roman Catholicism denounced by
Myshkin in, 27, 147; scandal scenes
in, 142–43, 145, 148–49, 162–63;
theme of, 136; Totsky in, 33, 145,
151–52, 155, 196n. 36; Vera
Lebedyev in, 165, 166; Yevgeny
Pavlovitch in, 146, 148, 164–67,
197n. 45; "young nihilists" in,
136, 153
imperialism, 102–4, 107–9, 112–13,
115–17, 122, 124, 127, 130, 131,
190n. 10, 192n. 26
incarnationist voice, 127–29, 135–51,
157, 163, 165
intersubjectivity, 14, 178n. 42
ironists, 22–23

James, Henry, 15, 192n. 35
Jameson, Fredric, 5, 7, 12, 19,
174–75n. 21
Jeanson, Francis, 77
Johnson, Samuel, 1
Jones, Malcolm, 145
Joyce, James, 20

Kant, Immanuel, 12, 139
Kavanagh, Thomas M., 115–16,
172n. 13, 178–79n. 54
Keats, John, 15
Kellman, Stephen, 73
Koc, Richard, 185n. 34
Koopman, Helmut, 182nn. 4–5
Kovacs, Arpad, 149–50, 156,
194n. 13, 194n. 19
Kozhinov, Vadim, 167–68
Krieger, Murray, 12, 13, 20, 143–44,
164–65, 176–77n. 35, 197n. 45

Lacan, Jacques, 12
language: Camus on, 188n. 26; ethical
importance of, 12, 176n. 29; incarnationist potential of language in
Lord Jim, 127–29; incarnationist
voice and referential signification of
Myshkin in *The Idiot,* 135–51, 157,
163, 165; and moral insubstantiality and duplicity, 192n. 22; in *The
Plague,* 84–86, 88, 91, 92, 96,
189n. 32; referential language,
29, 30, 135; Rorty on contingency
of, 22
Lazere, Donald, 186nn. 6, 17
Levenson, Michael, 113, 117–18
Levinas, Emmanuel, 11–12, 14,
176nn. 29–30
literary canon. *See* canon formation
literary criticism. *See* ethical literary
criticism
literary narratives. *See* narrative
Lord Jim (Conrad): affinity between
reader and Marlow in, 104–5,
191n. 15; alternative interpretive
possibilities of, 130–33, 192n. 30;
authorial presence in, 105,
190n. 8; Brierly in, 125, 126, 130;
capitalism and imperialism in,
102–4, 122, 123, 124, 130,
193n. 36; Chester in, 125–26,
127, 128; Gentleman Brown in,
190n. 11; incarnationist potential
of language in, 127–29; Jewel in,
129–30; Jim's decision to jump
ship in, 121–26; and Jim's importance to Marlow, 121–32,
193n. 36; Jim's romanticism in,
127, 193n. 37; Jim's voice and
moral consciousness in, 30, 104,
105, 121–32; and limits of language to express "truth," 103;
Marlow as narrative device in,

Lord Jim (Conrad) (*continued*)
193n. 35; Marlow's identification
with Jim in, 121–23; Marlow's
moral consciousness in, 28, 30,
33, 99–100, 102–6, 120–33,
193n. 35; Marxist analysis of, 5; as
modernist narrative, 124; moral
dialogue in, 33; natives' respect for
Jim in, 127; Privileged Man in,
132; relationship between *Heart of
Darkness* and, 105–6, 120–24, 127,
131, 132–33; shipwreck in, 110,
121, 123; Stein in, 127, 130; third-
person narrator of, 121, 123; trial
in, 122–28
Love's Knowledge (Nussbaum), 180n. 67
Lukács, Georg, 39, 40, 67, 82,
183n. 14, 184n. 20, 185n. 23,
185nn. 27–28
Lyrical and Critical Essays (Camus), 71,
75, 76

MacIntyre, Alasdair, 20–21, 24, 71
Magic Mountain, The (Mann): authorial
presence in, 27, 37, 46–47, 69;
Castorp and Ziemssen's death in,
64; Castorp in World War I in,
68–69; Castorp's acclimatization to
sanatorium's lifestyle, 54–55, 58;
Castorp's bourgeois ideology at
beginning of, 46–50, 54–55;
Castorp's departure from Berghof
at end of, 44–45, 68–69, 185n. 34;
Castorp's ethical development in,
37–38, 54–59, 62–63, 67–69,
183n. 7, 185n. 29; and Castorp's
finances and need to work, 47–48,
55; and Castorp's grandfather, 53;
Castorp's love for Chauchat in, 51,
54, 56–59, 65; Castorp's near-
death experience in, 62–63, 97;

Castorp's silence and gesture in,
65–66; Castorp's voice in, 30,
185n. 31; Chauchat and social standards of Haus Berghof in, 49;
Chauchat's voice and ethical position in, 38, 45–46, 54, 56–59, 62,
64, 66; competing pedagogic
voices in dialogue of, 32, 37, 38,
69; dialogue between Settembrini
and Naphta in, 38, 59–61, 182n. 5,
185n. 27; duel between
Settembrini and Naphta in, 67;
genesis of, 35–36; historical
urgency in, 38, 69; *Leitmotiv* in,
48–49; and lethargy at Berghof,
65–66; Naphta's suicide in, 67;
Naphta's voice in, 45, 59–61, 63,
64, 68; narrator's voice in, 38, 44,
46–47, 184n. 22; Peeperkorn's
physical presence in, 64;
Peeperkorn's voice in, 38, 45–46,
59, 63–66, 68; Peeperkorn's suicide in, 65; and reader's identification with Castorp, 48–49;
reciprocity between history and
consciousness in, 46–47; relationship of, to *Reflections of a Non-
Political Man,* 36, 37, 47, 51,
182n. 5; seance in, 66–67,
185n. 34; Settembrini as
Zivilisationsliterat in, 39–40, 41,
182n. 5; Settembrini-Castorp relationship in, 50–59, 64, 185n. 24;
Settembrini's bourgeois ideology
in, 50–51, 60, 184n. 23, 185n. 27;
Settembrini's ideological inconsistency in, 51, 53; Settembrini's
voice and ethical position in,
26, 27, 44, 45, 50–61, 63, 64,
65, 184n. 23, 185n. 27, 185n. 29;
social relations in, 58, 67, 184n. 20;

and social standards of Haus
Berghof, 49–50; theme of,
185n. 30; time in, 38, 44;
Walpurgis Nacht carnival in, 57–59;
"you" construction in, 184n. 22;
Ziemssen in, 49, 50, 54–55,
61–62, 64, 66–67, 68
Malbone, Raymond Gates,
190–91n. 13
Mann, Heinrich, 27, 39, 40, 183n. 9
Mann, Thomas: on aestheticism,
40–44; brother of, 27, 39, 40,
183n. 9; Camus compared with,
73; on conscientiousness, 38; as
critic and defender of Prussian
culture, 39, 43; criticisms of, 42;
on ethics and morality, 42; on
pedantry, 38; and politics, 43–44;
on *Zivilisationsliterat* (European lit-
erary man), 38–43, 67, 183n. 13.
See also Magic Mountain, The (Mann);
Reflections of a Non-Political Man
(Mann)
Marcus, Judith, 185n. 28
Marxist criticism, 5, 6, 19, 75, 139,
174–75n. 21
März (magazine), 39
Maurice (Forster), 10
McGinn, Colin, 172n. 5, 173n. 18
McLauchlan, Juliet, 192n. 28
Miller, J. Hillis, 12, 13–14,
177nn. 38–39, 192n. 30
Miller, Robin Feuer, 136, 149, 164,
195–96n. 28
Milton, John, 24, 28
modernist movement in art, 19
Monas, Sidney, 159
monologic text and monologism,
71–72, 140–42, 149–50, 195n. 19
moral criticism. *See* ethical literary
criticism

Murav, Harriet, 194n. 14
Myth of Sisyphus and Other Essays
(Camus), 71–72, 73
mythology, 20

narrative: authorial presence in, 27,
180n. 71; bridging between history
and, 188n. 28; and characters,
24–26, 27; and dialogue, 31–34;
and ethical literary criticism,
20–24; and ideological filters,
27–28, 31; instabilities in,
179n. 64; MacIntyre on, 20–21;
Nussbaum on, 21; pedagogic voice
and moral dialogue, 4–5, 24–34;
point of view or narratorial voice
of, 26–27, 180n. 67, 180n. 69;
readers' awareness of criticisms and
evaluations of, 27; Rorty on,
21–23; and time, 21; Woolf on
modernist narrative technique,
19–20. *See also* pedagogic voice;
and specific novels
Native Son (Wright), 10
Nausea (Sartre), 37, 71
Nazism, 78, 81
Nealon, Jeffrey T., 25
Nehamas, Alexander, 179n. 57,
185n. 25
New Criticism, 6
New York Times Book Review, The, 77
Newton, Adam Zachary, 176n. 29
Nietzsche, Friedrich, 12, 109
Nigger of the Narcissus (Conrad),
100–101
Norris, Christopher, 12–13, 176n. 34,
177nn. 38–39
Notebooks (Camus), 70, 74, 186n. 7,
187–88n. 25
Notebooks (Dostoevsky), 135–36,
137, 143

Notes on Life and Letters (Conrad), 101
"Nuptials" (Camus), 70
Nussbaum, Martha, 5–6, 10, 21, 25, 171n. 3, 172n. 9, 173n. 16, 179n. 57, 180n. 67

On Moral Fiction (Gardner), 6

Palmer, Frank, 25, 173n. 18
Paradise Lost (Milton), 24, 28
Parker, David, 32, 171n. 4
Parker, Emmett, 81, 188n. 30
Parry, Benita, 102, 190n. 10
Pecora, Vincent, 103
pedagogic dialogue, 180n. 74
pedagogic monologue, 180n. 74
pedagogic novel, 36–37
pedagogic voice: competing pedagogic voices in dialogue, 31–34; and constitutive signification, 29–31, 135; and moral dialogue, 4–5, 24–34; and referential signification, 29, 30, 135–51, 157, 163, 165; structural perspective on, 28–29; thematic perspective on, 28. *See also* specific novels
Personal Record (Marlow), 101
Petrey, Sandy, 29
Phelan, James, 179n. 64
philosophical novel, 36–37
Plague, The (Camus): abatement of the plague in, 95–98, 189–90n. 45; absolute versus contingent ethical position in, 82–83; allegory in, 80–81; authorial presence in, 27; burial of bodies in, 88–89; Camus's reply to Barthes on, 79; class struggle in, 89; compared with *The Fall,* 187n. 24; compared with *The Magic Mountain,* 97; Cottard in, 85, 86–87, 88, 90–91, 95–96,

187n. 25; critics on, 27, 70, 75, 76–82, 93, 94, 186–87n. 17; deaths of major characters in, 91, 92, 93, 94, 189n. 33; Grand in, 85–86, 88, 90, 94, 96, 97, 98; language in, 84–86, 88, 91, 92, 96, 189n. 32; memories of loved ones in, 88; moral dialogue in, 33, 94–98; narrator of, 26–27, 83–84, 188n. 27; Oran's description in, 83–84; Paneloux in, 87, 88, 89–92, 94, 97, 98, 189n. 43; publication date of, 76; Rambert in, 84, 89, 90, 93, 96, 97, 98; Rieux in, 30, 80–81, 84–86, 88, 89–93, 96–98, 188n. 25, 189n. 31, 189n. 33; Rieux's use of word *plague* in, 30, 84–85; Tarrou in, 86, 88–98; time in, 86, 87–89, 189n. 38; townspeople in, 83–84, 87, 95, 97, 188n. 29, 189n. 41, 189–90n. 45
Plato, 1, 102, 139, 171n. 1
poetics, 1, 12
political criticism, 7–9, 169, 174–75n. 21
Political Unconscious (Jameson), 5, 174–75n. 21
politics of identity, 169
Porter, Laurence M., 80
Posner, Richard, 10, 134–35
Prescott, Orville, 77
"Prodigal Son," 177n. 35
proniknovennoe slovo (penetrated word), 141–42
Putnam, Hilary, 173n. 16

Rader, Ralph W., 190n. 11
Rand, Ayn, 37
reading: and awareness of criticisms and evaluations of literary narrative,

27; Booth on, 17–18; dialogues
produced in act of, 25–26; ethics
of, 13–14, 177n. 39; and idcologi-
cal filters, 27–28, 31; and ironists,
22–23
realism, 72–73
Rebel (Camus), 73–74, 77
Reed, T. J., 183nn. 15–16
referential signification, 29, 30,
135–51, 157, 163, 165
Reflections of a Non-Political Man
(Mann), 35–44, 45, 47, 51, 67, 69,
73, 182n. 5
relativism, 9–11, 70–71
Republic, The (Plato), 171n. 1
Resistance, Rebellion, and Death
(Camus), 71, 72, 73
Ricoeur, Paul, 21
romanticism, 127, 130, 193n. 37,
194n. 13
Rorty, Richard, 19, 21–23, 69, 71,
174n. 18
Rzhevsky, Nicholas, 167, 196n. 32

Said, Edward, 12
Sartre, Jean-Paul, 27, 37, 70, 71,
77–78
Satan, 24, 28
Schwarz, Daniel R., 172n. 13,
180n. 72
Seamon, Roger, 177n. 35
Shakespeare, William, 15, 16
Shelley, Percy Bysshe, 1
Shryock, Richard, 189
Sidney, Sir Philip, 1
Sidorsky, David, 19
Siebers, Tobin, 7, 8
signification modes, 29–31
Singh, Frances, 112–13
Slattery, Dennis Patrick, 138,
196nn. 37–38

Smith, Jeremy, 197n. 45
socialist realism, 72–73, 75, 186n. 6
Spacks, Patricia Meyer, 175n. 26
Spender, Stephen, 77
Sprinker, Michael, 8, 193n. 36
Sprintzen, David, 87, 188n. 29
Stephanson, Raymond, 187n. 21
Stock, Irvin, 185n. 29
Stow, Simon, 7, 8
structuralist criticism, 6

Tarrow, Susan, 186n. 3, 187n. 17,
188n. 29, 189n. 42
themes, 13, 19–20, 23, 169, 177n. 35
Thody, Philip, 189n. 31
time: in *The Magic Mountain,* 38, 44;
and narrative, 21; in *The Plague,* 86,
87–89, 189n. 38
Tolstoy, Lev, 142
Tretheway, Eric, 103

universalization, 174n.21
univocality in exegesis, 3

Van Ghent, Dorothy, 192n. 35
verification of exegesis, 3
Vico, Giambattista, 20
voice: author's own theoretical voice
in narratives, 27, 180n. 71; Bakhtin
on, 28, 180n. 74; definition of textual voice, 180n. 69; incarnationist
voice, 127–29, 135–51, 157, 163,
165; narratorial voice or point
of view in narratives, 26–27,
180n. 67, 180n. 69. *See also* pedagogic voice; and specific novels

Wagner, Richard, 41
Wasiolek, Edward, 157
Watt, Ian, 105, 123, 190n. 8
Weigand, Hermann J., 48, 185n. 24

Whitman, Walt, 184n. 21
Wiegand, Hermann, 36
Williams, Raymond, 7, 19
Woolf, Virginia, 19–20
Wright, Richard, 10

Yale Review, 77

Zivilisationsliterat (European literary
    man), 38–43, 67, 183n. 13
Zola, Émile, 41

JOHN KRAPP is a teaching fellow of interdisciplinary studies at Hofstra University in Hempstead, New York. He leads courses that examine the intersection of intellectual history, literature, and philosophy, and has published articles in these fields. Krapp lives in Centerpoint, New York.